# CHURCHILL'S FORGOTTEN GENERALS

## *War and Military Culture in South Asia, 1757–1947*

www.helion.co.uk/warandmilitarycultureinsouthasia



**Submissions**
The publishers would be pleased to receive submissions for this series. Please contact us via email (info@helion.co.uk), or in writing to Helion & Company Limited, Unit 8 Amherst Business Centre, Budbrooke Road, Warwick, CV34 5WE

**Titles**

1 *'Swords Trembling In Their Scabbards'. The Changing Status of Indian Officers in the Indian Army 1757–1947* Michael Creese (ISBN 978-1-909982-81-9)
2 *'Discipline, System and Style'. The Sixteenth Lancers and British Soldiering in India 1822-1846* John H. Rumsby (ISBN 978-1-909982-91-8)
3 *Die in Battle, Do not Despair. The Indians on Gallipoli, 1915* Peter Stanley (ISBN 978-1-910294-67-3)
4 *Brave as a Lion. The Life and Times of Field Marshal Hugh Gough, 1st Viscount Gough* Christopher Brice (ISBN 978-1-910294-61-1)
5 *Approach to Battle. Training the Indian Army during the Second World War* Alan Jeffreys (ISBN 978-1-911096-51-1)
6 *The Indian Army in The First World War: New Perspectives* Edited by Alan Jeffreys (ISBN 978-1-911512-78-3)
7 *War without Pity in the South Indian Peninsula 1798–1813: The Letter Book of Lieutenant-Colonel Valentine Blacker* Edited and with introductory notes by David Howell (ISBN 978-1-912390-86-1)
8 *Of Islands, Ports and Sea Lanes: Africa and the Indian Ocean in the Second World War* Ashley Jackson (ISBN 978-1-912390-74-8)
9 *Ceylon at War 1939-45* Ashley Jackson (ISBN 978-1-912390-65-6)
10 *For The Honour of My House: The Contribution of the Indian Princely States to the First World War* Tony McClenaghan (ISBN 978-1-912390-87-8)
11 *'Terriers in India: British Territorials, 1914–1919* Peter Stanley (ISBN 978-1-912390-82-3)
12 *John Company's Armies: The Military Forces of British India, 1824–57* Peter Stanley (ISBN 978-1-804513-30-9)
14 *Churchill's Forgotten Generals: Victors in Burma* Raymond Callahan & Alan Jeffreys (ISBN 978-1804516-71-3)

# CHURCHILL'S FORGOTTEN GENERALS

*Victors in Burma*

---

Raymond Callahan & Alan Jeffreys

Helion & Company Limited
Unit 8 Amherst Business Centre
Budbrooke Road
Warwick
CV34 5WE
England
Tel. 01926 499619
Email: info@helion.co.uk
Website: www.helion.co.uk
X (formerly Twitter): @Helionbooks
Facebook: @HelionBooks
Visit our blog at https://helionbooks.wordpress.com/

Published by Helion & Company 2025
Designed and typeset by Mach 3 Solutions (www.mach3solutions.co.uk)
Cover designed by Paul Hewitt, Battlefield Design (www.battlefield-design.co.uk)


ISBN 978-1-804516-71-3

British Library Cataloguing-in-Publication Data.
A catalogue record for this book is available from the British Library.

# Contents

# Dedication and acknowledgements

Dedicated to the memory of my father Commodore David Jeffreys RN.

## Raymond Callahan:

This book is dedicated to my father who understood the loneliness of command, but sadly did not live to see this publication.

I want to thank my colleagues in this project, Alan Jeffreys and Daniel Marston. Alan was very supportive when a lengthy hospitalization slowed my completion of the essay on Claude Auchinleck. Dan, who had originally hoped to write the Auchinleck story, was very generous in sharing his thoughts and conclusions when I took up the task. Above all, I want to thank my daughter Sarah whose support saw me through surgeries, hospitalization, and the completion of this chapter on the Auk. I couldn't have done it without you, my wonderful daughter!

## Alan Jeffreys:

This book is dedicated to my father, who has discussed the loneliness of command with me. I am delighted to co-author a book with Raymond Callahan. It has been an absolute pleasure. I am grateful for the support of my colleagues at the National Army Museum. Many thanks also to my wife, Lorraine, and my son, Michael, who read my essay and corrected the grammar.

We would both like to thank Daniel Marston for writing the introduction and Nancy Owens for help with formatting the essays.

The authors have written in the English of their respective nationalities.

# Introduction

The first half of the 20th century was the high-water mark of the British Indian Army. In that time, it transformed from a colonial constabulary into one of the most modern and victorious armies in the histories of both the First and Second World Wars. As with other armies, it went through major changes, defeats, and experiences; in 1945, it stood as a victor in war and as an organization highly respected by both its allies and enemies.

The Indian Army's transformation is best encapsulated in reflections by an Indian Army officer and famous author, John Masters, on the closing days of the war in Burma in 1945:

> As the tanks burst away down the road to Rangoon ... it took possession of the empire we had built...Twenty races, a dozen religions, a score of languages passed in those trucks and tanks.When my great-great-grandfather first went to India there had been as many nations; now there was one – India... . It was all summed up in the voice of an Indian colonel of artillery. Now the Indian, bending close to an English colonel over a map, straightened and said with a smile, "O.K., George. Thanks. I've got it. We'll take over all tasks at 1800. What about a beer?"[1]

The three generals that are the focus of this book—Savory, Slim, and Auchinleck—experienced these key years of the Indian Army's transformation through both war and peace, success and defeat. Some key themes that contributed to the success of the Indian Army during the two world wars include embracing a learning culture; transformation of the identity of the army; expansion of its recruitment base; expansion of the officer corps to include members who had been previously deemed unfit for command; and most importantly, the role of key individuals.

The Indian Army's experiences in the First World War were similar to those of their compatriots—the ANZACS, Canadians, and other armies that served in the BEF on the Western Front and in the other peripheral theaters. All of these forces dealt with issues resulting from rapid over-expansion of forces, fighting a long, drawn-out industrial war, and learning and adaptation on the battlefield. The Indian Army, along with its British

1 John Masters, *The Road Past Mandalay: A Personal Narrative* (London, 1961), 312–313.

and Empire counterparts, achieved victory in 1918. By instituting a culture of learning and adaptation on the battlefield, the Indian Army went through a series of significant organizational, tactical, and operational reforms that enabled it to not only hold its own but also to emerge from battle in 1918 as a victorious and modern institution.

Auchinleck, Slim, and Savory experienced the carnage of the First World War in the so-called 'peripheral' campaigns of Gallipoli and Mesopotamia. While junior to mid-level officers, they grappled with challenges including learning and adaptation, the limitations of pre-war recruitment practices, logistical deficiencies, and modern warfare. While the Indian Army initially deployed to support the Empire in France, it was in Mesopotamia and Palestine, where the bulk of the army—600,000 in Mesopotamia alone—served, and where it achieved its greatest victories of the First World War.

In this theatre, these three officers had a particular opportunity to observe at close range one of the most significant reform initiatives undertaken during the First World War. Following the British Army's disastrous experience at Kut in 1916, the British overhauled the entire military situation in Mesopotamia, placing Lt. Gen. Sir Stanley Maude in command. Maude set out to reform the army: he improved logistical and sustainment systems, and undertook efforts to improve the quality of British officers. He ensured that all units—corps, divisions, brigades, battalions, and regiments—rested and retrained, and introduced dissemination of battlefield experience and lessons from the fighting in Mesopotamia, as well as from other theaters, throughout the force.

In his role as commander of Allied forces in Mesopotamia, Maude demonstrated that he was not only a solid administrator and reformer, but also an effective commander in the field. Even after Allied forces had turned the tide in Mesopotamia with the seizure of Baghdad, Maude's influence continued: the Indian Army stopped its advance and restored the fighting condition of its forces, and both lessons and training transformation continued in the Indian Army, as well as the British Army, in France. It seems likely that Auchinleck, Savory, and Slim were influenced by General Maude's ideas and leadership; all three would carry his core themes of learning and adaptation into their own careers, coming to full fruition when they were senior officers in the Indian Army during the Second World War.

They began almost immediately; as soon as peace came, all three officers had noted issues that had arisen in fighting the First World War that must be addressed in the coming years in order to prepare the Indian Army for any future modern peer war. Each continued to seek better solutions for the army—through debate, training, and most importantly, education—as they rose through the ranks and took on the roles required for Indian Army officers who wished to make an impact on the army, as students and directing staff at Camberley and Quetta staff colleges.

The Indian Army went through various transformations during the inter-war period, such as the expansion of the officer corps to include Indians. All three of the officers took part in the attending debates; they each recognized, to varying degrees, the need to prepare a properly balanced force for a future independent India, whenever that contingency might occur. They all clearly understood the interplay of 'war and society' in the Indian Army as a cultural institution, and continued to assess, analyze, and debate the 'lessons' gleaned from war, internal security duties, and operations on the North-West Frontier. They wrote various pieces or served on various committees that prepared and shaped the foundations for future reform initiatives that are inevitable in the opening stages of war.

Despite reform and training efforts, the Indian and British army were not ready when war broke out once again in 1939. Through the upheaval of the war years, the Indian Army's officers and men kept focused on the need to learn from the mistakes that were inevitable for any force finding itself in new situations and environments with inexperienced personnel. The army had a number of teething troubles as it grew in strength and experience, as it had in the First World War, but it also avoided some of the same pitfalls. By the end of 1943 it was able to point with pride to its ability to learn from mistakes and adapt to conditions.

The Indian Army's successes in Africa, the Middle East, Italy, and particularly the Far East could not have occurred without fundamental reforms, notably expanding recruitment of ethnic groups and classes far beyond traditional limitations, restructuring the officer corps to admit more Indian commissioned officers, and instilling a culture of professionalism. These reforms went hand in hand with the tactical and operational level reforms that occurred on the battlefields of the Second World War. By the end of 1943, the Indian Army had reached a level of performance characterized by consistent and reliable professionalism. Its success, particularly in contrast to earlier defeats in Malaya and Burma, reinforced the army's perceptions of itself as a truly professional force, and bolstered *esprit de corps* throughout the war and into the postwar period, even in the face of impending national independence and change.

The Second World War was a trying time for Auchinleck, Savory, and Slim, as each served in different and crucial roles. While all three re-learned their trade from battalion to Army level command throughout the war, their combined influence took on almost a 'triumvirate response' by 1943, as evidenced in the success noted previously. Each was placed into positions that would shape the army well beyond the successes of the battlefields of North Africa, Italy, and Burma: Auchineck served as Commander in Chief India twice; Savory became Director of Infantry; and Slim took command of the 14th Army in 1943.

In these roles, the three officers shaped and influenced the Army in all its elements —recruitment, officer expansion, training, logistics, and learning and adaptation—into one of the finest fighting formations in history. They knew that for the Indian Army to be successful, it needed to address all of the elements which make an army successful on the battlefield—and that many of those elements have nothing to do with the battlefield. They recognized the need to understand the 'societal' impact upon a wartime army, and to embrace initiatives which would enhance battlefield performance. Their successful leadership is apparent in historian James Kitchen's suggestion that "Megiddo [1918] thus stands alongside 14th Army's [Second World War] Burma operations…[a]s evidence that the twentieth century British led Indian Army was capable of organizing, fighting and winning a modern military campaign."[2]

2 James Kitchen, "The Indianization of the Egyptian Expeditionary Force," in Kaushik Roy, ed., *The Indian Army in the Two World Wars* (Amsterdam, 2011), 190.

The foresight of all three officers would extend beyond the victories of the Second World War; all recognized in 1945 that independence for India was looming on the horizon. Savory and Auchinleck in particular would be in the 'thick' of the difficult process of demobilizing the world's largest volunteer force, preparing and handing over the army to new independent entities, India and Pakistan. It was only fitting that Savory would submit the final Indian Army order on 14 August 1947, sadly in the midst of the communal civil war in northern India. The Indian Army did not crack under the strain of the societal rupture and the attending violence, and it is a testament to these three officers, their professionalism, drive for success, and most importantly forward vision of the role of an army, that helped the army manage these final difficult days.

The following chapters tell the story of these three extraordinary officers, who played crucial roles in forming, building, and leading one of the greatest and most successful fighting organizations in history—the Indian Army.

Professor Daniel Marston

# 1

# The Auk: Field Marshal Sir Claude Auchinleck

## Introduction

Claude John Eyre Auchinleck, the last Commander-in-Chief of the Indian Army of the British Raj, is nearly forgotten today. He lies in a cemetery in Casablanca. In London, replete with statues of generals, his is nowhere to be found – only a small plaque in the crypt of St. Paul's Cathedral. In Birmingham, a city he had no real connection to, there is a statue, erected by a real estate firm on whose board he served after retirement, now (thanks to redevelopment) facing a hotel parking lot. Yet Auchinleck played a critical role not only in the 1941-42 desert war against Rommel but, more importantly, in leading the Indian Army's great transformation during World War II as well as in maintaining its stability during the wrenching months of India's "Transfer of Power" in 1946-47 and during the trauma of Partition, when that army's failure would have made a calamitous situation infinitely worse. But he never wrote a memoir or offered any other account of the momentous events in which he played such as important role. And so, as the end of the Raj became a subject of polemical accounts, vivid popular histories (and bad movies), while serious historians fixated on the dramatic politics of the twenty-four months between VJ Day and 15 August 1947, the end of that remarkable institution, the Indian Army, was treated, like the division of the Raj's civil servants and office furniture, as a secondary matter. It wasn't. "The Auk" – his army nickname – was crucial to keeping the Indian army functioning and not murderously factionalized. He deserves a better memorial than he has so far received.[1]

1 A full-scale new biography would be a good place to start. The only substantial study, John Connell's *Auchinleck: A Critical Biography* (London, 1959) although well written and sympathetic is badly out of date and moreover concentrates overwhelmingly on his time as Commander in Chief in the Middle East.

## An Indian Career

Auchinleck was born in 1884 at Aldershot where his father, an officer in the Royal Horse Artillery, was then stationed. When his father was posted to India he became, briefly, a "child of the Raj" for a few privileged, sun-washed years. His subsequent path was a quite common one for members of his class (he was descended on both sides from Scotch-Irish and Anglo-Irish minor gentry) who staffed as soldiers and civil servants the ever-widening boundaries of Britain's empire. He attended Wellington College, a public school founded in memory of the Iron Duke, where his achievements were average. He then moved on to the Royal Military College at Sandhurst. He had hoped for the Royal Military Academy at Woolwich, where the British Army trained its gunners and sappers, but his mathematics scores were too low. When he entered Sandhurst, he was already destined for the Indian Army. The British Army had abandoned purchase of officers' commissions in 1871 but got the same result, restricting commissioned rank to men of the "right sort," by requiring Sandhurst graduates to be accepted by a regiment. This meant meeting the regiment's expectations about the availability of "private means" – officers were not expected to live on their salaries. The only regiment where the impecunious were accepted was the very *déclassé* West India Regiment, a professional Siberia, albeit a warm one. The Indian Army however did not require private means (being, at least comparatively, well-paid). A young officer, without private means, therefore, could set his sights on an Indian career. But first he had to surmount the hurdle put in place to keep that army – vital to the security of the Raj and the British empire's strategic reserve – from being encumbered with officers not only without private means but lacking in brains as well: he must have passed into Sandhurst with a high score on the admission exam. When Auchinleck entered that meant in the first forty-five. His score placed him forty fifth (he would graduate in the middle of his class). When he passed out of Sandhurst in 1902 there was nothing to indicate that the young man, a new second lieutenant, who would sail from Tilbury docks in London in March 1903 was in any way marked for a great future.

Newly minted officers joining the Indian Army did not however on arriving in India immediately join an Indian Army regiment. First, they spent a year with a British army unit stationed in India. This was explained as a way of allowing the neophyte time to acclimate to the subcontinent and make his rookie mistakes in the safe confines of a British unit rather than with Indian soldiers. But it is also possible that it actually represented the British Army view that it represented the gold standard of soldiering that a young officer ought to experience before going off to join the second eleven, an attitude confirmed by the less than welcoming atmosphere many new Indian officers encountered during their time with a British unit, especially if that unit was from a "good" (i.e., expensive) British regiment. Auchinleck however was fortunate in his posting to a battalion of the King's Shropshire Light Infantry one of those "county" regiments that were the British's Army's backbone. After his year with them (studying Indian languages among other things) he moved on to the Indian Army's 62nd Punjabis in April 1904. It was a regiment that neatly encapsulated the state of the Indian Army at that moment. That army was originally created by the East India Company as three separate forces based on its Presidencies of Bengal, Madras and Bombay. The Indian Army passed to the Crown in 1858 when the Company was abolished after the 1857-58 Mutiny that consumed its largest component, the Bengal Army, and shook British power in India to its roots. However, it remained a separate service with its own officer corps, customs and traditions, while undergoing a slow transformation in its structure. The maintenance of three separate armies became increasingly anachronistic and they were merged in 1895. More importantly, the basic composition of the Indian Army was changed by the rise of the "martial races" theory which shaped the army Auchinleck would know. The "martial races" were held to be the conservative, agricultural peasantry of northwest India and its mountainous frontiers – Sikhs, Punjabi Muslims, Garwahlis and the tribesmen from the Indo-Afghan border (plus Gurkhas from the client kingdom of Nepal). They had remained loyal to the Company in 1857 and made up the bulk of the forces that restored British power in 1857-58. They were held to be inherently more warlike and trustworthy – and untouched by the political currents beginning to swirl in India by the time Auchinleck began his career. The 62nd Punjabis were a good example of what this change in the nature of the Indian Army meant at its grassroots. Originally raised in Madras Presidency as the 2nd Madras Infantry it was part of the Madras Army that had played a major role in the rise of the Company's power in the second half of the 18th century. But as the center of gravity of the Company's power shifted north and west, it became a force largely of garrison routine – although it did serve in Burma as the Company expanded there and it remained unmoved by the 1857 explosion in northern India. Frederick Roberts, who won a VC in the Mutiny, and went on to become Commander-in-Chief, India (celebrated by Kipling as "Bobs Bahadur") had been the Madras Army's commander-in-chief but, as the high priest of the martial races cult, he felt that the Madrassi units had lost their martial virtues. The old south Indian units were therefore "reconstituted" and retitled, a process the 2nd Madras Infantry had undergone shortly before Auchinleck joined. It morphed into the 62nd Punjabis, with a few officers from its former incarnation and a completely different rank and file, Hindu peasants from South India giving way to Muslim peasants from the Punjab, the "garrison state" of the Raj.[2]

Pre 1914 soldiering in India was quite routine. The Indian Army was now not only recruited in northwestern India but largely focused on India's northwest frontier – conducting punitive expeditions regularly against its turbulent tribes, warfare that was small scale but intense. All Indian Army units rotated regularly to the frontier. Auchinleck however, and unusually, saw no action before 1914 because the 62nd Punjabis were deployed in the opposite direction – India's peaceful northeastern frontier. Since Lord Curzon, India's most imperious Viceroy since Lord Dalhousie before the Mutiny, sent a military expedition into Tibet in 1904, the Government of India had

2 The Indian Army's final reorganization scheme in 1922 retitled the 62nd the 1st Battalion, 1st Punjab Regiment.

maintained an outpost at Gyantse in Tibet close to the Indian border. There and in Sikkim, an Indian princely state on the Indo-Tibetan border, Auchinleck spent several unadventurous years. Then in 1914 India went to war and, though no one then knew it, the curtain began to come down on Kipling's India.

The 62nd went, first, to Egypt and was one of the units defending the Suez Canal when the Turks attacked it, unsuccessfully, in February 1915. Then it moved to the Aden Protectorate, threatened by Turkish forces based in Yemen to the north. Finally, in late 1916, it was transferred to Mesopotamia (now Iraq) where the Indian Army's major World War I campaign was going very badly. It had begun well enough. Indian Expeditionary Force "D" had landed at Basra, a primitive port at the head of the Persian Gulf in 1914. Its mission was to ensure the safety of the terminals from which oil from the fields of southwestern Persia, vital to the Royal Navy, was shipped. Then "mission creep" set in, driven by the ambitions of both the Government of India and the commander of the 6th Indian Division, Major General Charles Townsend. The result was a steady northward movement from the utterly inadequate Basra base, culminating in an overly optimistically conceived drive on Baghdad by the 6th Indian Division (which nonetheless almost got there). Stopped short of their objective, then forced to fall back on their supply base at Kut on the banks of the Tigris, the 6th was besieged there. At this point Auchinleck and the 62nd Punjabis joined the Mesopotamia Expeditionary Force.

It is a commonplace that the Western Front shaped the thinking of the British Army during the interwar years and strongly conditioned the Western Front survivors who rose to high command during World War II (especially Bernard Law Montgomery). The campaign in "Mespot" was the Indian Army's Western Front and it also taught some expensive lessons. The 62nd Punjabis had reached Basra at full strength: 12 British officers, 22 Indian VCOs (Viceroy Commissioned Officers, crucial to a unit's functioning) and 907 rank and file. A month later it had sustained 443 casualties, including half its British officers and VCOs, Somme level losses, in the first, badly managed attempt to relieve the 6th Indian. And there was more to come. A second attempt to break through the Turkish defenses south of Kut again failed and when it did the 62nd Punjabis were down to 8 British officers, 4 VCOs, and 235 sepoys. In addition to command failures, the logistic underpinnings of the campaign were calamitously weak. Much that was available at Basra, itself a shambolically bad base, could not reach the front because the only line of communication was the Tigris and there was not enough river transport. Medical care was medieval. Auchinleck was, much later, to anger Churchill by his caution about undertaking offensives until his logistics were adequate and his line of communications in good order – the long shadow of the attempt to relieve Kut, which surrendered at the end of April 1916.

The failure to relieve Kut and the obvious shambles at Basra that contributed so much to the disaster led to a major overhaul: the War Office took over from the Government of India, Basra got competent management, medical care was sharply improved, and motor transport began to replace 18th century modes. But, above all, the much-tried Mesopotamia Expeditionary Force got a new commander – Lieutenant General Sir Stanley Maude. Maude was a British Army officer in a theater where most of the troops were Indian, but he was perceptive enough to learn enough Urdu (the Indian Army's *lingua franca*) to speak directly to Indian soldiers. Slim, then a young British Army officer serving in Mesopotamia would later testify to Maude's galvanic effect on the bedraggled army: "to watch an army recovering its morale is enthralling".[3] That too was a lesson that would have consequences in the next war. Under Maude, a revitalized army took Baghdad in March 1917. Auchinleck, now a major, had a spell temporarily commanding his battalion, earning a DSO, (the award then recognized leadership and gallantry just below Victoria Cross level). Maude died in 1917 but the army he brought back to life continued its successful advance. War's end found it, and Auchinleck, amid the mountains of Kurdistan. Unlike Slim, Auchinleck left no written memorials to his career but by 1919 he was a brevet lieutenant colonel with a major decoration and clearly marked to go further. The divisional commander to whose staff he was posted in 1919 described him as a "tower of strength". It was a characteristic that would serve him well in the future.

For Auchinleck, the next twenty years were a slow but steady climb up the Indian professional ladder, He was offered a slot at the Indian Army's staff college at Quetta. The war had thinned the ranks of the Indian Army's British officers, allowing the survivors to move ahead a bit more quickly. Auchinleck's first (and, to date, most thorough) biographer speculated that he might have done better to have tried for a place at British Army's staff college at Camberley where he might have made contact with not only British Army contemporaries but with the invisible networks of ideas, influence, patronage (and enlightening gossip) that exist in all institutions. This is an important observation but also wisdom after the event when lack of such connections handicapped Auchinleck in the Middle East in 1941-42. In 1919-20 Indian Army officers lived in a world where the future of the Raj seemed secure and their careers consequently would be as part of it (in any case, Auchinleck would spend a year at the Imperial Defence College in London in 1927-28 where he came into contact with British Army officers on their way up, especially John Dill, a future CIGS). After his year at Quetta and a long home leave, his first since 1912, (during which he married Jessie Stewart, from a minor Scottish gentry family – a background similar to his own) he returned to India to move smoothly though a series of command and staff appointments as well as command of a major punitive expedition against the Mohmand tribe on the perpetually unquiet NorthWest Frontier (which for generations had served as a training center, with live fire, for the Indian Army). By 1938 he was Deputy Chief of the General Staff at Army headquarters in Delhi and clearly tabbed to go still higher. The Indian Army was at that point already in the throes of a major personnel change and about to confront an even more complex challenge – modernization. The personnel change was "Indianization", awarding King's Commissions to Indians thus giving them equal status with British officers. This fundamental change had been forecast in 1917 – the military counterpart to the declaration by the Secretary of State for India, Edwin Montagu, that

3 William Slim, *Unofficial History* (New York, 1962), p. 42.

Dominion status (i.e., self-government) was the political goal of British policy in India. The elite Indian Civil Service already had Indian members (not too many, however). Implementing Indianization in the Army was a slow and halting process. There was outright opposition on the ground that Indian officers could not show the leadership qualities British officers did. There was also concerns about British officers (and British rank and file serving in India) coming under Indian command. Those concerns, some clearly racial, however were overborne by the clear political necessity for the commissioning of Indians to march in step with political change. An unsatisfactory compromise was therefore reached. Eight units were chosen to be "Indianized," and once Indian commissioned officers were posted to them, no more British officers would be. Thus, their officers would slowly become completely Indian from the bottom up and no British officer would have to serve under an Indian. There were many problems with this scheme – not the least being its racism – not inaptly described as the creation of "Jim Crow regiments". But, once begun, change was inexorable, and, after an experiment with sending Indian cadets to Sandhurst in the 1920s an Indian military academy was opened in 1932 at Dehra Dun in the Himalayan foothills. Auchinleck disliked the "eight units" scheme and felt British and Indian officers should meet socially as well as serve together professionally. But he did not have the power to turn his view into policy – yet.[4]

The second great issue facing the Indian Army was modernization. In 1938 all cavalry regiments were still horsed; transport was still a matter of mules and camels. The few tanks in India were light tanks belonged to British units. Modern aircraft – and anti-aircraft defence – were nowhere to be seen. As yet, India's role in any future war was uncertain but that it would be involved in the war that loomed in Europe was certain, given the Indian Army's longtime role as an imperial strategic reserve. In 1938, the Commander-in-Chief, General Sir Robert Cassels (with whom Auchinleck's relationship went back to the Mesopotamian campaign) appointed a Modernization Committee under Auchinleck's chairmanship. The committee recommended a reorganization and reequipping of the Army to ready it for overseas deployment, a recommendation Cassels accepted in toto. Then the Modernization Committee's work was overtaken by the high-powered Chatfield Committee dispatched from London under the chairmanship of Admiral Lord Chatfield to assess the Indian Army's requirements for modernization. Auchinleck became the Indian Army member of Chatfield's committee, which reported in January 1939. Its recommendations were obvious and paralleled those of the Modernization Committee. The problem lay in the areas of finance and production. The Government of India which already spent more than a third of its revenue on the Army could not afford more; the British government would have to pay (no one yet had an inkling how much that would ultimately turn out to be). Even if funds were made available however India could not produce tanks, trucks, field guns or any of the huge panoply of equipment a modern army required. That, too, would have to come from

4 Pradeep Barua, *Gentlemen of the Raj: The Indian Army Officer Corps 1817-1949* (Wesport, CT, 2003) is the best guide to the tangled history of Indianization.

Britain at a time when the demands of the British services were sharply accelerating. Throughout the war the Indian Army, compared to the allied forces that fought in the Mediterranean and Western Europe, was an equipment poor force (Slim's splendid XIV Army mastered imaginative improvisation as a result).

Auchinleck's term as Deputy Chief of the General Staff ended with his time on the Chatfield Committee. He then took up his next command, 3rd Indian Division. His first task was training his division for modern, mobile warfare without any of that equipment necessary for that type of warfare. "A great part of the division's training, therefore, was bound to consist of imagination and improvisation." [5]- a situation in which the Indian Army units were to find themselves frequently in the years ahead. Auchinleck was only to labor for a few months at making bricks without straw however before he was summoned to Delhi to be told by Cassels that he was to return to Britain to assume command of a corps.

## Auchinleck's War – England and Norway 1940

Auchinleck had been called back to Britain to command a new corps, IV Corps, scheduled to move to France to join the British Expeditionary Force in 1940. He landed in a country not quite sure, despite blackout regulations, that it was actually at war. Neville Chamberlain had not wanted to go to war and neither he nor his cabinet were (despite the presence of Churchill, recalled to office when war was declared) really suited temperamentally to waging one. Auchinleck, who the Chief of the Imperial General Staff, General Sir Edmund Ironside, had brought home to raise and command the new corps, considering him "the best India had," filled his diary during the months of what Churchill aptly christened the "Twilight War" with complaints about the fecklessness of Chamberlain's cabinet on military matters.[6] Auchinleck had only gotten the process of forming his headquarters and shaping up his new corps started when his career took an abrupt swerve. On April 9 the Germans invaded Norway. Chamberlain's cabinet had been, rather desultorily, discussing, since the previous autumn, action to block shipments of Swedish iron ore to Germany, actions which would lead to violations of Norway's neutrality since, when the Baltic froze, the ore went by rail to the ice-free Norwegian port of Narvik, thence by sea, within Norwegian territorial waters to the Baltic and thence to Germany. Churchill, again First Lord of the Admiralty and anxious (as no one else in the cabinet seemed to be) for offensive action against Germany had relentlessly argued for it. Finally, the cabinet agreed – but too late. Forestalled by the Germans, Chamberlain's government then rushed to support the Norwegians. But the resulting operation was shambolic, making the planning and

5 Connell, *Auchinleck*, p. 73.
6 Connell, p. 86, fn 1. Ironside added that Auchinleck "was not contaminated by too much Indian theory." He did not explain what he meant by this curious comment.

execution of the 1915 Gallipoli expedition look not so bad.[7] The situation was already beyond redemption when, late on the evening of 28 April, Auchinleck was summoned to the War Office and told he was to take command of the force which had been sent to retake Narvik, seized in an audacious surprise attack by the Germans at the beginning of their assault on Norway. With southern and central Norway already in their hands and German troops pushing steadily north, enjoying air superiority and able to reinforce at will, the Germans held all the cards. The allied force (British, French and Polish) that had been rushed to the area was stalled in the face of the stubborn defense mounted by tough, well-led German mountain troops, not to mention lack of anti-aircraft defense (among many other things) as well as a dysfunctional command structure. Auchinleck could remedy that but could do nothing about the complete lack of what he needed to conduct the operation London wanted. In a message on 17 May, by which time Churchill had become prime minster and the German offensive in the West had already shattered both the nerve of the French government and any hope for additional resources for the Narvik forces, Auchinleck received a signal telling him that further help would not be forthcoming but adding: "Northern Norway is not to be abandoned unless militarily inevitable…"[8] Auchinleck's response to this was clear and unequivocal, and would remain a constant whether addressing the Chiefs of Staff or the prime minster for the next three years: "…l will do my very best to do what is wanted, but I will not pretend to be able to do anything for which I think the means are inadequate."[9] Auchinleck took Narvik, demolished those port facilities not already destroyed by the fighting and oversaw a well-planned and conducted evacuation (like Gallipoli, the withdrawal was the smoothest part of the story). As he prepared to leave Norway he wrote a letter to the CIGS, General Sir John Dill one of his few close British Army friends, who had taken over from Ironside (pushed gently aside by Churchill) in which he analyzed the failures in Norway: "I feel we are much too slow and ponderous in every way…"[10] It was a perceptive comment, to be echoed by others about the British Army.[11] One other facet of Auchinleck's approach to command became apparent during the Narvik campaign: his willingness to remove officers not performing well in the field. He sacked the commander of the rearguard force south of Narvik trying to hold off the advancing Germans who he felt was not performing up to the demands of field command. The officer was a Guards lieutenant colonel. Auchinleck did not know the British Army well, but Mesopotamia and the frontier had taught hard lessons about leadership.

7 The best account of this doomed campaign is John Kiszely, *Anatomy of a Campaign: The British Fiasco in Norway, 1940* (Cambridge, 2017).
8 Connell, p. 121.
9 Ibid., p. 122.
10 Connell, p. 141.
11 General Sir David Fraser, looking back in his *And We Shall Shock Them: The British Army in the Second World War* (London, 1983) pronounced the army in the early stages of the war "over deliberate, slow, reactive." p. 53.

By early June he was back in Britain, where he wrote a very candid assessment of his time in Norway (which, when published in 1947, had been carefully bowdlerized and then was downplayed in the official history).[12] But Norway faded into the background. Auchinleck was rapidly given another command, V Corps whose three divisions covered southern and western England at a time when invasion was presumed imminent and no division in the British Army – at this point there were thirteen – was fully ready for it. The units saved from Dunkirk's beaches needed re-equipping (they had left about ten divisions worth of equipment behind). Those divisions that had not been through the furnace had never been fully equipped. Only the newly arrived 1st Canadian Division had its full complement of men and equipment, and it was newly raised and not yet fully trained. Auchinleck barely had a month at V Corps however before an upheaval in the army's high command moved him on.

When Churchill replaced Ironside with Dill in May he made "Tiny" Commander-in-Chief, Home Forces, responsible for Britain's land defenses against invasion. By mid-July it was clear to the prime minster that Ironside needed to be replaced by someone with more recent combat experience.[13] His choice was Lieutenant General Sir Alan Brooke who had commanded a corps in the BEF and then was named to command the "second BEF" being built up in France after Dunkirk, a doomed venture ended by the French decision to seek an armistice. Brooke got through another successful, if fraught, evacuation, this time from Brest and then took over Southern Command which would face any German invasion. When Churchill gently sacked Ironside for the second time, Brooke took over Home Forces and Auchinleck moved up to Southern Command. He handed V Corps over to Lieutenant General Bernard Montgomery who had commanded a division in Brooke's corps in the BEF and for whom Brooke would always act as a patron (and, often, a guardian angel). Thus, was forged one of the most fraught relationships of the war between senior British commanders.

Montgomery was a man of talent and drive but also of marked egocentricity (and personal eccentricity). One of his most marked characteristics was his disdain for control by superiors in rank who he did not regard as up to his standards – and none (except Brooke) ever seemed to be. Montgomery, when at Sandhurst, had aspired to the Indian Army but the criteria had changed from Auchinleck's time: instead of entry ranking it depended on graduation order. In Montgomery's time it was top thirty-five – he ranked thirty sixth. Thereafter he seems to have had a rather jaundiced view of the Indian Army. He now found himself reporting to an Indian Army superior and, as a member of his V Corps staff commented when Auchinleck left: "It is a great achievement for a man from the Indian Army to get Southern Command, as such plums are usually the preserve of the British Services." [14]

12 Auchinleck's *Despatch* was published in the official *London Gazette* on 10 July 1947. The offfical history is T.K. Derry *The Campaign in Norway* (London, 1952).

13 Once again Ironside was let down gently – a field marshal's baton and a peerage. Churchill had known Ironside before the war and seems to have liked him, despite his obsolescence.

14 Connell, p. 158.

Auchinleck at first seemed to regard Montgomery as a competent subordinate, if one with slightly amusing eccentricities. He recalled years later:

> Monty had 5th Corps...I used to go listen to his lectures...all very inspiring and made me feel a bit inadequate. But I doubt if runs before breakfast really produce battle winners...[15]

The relationship soon soured. Montgomery was no respecter of established channels if they frustrated his intentions. To get officers he wanted for V Corps he began to do end runs around Auchinleck, going directly to the War Office to "pinch" officers from other formations, a tactic which, predictably, led to blowback. Auchinleck's letters to Montgomery moved from "My dear Monty," to the frostier "My dear Montgomery" and an order to stop freelancing. Before things could go further, Montgomery escaped from Auchinleck who was told in early November that he was to return to India, to succeed Sir Robert Cassels as Commander-in-Chief. Since Cassels was an Indian Army officer, he would customarily be followed in office by a British Army officer. But India's position in Britain's war effort had changed dramatically in May-June 1940 and the person Ironside had called "the best India had" was clearly the obvious choice. Shortly after Christmas 1940 Auchinleck left for the long (and in those days very uncomfortable) flight to India. In a real sense, he was going home.

## India and Iraq

The India to which Auchinleck returned, after less than a year's absence, was beginning, slowly, to change in response to the demands of total war – a change that would steadily accelerate eroding the Raj as it did. Two Indian divisions, 4th and 5th, had already gone to the Middle East (and a brigade to Singapore). Pre-war plans for a slow, controlled expansion had already been torn up by London's decision as France collapsed to order open-ended expansion of the Indian Army – as many formations as could be raised and as rapidly as possible. The 1940 expansion program, underway when Auchinleck returned, called for five divisions (a sixth was subsequently added) plus an armored division. At that point there was not a single modern armored fighting vehicle in the subcontinent, only eight modern anti-aircraft guns, and the air power available (RAF and the fledging Indian Air Force) was a collection of museum pieces. India's industrial base, small but growing, was being geared up for war. The Eastern Group Supply Council, based in

15 Connell, p. 162. It is interesting that Lieutenant General Sir Francis Tuker, a brilliant Indian Army divisional commander, writing in Oct. 1958 offered a similar view: "If Monty, instead of making his officers run 7 miles a day, had made them turn out and train themselves on the ground, and teach themselves and their man a little battle skill, they would have got the same physical exercise and learnt to use their brains." Quoted in Raymond Callahan, *Churchill and His Generals* (Lawrence, KS, 2007), p. 143.

Delhi, had been formed to relieve pressure on both British industry and shipping by producing as much war material as possible "locally", i.e., in British dominions and colonies east of Suez. India, which on the eve of war was spending nearly sixty percent of its government revenue on defense could not fund the massive expansion of its army and its overseas deployment so Britain would have to do so. This marked the beginning of the problem of India's "sterling balances," giant IOUs held in London for postwar payment, that, by 1944, would deeply concern Churchill. Finally, the frantically expanding army needed officers, and an expanded recruitment base, since there was a limit to the men available from the traditional "martial races." Auchinleck was not involved in the Raj's finances, but he was deeply concerned with expanding the army's officer corps, equipping the ever-multiplying units, and widening recruitment.

Auchinleck told the Secretary of State for India, Leo Amery, in a long letter on 17 March 1940, that "Equipment and officers are the two bottlenecks and likely to remain as such…" adding "I do not think one can keep troops in an unequipped state indefinitely."[16] Just how underequipped new Indian units were is shown by a glance at the 1st Sikh Light Infantry, formed in January 1941. The unit's transport was made up of the Adjutant's car and a mix of bicycles, camels and requisitioned civilian buses. Air rifles had to be acquired from the local bazaar for marksmanship training, while for maneuvers the battalion was "armed" with the bamboo poles normally used to support mosquito netting. When Slim began training his first brigade command, intended to serve as a motorized infantry brigade in the Middle East, he not only had no vehicles but none of the sepoys knew how to drive, and carts drawn by draft animals had to stand in as trucks. By September 1941 the equipment received for the divisions of the 1940 expansion programs amounted to about a third of the needed field artillery, a quarter of the anti-tank guns and four percent of the anti-tank rifles.

Officers were also a massive problem. The pre-war regulars, with their language skills and knowledge of the customs and traditions of their men simply could not be replicated quickly. Some British personnel could be found and commissioned in India and some cadet officers sent out from Britain but neither sources would be adequate to fill the commissioned ranks of the burgeoning Indian Army. The only solution was more Indian officers. Here Auchinleck was decisive. He ended the ghettoization inherent in the "eight units" scheme. Indian officers became eligible to be posted to any unit. "Of one thing I am quite sure – we can no longer afford to differentiate between Englishman and Indians in the matter of pay, etc. when both are doing the same job side by side," he told Amery.[17] There was a world of change contained in that "etc." What he was insisting on was "equal treatment regardless of colour."[18] Claude Auchinleck, with the pressure of war at his back, finally made a success of Indianization. In 1939 there were

16 Connell, p. 188.
17 Connell, p. 189.
18 Quoted in Daniel Marston, *Phoenix from the Ashes: The Indian Army in the Burma Campaign* (Westport, CT, 2003), p. 48.

577 Indian officers; in 1945 there were over 15,000. Auchinleck also presided over the burial of the "martial races" paradigm in recruiting, telling Amery "we must broaden our basis...This I hope to do by reviving old units such as the Madras Regiment and raising new regular...units to represent...Bengal, Assam and Bihar".[19] Auchinleck's first stint as Commander-in-Chief was short but long enough to launch fundamental change in the army he had served in for nearly four decades – change that would be foundational to that Army's success over the next four years. It would also change in a fundamental way the machinery of the Raj – a milepost on the road to 1947.

After barely six months in India, Churchill moved Auchinleck to Cairo to become Commander-in-Chief, Middle East in place of General Sir Archibald Wavell, who would move to Delhi to take over command in India. Behind this switch lay the increasing centrality of the Middle East in British strategy for the prosecution of the war. Since the Mediterranean and Middle East would become the most important area of British and imperial military effort in the European theater 1941-1944, it is easy to forget that, prewar, it was assumed that it would be a matter of secondary concern. British and French staff planners assumed that, as in World War I, a Western Front would be their focus. Together the two empires dominated the southern and eastern Mediterranean littoral, and the landscape from Morocco to Syria while their navies easily outweighed that of Italy. Then, in a twinkling of an eye, everything changed. The collapse of France and Italian entry into the war in May-June 1940 was a huge strategic revolution. French North Africa and the Levant suddenly were not terribly friendly neutrals. The large modern French navy had become a potential menace, should its weight be ranged with the Axis. Anti-British nationalists in Egypt and the Arab world suddenly were energized by the heady prospect of a British collapse while the British Commander-in-Chief in Cairo faced the need to sustain British power with resources for which "inadequate" is much too weak a word. A huge question was suddenly before Churchill's war cabinet: could the British position in the Middle East be sustained? There was a suggestion that the answer was "no", quickly squashed by Churchill (seconded by the pugnacious Admiral Andrew Brown Cunningham, the Mediterranean Fleet Commander, who felt abandoning the area, on the heels of defeat in France, would produce a "landslide" in territory and prestige). And so, the die was cast. That decision – seldom discussed – shaped not only Britain's war effort (and much of the eventual Anglo-American alliance's) for the next three years but India's as well. The assumption that India would provide the bulk of the troops needed to maintain the British position not only drove the breakneck expansion of the Indian Army but focused its training almost exclusively on the needs of a theater where mechanization was crucial (with serious consequences 18 months later when Indian units, trained for the wrong war, faced the formidable

19 Connell, p. 189. Auchinleck's own regiment 1/1 Punjab, although recruited in his time from the martial races, had its historical roots in the 2nd Madras Infantry of the East India Company's Coast or Madras Army.

Imperial Japanese Army in Malaya and Burma).[20] It also made Iraq a central concern for Delhi, and it was Iraq that would become the issue that would lead to Auchinleck's move in June 1941 from Delhi to Cairo and a fraught fourteen months as commander-in-chief of not only what had become Britain's major theater but of the one with which Churchill was most deeply entangled.

Iraq was the scene of the Indian Army's major World War I campaign, a campaign in which Auchinleck served and first attracted the notice of his superiors. Postwar, although Iraq was turned into a client state under a British selected monarch rather than the Indian province Delhi had hoped for, the Indian Army provided most of the garrison there and dealt with the 1920-21 revolt against continuing British control. Even after Iraq became first, an Arab kingdom under a British mandate and then an independent state (albeit with permanent British airbases), India continued to regard it as a strategic interest. There were two reasons for this: Iraq was a vital staging post on the imperial air route to India and beyond, and the oil shipping terminals at the head of the Persian Gulf remained, as they had been in 1914, vital to Britain. In addition, a pipeline from the oil fields of northern Iraq, linked them to Haifa in British Palestine. Opened in 1935 it was crucial to British operations in the Mediterranean and Middle East. As Arab nationalism grew stronger in the 1930s, strengthened both by British policy in Palestine and German and Italian propaganda and funding, a reliably friendly Iraq seemed less likely, and India began to consider a possible future intervention there. By the time Auchinleck became commander-in-chief, there was a draft plan for that contingency – christened "Sabine" – in existence. As Spring 1941 advanced Auchinleck's concerns about Iraq deepened. The government of the pro-British Regent (the King was a minor) was under mounting pressure from the Iraqi army whose officers, although British trained and equipped, were increasingly anti-British and pro-Axis (since, at that point, the Axis looked very likely to win the war). In mid-March Auchinleck writing about the mounting crisis in Iraq to Wavell, under whose command Iraq fell, noted that "…with events moving at the pace they are, the notice we should get may be very short." Auchinleck at that point had a plan to intervene in Iraq and had named a force commander, Major General Edward Quinan, adding "I propose to give him Slim as his BGS and I think the combination should be a good one."[21]

20 Australia, New Zealand and South Africa later contributed troops to the Mediterranean theatre but in 1940 they had only begun to expand their armies from exiguous pre-war establishments. And, unlike the Indian Army, freely disposable by Whitehall, the Dominions were independent actors quite capable of negotiating over the use of their troops, a power Australia in particulalr was quite prone to use. The Indian Army came with no strings attached.

21 Letter, Auchinleck to Wavell, 13 March 1941, Timothy Bowman (ed.), *The Military Papers of Field Marshal Sir Claude Auchinleck, Vol. I: 1940–42* (Woodbridge, UK, 2021), p. 113. Slim, who had been wounded commanding his brigade in Ethiopia, had been working at Army Headquarters on contingency plans for intervention in Iraq. (BGS: Brigadier General Staff)

Auchinleck pressed constantly for more vigorous action in Iraq, action that would be under India's control, since the troops would have to come from India. Wavell, dealing with commitments in Greece and the Western Desert where the Germans had arrived to prop up the Italians, quickly erasing British gains there and besieging an Australian division in the Libyan port city of Tobruk, wanted no part of intervention in Iraq. While not offering to relinquish control to India, he argued for negotiation and compromise, telling London to Churchill's mounting exasperation, he simply had nothing to spare for yet another campaign.[22] In the end, events forced the adaption of Auchinleck's policy. Encouraged by apparent British hesitancy and a promise of German support, the Iraqi army moved against the sprawling RAF base at Habbaniya, west of Baghdad. A training facility rather than an operational base, it was "defended" by an assortment of obsolescent aircraft and by the locally raised, British officered and lightly armed Assyrian Levies – as well as miles of chain link fencing. It must have seemed the softest of targets to the Iraqi division that moved against it. Instead, an improvised defense – and the ineptitude of the Iraqi commander – led to the base holding out in one of war's fascinating minor episodes. Churchill, overruling Wavell's hesitations, ordered him to get a relief column from Palestine moving across the desert to Habbaniya – and then Baghdad – or resign. Auchinleck activated India Command's plan: half a battalion of British infantry was airlifted from Karachi, via two refueling stops in the Persian Gulf, to Shaiba near Basra, the other RAF base that had been retained under the Anglo-Iraqi treaty that ended the British Mandate. Mounting this airlift involved borrowing civilian airliners from Imperial Airways to supplement the obsolete bombers used as transports in India. Meanwhile, the lead brigade of the 10th Indian Infantry Division, already embarked at Karachi for Malaya, was redirected to Basra. No Iraqi opposition was encountered to either move and the Iraqi revolt quickly collapsed. It was the beginning of what would become a British military occupation of Iraq, Syria and Iran, carried out largely by the Indian Army, that lasted to the war's end.[23]

Auchinleck's promptitude in responding to the Iraq crisis had a decisive impact on his own career. It decided Churchill on the future of Middle East Command, The prime minster had never warmed to the taciturn Wavell, comparing him (according to which version of the anecdote one accepts) to the chairman of either a suburban golf club or a local Tory constituency association. His reservations deepened in the Spring of 1941 as defeat after defeat hammered British forces in the theater: Rommel's first offensive swept away most of the gains of "Compass", the 1940-41 winter offensive against the Italians. Then came the withdrawal from Greece, the loss of Crete, the Iraqi crisis and

22 According to Auchinleck's official biographer, Wavell was being urged to this course by the Arabists in various Cairo bureaucracies who feared widespread unrest in the Arab world if Britain took forceful action in Iraq.

23 There are good recent accounts of this largely now forgotten episode in Ashley Jackson's *Persian Gulf Command: A History of the Second World War in Iran and Iraq* (London, 2018) and Robert Lyman's *First Victory: Britain's Forgotten Struggle in the Middle East, 1941* (London, 2006).

the growing need to move against Vichy Syria (whose airfields had been made available to the Germans during the Iraq episode) – another task Wavell was reluctant to undertake. Then there was the Western Desert where an offensive to push back Rommel and relieve the besieged Australian division in Tobruk was a high priority for Churchill. The Middle Eastern theater had become increasingly vital to the prime minster. It was the only theater where British troops confronted Germans; the only theater where British victories could both raise morale on the home front and British credibility with their vital American ally (and FDR had already expressed some skepticism about the depth of British commitment there). Wavell, on the other hand, was obviously tired. He had done a remarkably deft job of juggling his multiple campaigns and the paucity of his resources was scarcely his fault. But there was a fundamental incompatibility between the temperaments of the prime minster and the general. Wavell would later say that Churchill never liked him, but it is also true that Wavell had never been hesitant about making clear how annoying he could find the prime minster. In 1940, when the Italians invaded Britain's indefensible Horn of Africa colony, British Somaliland, the heavily outnumbered garrison of mostly Indian and African troops conducted a credible withdrawal to the port of Berbera and a successful evacuation. Looking at the light casualities, Churchill queried whether the troops had fought hard enough. Wavell's response was both decisive and deeply wounding: "a big butcher's bill is not necessarily evidence of good tactics."[24] Sir John Dill, then CIGS, later said he had never seen Churchill so angry. The relationship between the prime minster and his Middle East commander lurched steadily downhill thereafter. By the time of the Iraq crisis Wavell was on borrowed time. Dill warned Auchinleck on 21 May that Churchill had lost confidence in Wavell "if he ever had any."[25] Then came the ragged launch of his attack on Vichy Syria – another improvised campaign Wavell had been pushed into. Much more significant was the failure of "Battleaxe", the first British offensive against Rommel. Launched on 15 June, it had failed by the 17th. On the 21st Churchill relived Wavell and appointed Auchinleck Middle East commander. It was his birthday, and the day Hitler invaded Russia. Wavell, denied a request for home leave, left for Delhi to replace Auchinleck.

In long retrospect there are some curious aspects to the command change of June 1941. Churchill did not actually know Auchinleck. He is mentioned, once in passing, in *The Gathering Storm* and not at all in *Their Finest Hour*, even though he commanded the defenses of that part of the coast deemed most threatened throughout the memorable Summer of 1940. There is no record that he ever met the prime minster. But, on 15 June 1940, the prime minster sent a note to Anthony Eden, the Secretary of State for War, that is very interesting in light of what was to happen a year later: "I hope before any fresh appointment is given to General Auchinleck, the whole story of the slack and feeble manner in which operations at Narvik were conducted, and the failure to make an earlier assault on Narvik town, will be considered. Let me know the dates when

24 Raymond Callahan, *Churchill and His Generals* (Lawrence, KS, 2007), p. 32.
25 Connell, p. 237.

General Auchinleck was in effective command."[26] Clearly, before the Iraqi episode the only time Auchinleck had appeared on Churchill's radar, he had not made a favorable impression. And Churchill was not generally an admirer of the Indian Army.[27] It is more than doubtful if he paid much attention to what Auchinleck did during his six months as Commander-in-Chief, India. Moreover, even when he soared in Churchill's estimation for his handing of the Iraq crisis, Dill, who did know him, felt he was not the person the prime minster had decided he was. When Dill returned to the War Office on 19 May 1941 after a Downing Street meeting with the prime minster, he told his closest confidant, Major General Sir John Kennedy, the Director of Military Operations, that he had told Churchill that "for all his great qualities and his outstanding record on the Frontier, he was not the coming man of the war, as the Prime Minster thought".[28] Churchill, increasingly desperate for a victory (over Germans) and disenchanted with Wavell, seized upon the only general who had shown aggressive drive (did he even remember his minute to Eden?). Dill liked and respected Auchinleck but clearly didn't think him the perfect fit for the most demanding post any British general could hold in mid-1941. It was not the firmest of foundations.

## The Desert

When Auchinleck arrived in Egypt, it was perhaps symbolically appropriate that there was no one to greet him at the airfield, so hurriedly had Churchill's decision been carried into effect and so effective was the secrecy surrounding it. It was symbolic in another way as well – Auchinleck, an Indian Army officer, was taking over a theater in which British Army officers predominated and as already noted, he had little experience with the British Army and certainly was not plugged in to those invisible networks that are so important to success (and sometimes survival) in any large, complex and long-lived institution.

Initially Auchinleck, who came to Cairo with only a secretary and two ADCs depended entirely on Wavell's staff. Lieutenant General Arthur Smith (a very establishment figure – Eton and the Guards – a world away from Wellington and the Punjab Regiment) stayed on as chief of staff, always a key appointment. But it was not only that Auchinleck was moving from Indian Army headquarters with its long-established

26 Kiszely, p. 273.

27 I have discussed Churchill's views (and prejudices) about the Indian Army in *Churchill and His Generals*, passim.

28 Bernard Fergusson (ed.), *The Business of War: The War Narrative of Major General Sir John Kennedy* (New York, 1958), p. 119. Dill never said who he thought the "coming man" was. At that point in the war, perhaps he had no one in mind. One of the great gaps in our knowledge about the making of British military policy and strategy in 1940-41 is represented by Dill. He died in 1944, leaving no grist for historians' mills. In the absence of any diary, letters or any other private papers there has never been a full study. Kennedy's record is the closest we are able to get to the thinking of the professional head of the British Army in 1940-41.

procedures and clear lines of command to Cairo where the command structure was much more complex due to the presence of Dominion units and new, improvised organizations (often of marginal value to the Command's main efforts).[29] And the already sprawling command was still growing. During Auchinleck's fourteen months in Cairo, while the focus of London (and subsequent historians) was on the Desert war against Rommel, the 8th Army, fighting that war, was far from the only Army for which Auchinleck was responsible. In November 1941 a Ninth Army commanded by Lieutenant General "Jumbo" Wilson was created, based on recently occupied Syria (whose Vichyite administrators were being as uncooperative as possible). It was responsible for preparing to meet a possible German drive through Anatolia into the Middle East. Then, in January 1942, another Army, the 10th, was fashioned out of the Indian forces that were occupying both Iraq and, since August 1941, Persia (as it was then still called). Together these two armies constituted the "Northern Front" called into existence by the German invasion of Russia. Throughout Auchinleck's tenure Germany was on the offensive in Russia and in 1941-42 it still looked like they might well succeed in driving Russia out of the war. Then the British position in the Middle East might well be challenged by the Wehrmacht driving through Turkey or the Caucasus – or both. We know that it did not happen, but Auchinleck had always to consider that it very well might. Britain was committed to support Turkey and a supply route to Russia was being planned to carry supplies from Basra by rail north to Russia (a route later christened the "Persian Corridor"). And there was still oil and the air link to India to defend. If the worst happened, neither Jumbo Wilson's Ninth Army nor Edward Quinan's Tenth were really trained and equipped as yet to meet the challenge. Slim, who became commander of the 10th Indian Infantry Division shortly after it landed at Basra, and led it through the Iraq and Syrian campaigns, as well as the nearly bloodless occupation of Persia, later wrote that, if the panzers came over the horizon, his division would have been a "soft-skinned orange flung in front of a steamroller" – and Slim's division was, in terms of leadership, experience and training, one of the 10th Army's best.[30] When Auchinleck left Cairo in August 1942, Stalingrad lay months in the future and German armies were deep in the Caucasus. Later accounts focused on how he handled 8th Army but at the time Auchinleck could never forget the two underequipped armies on his Northern Front. He had to keep looking over his shoulder.

29 The best picture of wartime Cairo is Artemis Cooper's very readable *Cairo in the War 1939-1945* (London, 2013). A good example of the improvised organizations that grew so lavishly in Cairo's hothouse atmosphere is the original SAS, beloved of pop historians and creators of TV series, but quite marginal to Middle East Command tasks.

30 W.J. Slim, *Defeat into Victory* (London, 1956), p. 3. A young Indian Army officer, John Masters, serving in a Gurkha battalion in Slim's division, later noted, caustically, that the British government had, under the treaty that ended the Mandate, been supplying the Iraqi Army with modern equipment unavailable in India. That situation changed all too slowly, as the Indian Army grew very rapidly. John Masters, *The Road Past Mandalay* (paper ed., New York, 1963), p. 17.

Finally, there was the sort of campaign he was taking over. The Desert War had begun when Italy entered the war in June 1940 and British armored cars began harassing the Italian forces on the frontier between Egypt (nominally independent and officially neutral) and the Italian colony of Libya. Then, in December 1940, after the reluctant Italian generals, prodded by Mussolini, had advanced, in overwhelming strength, into Egypt, and, after sixty miles, stopped, dug themselves into a series of entrenched camps stretching from the Mediterranean south into the desert – and waited. In December 1940 Wavell launched what was intended as a limited offensive by the newly constituted "Western Desert Force" under Lieutenant General Richard O'Connor, comprising two divisions, 7th Armored and, initially, 4th Indian, replaced later by the 6th Australian. When the limited attack became an all-out offensive Italian resistance collapsed. In ten astounding weeks O'Connor, operating on a logistic shoestring, destroyed ten Italian divisions, taking 130,000 prisoners and making the British masters of Cyrenaica (eastern Libya) while incurring less than 1000 fatal casualties. A defeat that sweeping, it was feared in Berlin, threatened the stability of Mussolini's regime and so the Germans rode to the rescue, sending a "blocking force", soon to be famous as the Afrika Korps, under an unknown divisional commander, Ewin Rommel, the future "Desert Fox". Quickly showing both his tactical aggressiveness and willingness to gamble, Rommel attacked before his forces were completely assembled – and well before his supervisors in Berlin thought prudent – sweeping the British forces in Cyrenaica (new to the desert and clumsily commanded) back into Egypt and penning an Australian division into a small port town of Tobruk. The subsequent effort to relieve Tobruk was the proximate cause of Auchinleck's arrival in Cairo. Mounted by the newly created 13th Corps (into which the Western Desert Force had morphed) it failed within two days. Churchill in great need of a victory after 1941's dark Spring, as related, removed Wavell. But the problem remained – twice in the four months since his arrival Rommel had handily beaten British forces that outnumbered him. Could the problem be with how the British fought? That would be the great question facing Auchinleck for the next fourteen months.

The first point to understand about Auchinleck's army in the Western Desert is that it was a coalition, not a homogenous force. There were three Australian divisions, whose government had a prickly sense of independence, and New Zealand's sole division. While the New Zealand government was less obstreperous than Australia's, the New Zealand commander, Lieutenant General Bernard Freyberg, V.C., was a force to be reckoned with. Not only was he a figure of legendary courage, personally known to, and liked by, Churchill (who had helped him to his commission in 1914) but he also represented the New Zealand government in Cairo. Then there were the South Africans. Jan Christian Smuts, the South African prime minster, a Boer War guerilla leader who had become a pillar of empire, had brought his country into the war at the cost of a major political crisis that left white South Africa deeply divided. Smuts was a very close personal friend of Churchill who placed a very high value on his opinion. If the Australians had to be handled carefully because of Canberra's concerns (going back to Gallipoli in 1915) about British commanders, the very casualty sensitive South Africans were another component of the Desert Army quite capable of exerting a latitude not generally accorded divisional commanders. Major General Dan Pienaar (a policeman pre-war) of the 1st South African division simply ignored orders he disliked. Only the British and Indian Divisions were unreservedly at Auchinleck's disposal. Then there was the question of exactly how this imperial coalition was to manage itself on the battlefield.[31]

That battlefield put a premium on armored mobility. The Dominion and Indian divisions were all infantry formations, albeit given (unarmored) mobility by trucks. The armor was all British and the British Army had entered the war with an unresolved argument about the use of the tank: whether it worked best in combination with infantry and artillery in a "combined arms" approach (as had happened at Amiens in 1918 and as the Germans consistently operated) or as an "independent" force, as the interwar "apostles of mobility" like J.F.C Fuller and B.H. Liddell Hart had urged? This unresolved argument had led to two different types of tank design: infantry tanks – slow, well-armored – and "cruiser" tanks – faster, with less armor, intended for independent maneuver warfare. By 1941 both types were under gunned, and the cruisers were under armored as opposed to the German tanks they faced. Both types were also prone to mechanical breakdowns (the first American tanks to reach the Desert were both under gunned and lightly armored but prized for the reliability of their engines). Finally, British armored units were handicapped by a fundamental misunderstanding of German tactics. The panzers travelled with a screen of anti-tank guns, the best known being the famous "88". When British armor attacked, the Germans drew it onto the accompanying posse of tank killers; Rommel's tanks were not as deadly to British armor as those anti-tank guns.

When Auchinleck took over in Cairo therefore he was not only confronting the dual responsibility of defeating Rommel (with an anxious prime minster urging him on) while keeping a wary eye on the Northern Front and doing so in a setting dominated by a service with which he was unfamiliar (and problems of coalition war he could not remedy) but the army with which he was supposed to defeat Rommel suffered from problems ranging from tank design to flawed tactical doctrine that could not remedied easily – and certainly not quickly.

He received two letters of advice as he settled in. One from Dill, the other was from Lieutenant General Sir Hastings Ismay, Churchill's personal chief of staff – and the only Indian officer operating at the heart of British decision making in Whitehall. Dill's letter was rather depressed, telling Auchinleck that he could expect pressure from London, wondering out loud whether some of his own decisions had been correct and finally telling Auchinleck that he could resign if he felt an unwise "course of action" was being forced upon him, Reading this now it becomes easy to see why Churchill, about this time, began to convert dissatisfaction with Dill to a search for a successor, a process that would make the infinitely more formidable Alan Brooke CIGS by the year's end.

31 All the Dominion armies were trained on the same lines as the British Army but, while this facilitated interoperability, it did not alter the fact that they were armies of independent nations drawn from societies that had become different from Britain in very important ways, or, in the case of South Afrikaners, had never been in the least like it.

Ismay, who had known Auchinleck since, as Majors, they had adjacent offices at Indian Army headquarters in 1923, urged him to send the prime minster "long and private" letters, outside normal official channels to cultivate a relationship that could help smooth over the inevitable differences that would arise between London and Cairo. It was very good advice, and very much in keeping with Ismay's own modus operandi, but there was a problem that no amount of personal rapport could easily surmount: there were a range of pressing issues whose solution needed a British victory over Rommel – a victory the army Auchinleck took over in June 1941 was not yet in a position to deliver.

London expected the new broom in Cairo to develop an offensive plan that would quickly sweep Rommel back and relieve the besieged Australians in Tobruk. Auchinleck felt that the need for training and preparation meant that no major attack could be mounted until the autumn. That was argued over the first few months of Auchinleck's tenure. Eventually Auchinleck made a very quick visit to London where, at a heated meeting of the War Cabinet's Defence Committee, he carried the day. Churchill reluctantly accepted the delay, remarking that even if Auchinleck was wrong, he was clearly the best man for the job in Cairo. Something else happened at that meeting that sign posted the prime minster's fundamental ambivalence about the army from which Auchinleck came (and which was at that point contributing more troops to the Middle East than either Britain or any of the Dominions). After the meeting, during a discussion of reinforcements for the Middle East, Auchinleck pointed out to Churchill that India had organized and trained personnel for an armored division but lacked most of the equipment for it, especially tanks. The prime minster responded "But, General, how do you know that they wouldn't turn and fire the wrong way?"[32] It was an astounding remark but redolent of the period when Churchill was a young man, when veterans of the 1857 Mutiny by many units of the East India Company's Bengal Army were still plentiful.

The battle for preparation time won, Auchinleck returned to Cairo to deal with the planning for operation Crusader, the British Army's first major offensive against the German Army. The Western Desert Force had grown into a two corps army and was therefore rechristened 8th Army. Finding a commander for it was one of Auchinleck's first tasks. The only British general, at that point, who had successfully commanded a major mobile operation was Lieutenant General Sir Richard O'Connor who had brilliantly led the Western Desert Force in 1940-41. Unfortunately, he had been taken prisoner in Rommel's first offensive in the Spring of 1941. Auchinleck's knowledge, after nearly 40 years in India, of the British Army was not extensive and his recent time in Britain had not remedied that – it had been quite brief. Moreover, he had moved so rapidly through so many commands (IV Corps, Norway, V Corps, Southern Command)

32 Connell, p. 274 fn. 1. Because it was a remark in coversations, it does not appear in any official documents, but Connell published it in 1959, and it has never been denied. Moreover, it tracks with so many other remarks Churchill made about India and its army that its credibility seems secure.

at a time when the British Army was in flux that he had not had an opportunity to really form careful judgements on the many officers whose paths crossed his. His choice therefore was really among lieutenant generals already in the Middle East and only one of them had conducted a successful campaign – Lieutenant General Alan Cunningham, who had led the recent campaign that destroyed Mussolini's East African Empire. That campaign had really been against distance and terrain – a feat of logistic improvisation – that encountered little significant resistance from the crumbling Italian colonial units or the increasingly demoralized Italian regular formations.[33] The Afika Korps would be a very different matter. Auchinleck made perhaps the best choice he could in the circumstances when he settled on Cunningham, but the event would prove it was a mistake. Perhaps it would not have been had chance not intervened. The corps (XXX) that would control the armor in Crusader was to have been commanded by Lieutenant General Vyvian Pope, an officer of the Royal Tank Regiment, the British Army's armor specialists, who had been the Director of Armored Fighting Vehicles at the War Office, as strong an appointment to command the armor as could be made. However, shortly after arriving in the Middle East he and key members of his staff were killed in a plane crash. A replacement was found by taking the commander of the 1st Armored Division, then en route to the Middle East, from his ship at Cape Town and flying him to Cairo. Major General Norrie Willoughby was a cavalryman ("born on a horse" was the dismissive appraisal of one staff officer in Cairo) who had no real experience with armor.

As a flawed command team was assembled Auchinleck was also dealing with one of the other peculiarities of his sprawling command: the semi-autonomous status of the Dominion units in this case, the Australians. The 9th Australian division had held Tobruk against Rommel since April and, in mid-Summer the Australian government wanted it relieved and reunited with the other two Australians divisions in the Middle East in an Australian commanded corps. The naval effort involved in this would be considerable and moreover the operation would have to be carried out during the moonless nights in September and October, just as preparation for Crusader were at their peak. Nonetheless the Australian Government remained adamant, a reflection both of the state of Australian politics and of Australian suspicions, born in 1915, that both the British government and British commanders were cavalier with Dominion, and especially Australian, lives. The relief was carried out successfully but not without leaving Auchinleck with the feeling that he really did not fully control the Dominion contingents, which, at that point, represented most of his fighting formations, a problem that would recur.[34]

33 There is a good account of this now forgotten campaign: Andrew Stewart, *The First Victory* (London, 2016).

34 The Dominion contingents (three Australian, one New Zealand and two South African) made up most of Auchinleck's infantry. There were two British infantry divisions – one however was garrisoning Cyprus. All the armor was British. In fact, the largest single contributor of forces to Middle East Command at that point was India.

"Crusader" began on 18 November to high hopes especially on Churchill's part. Eighth Army fielded more armor than its opponent. Cunningham's plan however was seriously flawed. XIII Corps – largely infantry – would advance on Tobruk, by passing the German-Italian defenses on the Egyptian-Libyan frontier. The other corps, Norrie's XXX Corps – containing the armor – would advance to a point in the desert, south of XIII Corps, and await Rommel's reaction, thus, of course, surrendering the initiative. Rommel dislocated the plan immediately by not reacting. Focused on his own impeding attack on Tobruk he at first did not realize that a major British offensive had been launched. With Rommel momentarily quiescent Norrie sent his three armored brigades forward on a three divergent axis of advance. Then Rommel woke up. There followed several days of confused armored engagements. Norrie's three brigades, once dispersed, never again reunited but fought three separate battles in which the experience and tactical skill of Rommel and his subordinate commanders resulted on a very rapidly diminishing stock of British tanks, while the sheer confusion generated by the complex, ever changing tactical situation caused the inexperienced Cunningham to lose both his control of his army and his confidence in its prospects. Thinking the attack should be broken off, he asked Auchinleck to fly up from Cairo to confer. On the evening of 23 November 1941, in Cunningham's command caravan Auchinleck listened to an obviously exhausted Cunningham describe 8th Army's tank losses and concern that the defense of Egypt, the Canal and the Middle East position as a whole might be endangered if 8th Army was destroyed. Perhaps breaking off the attack and retiring into Egypt was the prudent course – live to fight another day? Auchinleck quickly made one of the most important decisions of his career. He was from a service with no familiarity with armored warfare, but he sensed that if 8th Army had been so heavily battered, Rommel's army must have suffered badly as well. Ordering the offensive to continue he flew back to Cairo thinking about a new commander for 8th Army since it was clear that Cunningham no longer had the energy and resilience for the job. He needed a new broom – and quickly. Here his unfamiliarity with the British Army was again a handicap. There were lieutenant generals in Britain, but most were unknown to him. The 8th Army corps commanders were handling a confusing and precarious tactical situation. He wisely did nor want Jumbo Wilson. Almost by default he looked at his staff in Cairo and settled on his deputy chief of staff, a junior major general, Neil Ritchie. It was a fateful choice. Ritchie was, in fact, junior to both his corps commanders and although a very good staff officer had never commanded a large formation in combat. Perhaps that mattered less in Auchinleck's calculation since he planned to spend as much time as he could at 8th Army headquarters to monitor the situation. In the short term it worked. British leadership was suddenly much firmer, even if, at the tactical level, British armor was no more deftly handled. But the New Zealanders (who Rommel felt were the best soldiers he ever faced) battered their way toward Tobruk and the attrition imposed on Rommel's German formations eventually forced him to retire westward, cautiously followed by the 8th Army. By year's end 8th Army was back at the point where O'Connor's offensive had ended nearly a year before. Auchinleck had won the first British battlefield victory of the war over the German army but, in deciding to leave Ritchie in command of 8th Army, he inadvertently sowed the seeds of the problem that would upend his career as a theater commander. But in the aftermath of Crusader, he had plentiful issues to manage, so it was easier to assume that the issue of 8th Army leadership had been settled.[35]

As Auchinleck's intervention tipped the scales against Rommel, the larger war had changed dramatically with the entry of Japan, which made the United States a full-fledged belligerent. As Churchill saw, this guaranteed ultimate victory but for Auchinleck, it meant an immediate loss of resources. RAF units moved east; two of the three Australian divisions were immediately called home, while units enroute from Britain to the Middle East (like the 18th Division) were rerouted to meet the crisis in Malaya. Interestingly the very experienced 4th and 5th Indian divisions remained in the Middle East while India rushed half trained formations to Malaya and Burma, but India did not, of course, enjoy the latitude the Dominions had.

On the other side of the hill, the pressure on Rommel's supply lines relaxed as a series of losses in December sharply reduced the Royal Navy's ability to operate aggressively in the central Mediterranean, while Luftwaffe pressure on Malta increased. The result was that force reconstitution for the Afrika Korps could move quickly. On the British side the units that had carried Crusader to a successful conclusion were pulled back to rest and refit, being replaced by new, inexperienced formations. The scenario that facilitated Rommel's first success was thus recreated and he duly seized the opportunity offered, counter attacking in January 1942 and, once again, tumbling the British into a chaotic retreat that ended just west of Tobruk, a position that came to be known as the Gazala Line.[36] Then there set in again the dynamic that Auchinleck had had to deal with before Crusader: pressure from London, especially from the prime minister, to resume the offensive, pressure Auchinleck steadfastly resisted. As in Norway and before Crusader he did not want to attack until his forces were ready. This argument was carried out at long distance since Auchinleck, after his experience in August 1941, steadfastly resisted pressure to return to Britain for discussions. The core of the problem was that both the prime minister and his Middle East commander-in-chief had good arguments. Churchill, looking at a global war, saw a series of devastating defeats in Malaya and Burma and an impeding crisis in Indian politics, as well as openly expressed doubts by Britain's American ally about its Mediterranean commitments (as well as its handling of the Indian Congress Party's demands for self-government). He faced as well rising discontent in Parliament about the

35 The literature on the Desert War is voluminous. The best succinct account of Crusader is Michael Carver's *Tobruk* (London, 1964). Carver served on Norrie's XXX Corps staff in 1941-42. After information on the intelligence available to British commanders from Bletchley Park's breaking of the German Enigma codes became public, Carver updated his account: *Dilemmas of the Desert War* (London, 1986).

36 During the hasty withdrawal of 8th Army, the 7th Indian Brigade, commanded by Brigadier Harold Briggs, was cut off in Benghazi. Briggs' extrication of his brigade was a remarkable feat – a major step in a career that would end in Malaya a decade later when he organized the ultimately successful British counter-insurgency effort there. Compton Mackenzie's *Eastern Epic* (London, 1951), pp. 300-310 describes 7th Indian Brigade's epic escape in full.

management of Britain's war effort that culminated in a vote of no confidence in January 1942. He won that easily, but his margin disguised a continuing undercurrent of concern. When would the tide begin to turn? So much could be either solved or greatly alleviated by victory. Only Auchinleck could give him that victory.

Auchinleck, on the other hand, was very close to the realities of a war more complex than any British theatre commander would have to deal with subsequently. He had two widely separated fronts to deal with. The Northern Front was only potential and the German failure before Moscow in December 1941 had provided breathing space, but only that. The expectation was that, come Spring 1942, the German advance would resume. To face the consequences of German success in Russia, the two armies sprawled across Syria, Iraq and Persia were poorly equipped and, in Quinan's 10th Army, his Indian formations were not only not yet fully trained but not fully equipped either. It is difficult, but necessary, to now remember that what never happened seemed, at that moment, a very real possibility. Throughout his time in Cairo, Auchinleck could never forget his Northern Front. Then there were the problems of the coalition he commanded. He could give orders to his British and Indian units, but he could not be sure his Dominion commanders would not balk if they felt the risks to their troops were too great (both Leslie Morshead of the 9th Australian division and Dan Pienaar of the 1st South African would at points do so while Bernard Freyberg was always an ally, not a subordinate). There was a political dimension to dealing with Dominion formations that was simply inescapable. Then there were the problems with equipment: British tanks were still undergunned and British anti-tank guns not powerful enough while British signals equipment (vital to affective command and control) was also deficient in important ways. Churchill could itemize equipment sent to the Middle East; Auchinleck could respond with careful explanations of the problems with materials months in transit with accompanying deterioration, modifications necessary for desert warfare, and the training time for units confronted with unfamiliar equipment. The prime minister could (and wearyingly often did) cite total ration strength in the Middle East and query why the "teeth" arms were so badly outnumbered by the "tail" of supporting services. The commander-in-chief could only point to the need to build a modern supporting infrastructure for a modern, mechanized army based in an area where no such infrastructure previously existed and then to the need to sustain that army in a barren desert through months of sustained combat.

Finally, there was the problem of how Auchinleck's armies actually fought. It was becoming clear that "victory by tanks alone" was not a viable approach. At the beginning of "Crusader" the British 22nd Armored Brigade, made up of cavalry units recently transitioned to armor, launched what one observer called a cavalry charge in tanks whose "exciting courage…was only curbed by the rapidly decreasing stock of dashing officers and tanks."[37] Rommel's edge in the Desert War was partly his own leadership qualities and tactical flair but partly also the fact that the Germans had standardized

37 Robert Crisp, *The Brazen Chariots* (New York, paper ed., 1961), p. 31.

and well-rehearsed combined arms tactics while the British were still groping their way toward them. In particular, the German use of their anti-tank guns offensively was doing serious damage to British armor whose aggressiveness played directly into German strength. Auchinleck was handling a flawed instrument but there was no time to completely retrain 8th Army – the pressures of the war situation were too intense and only became more so as the plight of Malta became more pressing. In the Spring of 1942, the tiny island became the most bombed area on the planet. British sea and air power based on Malta could exert crucial pressure on Rommel's supply line. As Malta was pounded into near quiescence, Rommel's logistic situation became steadily healthier. The increasingly fraught exchanges between the prime minster and Auchinleck came to focus on the need for a British offensive that would drive Rommel far enough westward to allow the RAF to acquire and operate from airfields that would allow protection for a relief convoy to reach Malta which was on the verge of starvation. On 10 May 1942 – the second anniversary of his arrival at Downing Street – Churchill ordered Auchinleck to attack in time to facilitate coverage of a convoy to Malta during the moon dark period in June. Auchinleck accepted what amounted to an ultimatum and agreed to an attack on Rommel – who, however, had also been planning an offensive and on 27 May his German-Italian army rolled forward, led as usual by the Afrika Korps. Auchinleck and Ritchie had considered a straight frontal attack by Rommel on the Gazala line his most likely move – a curious misreading of how Rommel operated. But even if he swung around the open desert flank (which in fact he did) Ritchie's two armored divisions, (which together greatly outnumbered Rommel's tank strength) were thought well positioned to counter him, and the newly arrived American "Grant" tanks were more than a match for most of Rommel's armor.

Just as Rommel's January 1942 counterattack had, in many ways, replicated what he had done in March 1941, the decisive opening days of his offensive replayed the opening of Crusader. Then the British armor had been allowed to disperse its efforts and had never successfully reunited. In the opening days of the Gazala battle the speed and ferocity of Rommel's drive into the rear of 8th Army knocked its armored units off balance and, in the considered judgement of one well qualified observer, the 8th Army never regained that balance. There followed nearly three weeks of very confused fighting in which 8th Army, superior to Rommel in so many categories, but not in command structure, was defeated in detail. Lieutenant General Sir Francis Tuker of the 4th Indian later called it the worst managed battle in British military history, and, in long retrospect, it is hard not to agree. The 8th Army's commanders spent a great deal of time and effort conferring, a command by committee style that had its roots in the Western Desert Force of 1941. The result was that Rommel remained a jump ahead. Some of the British decisions were simply incoherent. Ritchie had two excellent, well commanded Indian Divisions, Francis Tuker's 4th and Harold Brigg's 5th, available. But they never fought as divisions (something the Dominion formations almost invariably did) but were scattered about by brigades and sometimes single battalions, often committed to "boxes" – stand alone defensive positions scattered about the battle area and usually quite easily overrun by the Germans. Auchinleck pointed this out to Ritchie to no avail. In the end, on 14 June,

Ritchie ordered the 8th Army to retire to the Egyptian frontier. But at that point the 8th Army was in serious disarray. Pienaar was directed to hold a section of the frontier defenses. He decided not to even try but continued to withdraw until he reached the defensive line taking shape at El Alamein. Lieutenant General W. H. Gott of XIII Corps ordered Major General "Pete" Rees, whose 10th Indian Division had arrived from Iraq to bolster 8th Army (and then lost units scattered in indefensible boxes) to hold a position on the frontier which Rees thought could not be held by his division without support. Gott, clearly rattled at this point, promptly sacked him for lack of determination, only to have to authorize his successor – only six hours later – to withdraw to save 10th Indian from being cut off.[38] As the 8th Army's withdrawal accelerated Rommel's attention turned to Tobruk. Churchill had wanted assurances that it would be held, which Auchinleck gave. He had never intended Tobruk to again stand a siege. He planned for 8th Army to hold positions on the Egyptian frontier and keep communications to Tobruk open. When it became clear that 8th Army's withdrawal would not stop on the Egyptian frontier, Auchinleck accepted that Tobruk might be "isolated" temporarily but that too was quickly shown to be a pipe dream. An 8th Army counter offensive would not happen quickly – indeed the most pressing question was whether the retreat could be halted rapidly enough to save Egypt – and then Suez Canal. Tobruk, as Auchinleck knew, was in no position to stand a siege. Its defenses had not been maintained; many of the defensive minefields had been dismantled to provide mines for the Gazala Line. Instead of Morshead's tough 9th Australian the garrison was made up of the new, inexperienced 2nd South African Division, understrength, and commanded by the newly promoted, inexperienced Major General H. B. Klopper who had an assortment of other units, including one of Tuker's 4th Indian Division's brigades, pushed into Tobruk by the course of the battle. At dawn on 20 June the Afrika Korps, Rommel riding with the vanguard, and following the design for the attack that he had planned to use when Crusader interrupted him, broke into Tobruk. By mid-afternoon Klopper had lost control of the battle. The next morning, he surrendered Tobruk with 33,000 men and mountains of stores. The 11th Indian Brigade fought stubbornly on until assured by one of Klopper's staff that Tobruk had actually surrendered hours before. Churchill (and Brooke) were in Washington, and actually at the White House, when the news reached them. FDR handed the prime minster a message containing the bitter details. It was clearly a moment of maximum disappointment and acute embarrassment for Churchill: "Defeat is one thing; disgrace is another," he would write bitterly in his memoirs, recounting that moment.[39]

38 Rees, who had succeeded Slim in command of 10th Indian would later command, very successfully, 19th Indian Division in Slim's XIV Army in Burma. After Gott sacked him, Auchinleck gave him the job of organizing the defences of the Nile Delta region in Egypt in case Rommel broke through the Alamein line. No one raised the issue of Pienaar's disregard of Gott's orders. The three Indian divisions (4th, 5th, 10th) lost, between them, four brigades mostly consumed in tryong to hold "boxes" dotted about the desert.

39 Winston Churchill, *The Second World War, Vol. IV, The Hinge of Fate* (Boston, 1950), pp. 382-383. The stand of the 18th Indian Brigade at Deir el Shein is described at length in P.C.

At the same time, however, there was taking place in the desert an event that would salvage the situation. Realizing that the battle had escaped Ritchie's control, Auchinleck flew up from Cairo and about 7 pm on 25 June took command of 8th Army. He told a staff officer accompanying him: "The British pride themselves on being good losers. I'm a damn bad loser. I'm going to win."[40]

The ensuing month saw Auchinleck do just that: he halted Rommel's headlong drive toward Cairo and Suez and laid the foundation for what Montgomery was able to do at the end of August – defeat Rommel's last offensive in the battle of Alam Halfa. At first it did not look like the change of command would make much difference. At Matruh, between the frontier and the Alamein position, Rommel again pulled off a remarkable tactical success: the Afrika Korps, with about sixty tanks and some 2500 bone weary infantry out maneuvered, and bluffed, two British corps (Gott's XIII and the X Corps, commanded by Lieutenant General W. G. Holmes, newly arrived) into precipitate retreat despite the fact that Gott's tank strength exceeded that of the Afrika Korps. Rommel bagged more than 6000 prisoners and additional mountains of stores. Indeed, at that point, Rommel was sustaining his offensive on captured trucks, fuel and rations.

The crucial moment came on 1 July. The last of the 8th Army had barely reached the Alamein position when the Afrika Korps attacked it. Rommel's few thousand exhausted German infantry and 55 tanks were heavily outnumbered by the defenders. His 90th Light was supposed to swing south of the Alamein box and cut the coast road east of it. However, the Alamein box was garrisoned by the 1st South African – Pienaar had found a position where he felt comfortable – whose massed artillery stopped the attack in its tracks. Even Rommel's personal intervention could not get 90th Light moving again. South of 90th Light, the Afrika Korps' two Panzer divisions (15th and 21st) with 55 tanks was aimed at a supposed gap in the British line which would allow it to swing into the rear of the British armor, concentrated in Gott's XIII Corps. With over 100 tanks, 40 of them powerful Grants, Gott outnumbered the Afrika Korps badly. However, the gap was not an open door. The 18th Indian Brigade was there – holding a shallow depression in the desert called Deir El Shein. Rushed up from the new 8th Indian Division in Iraq as part of the scramble to reinforce 8th Army, it had an acting commander, two of its three battalions were new to combat, and it was supported by a scratch force of gunners and nine infantry tanks whose crews had been hastily assembled from replacement depots. In a day long battle the brigade (Sikh, Gurkha and British battalions) and its supporting arms were destroyed but Rommel's panzer divisions were fought to a standstill. Rommel tried again on 2 and 3 July but to no avail. He had finally been brought to a halt. The most critical moment in the desert war had passed. Perhaps the most critical moment for the prime minster as well. He had won a vote of confidence

Bharucha, *The North African Campaign 1940-1943* (Calcutta, 1956), pp. 547-551. This is a volume in the Indian official history.

40 Quoted in Correlli Barnett, *The Desert Generals* (London, 1960), p. 184.

on 2 July 475-25 (twenty-seven members abstained however). Clearly, the concern was even more widespread than in January. One well informed MP wrote that if Rommel had not been stopped "Winston would have fallen".[41]

Clearly much would depend on how soon and how successfully the British could resume the offensive in the desert. Rommel had now been forced onto the defensive. His men were exhausted, his supplies as well, and his stock of trucks, even with the captured British vehicles available, was diminishing by about thirty a day as the RAF, operating from well-stocked bases close to 8th Army, pounded him round the clock. The opportunity to go over the attack was immediately grasped by Auchinleck. During July he launched four attacks on Rommel's now entrenched army. Much of Rommel's front was manned by Italian formations, as exhausted as the Afrika Korps and less resilient. His German units were kept busy propping up their allies. Auchinleck's attacks were however, despite the weakness of Rommel's army, failures. One of them destroyed an Italian division, but the other three were fiascos: two New Zealand brigades, as well as an Australian and a British brigade suffered heavy casualties. The New Zealand Division (operating under an acting commander, Freyberg having been wounded during the retreat to the Alamein line) decided that they simply could not depend on adequate support from the armored units, which were all British. Many years later the British official historians put their finger on the core of the problem: the failure to achieve an effective integration of different arms on the battlefield – lack of combined arms tactics.[42] Auchinleck had long realized this and was thinking about reorganizing British armored divisions to include an infantry brigade. But the overriding need at the end of July was a period of rest in which replacements and reinforcements could be absorbed and any reorganization and retraining could occur. On 31 July, Auchinleck told Churchill that it would be at least six weeks before 8th Army could resume the offensive. It was the beginning of the end for Auchinleck in the Middle East. Churchill felt that his fate was tied to Desert War. Moreover, he had recently won his long struggle to persuade the reluctant Americans to accept his preferred strategy – an amphibious assault on Vichy controlled Morocco and Algeria, christened "Torch," as the first Anglo-American offensive of the war. Success in the desert war would consolidate that success in shaping alliance strategy. Since Churchill knew that Stalin had reason to believe he had been promised a Second Front in Western Europe in 1942 he decided to break the news of Torch to Moscow personally and, en route, to confer with Auchinleck in Cairo about renewing the attack on Rommel. For Britain's only active field army to pause any offensive operations until September as the Russians retreated before the German summer offensive while the Anglo-American Torch landings could not happen until late autumn, was not acceptable to him. Churchill needed a victory over Rommel. Brendan Bracken, one of his closest associates, told the prime minster's doctor, at about this time, "the Prime

41 Quoted in Paul Addison, *The Road to 1945* (London, 1975), p. 208.
42 Major General I.S.O. Playfair, *The Mediterranean and Middle East* Vol. III (London, HMSO, 1960), p. 352.

A group of British officers, including Brigadier Auchinleck (on the right) during the Mohmand Expedition, 1935. Auchinleck commanded the Peshawar Brigade. (National Army Museum 1960-06-123-1-92)

General Auchinleck decorating Subadar Major Ahmed Khan, 4th Battalion, 7th Rajput Regiment with the Order of British India, 1st Class on 22 December 1944. (National Army Museum 1951-05-54-238)

Auchinleck as Commander-in-Chief India. (National Army Museum 1976—03-94-89)

General Auchinleck addressing troops during a tour of India whilst Commander-in-Chief India, c. 1944. (National Army Museum 1957-10-9-1-83)

Field Marshal Auchinleck inspecting members of the Women's Army Corps (India), c.1946. (National Army Museum 1969-10-591-169)

Field Marshal Sir Claude Auchinleck in full dress, c. 1947. (National Army Museum 1966-02-106-4)

**S. I. A. O.** 632 **August 1947**

**SPECIAL INDIA ARMY ORDER**

**INSTRUCTIONS, ETC.**

**S. I. A. O. 79|S|47. Discontinuance of India Army Orders.—**

This is the last India Army Order.

No. 7040|49|AG (Co-ord 2).

R. A. SAVORY, *Lieut.-General,*
*Adjutant General in India.*

Auchinleck
F.M.

RASavory
Lt. Gen.

**L81IAO—00,000—14-8-47—GIPS**

The last Special India Army Order signed by Field Marshal Sir Claude Auchinleck and Lieutenant General Sir Reginald Savory. (National Army Museum 1951-05-87-1)

Minster must either win his battle in the desert or get out."[43] Churchill did not arrive in Cairo determined to sack Auchinleck; he came determined to see the 8th Army attack as soon as possible. The fact that Auchinleck, as in Norway, before Crusader and before the Gazala battles, stuck to his belief that attacks should only be launched when the state of preparation gave a good chance of success, tipped the balance against him. On 8 August Colonel Ian Jacob of the prime minster's staff carried the news of his dismissal to Auchinleck at his desert headquarters. Jacob, who came from a family that had served in the Indian Army since 1816 (his father had been its commander-in-chief) told his diary that he felt as if he were going to murder an unsuspecting friend. Churchill offered Auchinleck a soft landing (as he had done with Ironside). He had finally come to accept that the responsibilities of the Middle East Commander-in-Chief were far too vast. Therefore, a new command, Persia and Iraq Command, was to be created that would assume responsibility for not only those territories but for the Northern Front as well. The prime minster urged Auchinleck to accept that appointment. Auchinleck, after reading the letter took Jacob for a walk, told him he felt retirement was better than any face-saving job for unsuccessful generals. He saw Brooke and Churchill the following day, briefed his successor Lieutenant General Sir Harold Alexander (who, when he and Auchinleck were both brigadiers, had fought under Auchinleck's command in a 1935 campaign against one of the more formidable tribes on British India's Northwest Frontier). We know little about any of these conversations. Brooke described his as "stormy and…unpleasant."[44] Churchill described his, which lasted an hour, as "at once bleak and impeccable."[45] There seems to be no record of Auchinleck's conversation with Alexander, but it must, given Alex's urbanity, have been easier. Before he was told of his own supersession, Auchinleck had discussed with Brooke a new commander for 8th Army and agreed with the CIGS' suggestion of Montgomery. Churchill had however, on the basis of a single conversation, decided to name Gott, widely known and admired in 8th Army but very tired after two years of desert fighting and whose performance as a corps commander had not been outstanding. Then fate intervened in the form of a roving German fighter that shot down Gott's plane as he was flying back to Cairo from the desert. Gott's death cleared the way for Brooke to install his favored candidate. His protégé Montgomery flew into Cairo early on 12 August. He met immediately with Auchinleck. No contemporary record of their meeting seems to exist and when

43 Lord Charles Moran, *Churchill: The Struggle for Survival 1940-1965* (Boston, 1966), p. 79.

44 Alex Danchev and Daniel Todman (eds.), *War Diaries 1939-1945: Field Marshal Lord Alanbrooke* (London, 2001), pp. 296-97. Diary entry 9 Aug 1942.

45 Churchill, *Hinge of Fate*, p. 468. In a career as lavishly documented as Churchill's it is unusual to find a significant meeting that left no trace. Possibly Churchill used it to urge Auchinleck to accept the new Persia and Iraq Command. Ian Jacob had been instructed to urge this on Auchinleck when he gave him his letter of dismissal – and he did so again when he saw him briefly on 9 August. Even after the "bleak" hour Churchill hoped Auchinleck might accept. He gave him extra time to mull the offer. Only when he returned to Cairo after his visit to Moscow did he accept that Auchinleck's refusal was firm.

Montgomery's *Memoirs* were published fifteen years later, Auchinleck, in a letter to the London *Times*, challenged the veracity of Montgomery's account of it. The following day Montgomery flew up to 8th Army headquarters, decided to assume command before the scheduled date of 15 August – and began constructing his legend. Auchinleck flew home, to India.

Auchinleck's thirteen months in Cairo are hard to evaluate. Churchill (who had had little contact with Auchinleck and had criticized him at the end of the Norway campaign) when he lost whatever confidence he ever had in Wavell, appointed Auchinleck Commander-in-Chief, Middle East, on the basis of the alacrity with which he responded to the Iraqi revolt. But, as Commander-in-Chief, India, Auchinleck had both a personal connection with Iraq where he had spent World War I and headed a military machine that regarded Iraq as an outwork of India's defense and had long planned for intervention there. India, moreover, was not overseeing any active operations while Wavell had multiple balls in the air. What Churchill saw however was vigor in Delhi as opposed to hesitation in Cairo. Dill, whose standing with Churchill was rapidly eroding, was, if Kennedy's memoirs are correct, dubious about sending Auchinleck to Cairo. Why? We don't know. Dill knew him and also knew that he had had little contact with the regular British Army with which he would now have to work. Was that behind his concern? Whatever gave Dill pause it was not reflected in the letter he sent to Auchinleck after his appointment, a letter which can be characterized largely as a lament for his own problems with Churchill, ending with the reminder that if Auchinleck felt himself being pushed to take a course of action, he felt unwise, he could always threaten to resign. Auchinleck not only knew little about the complex organism he was taking command of, he had no powerful ally in London (as Alexander and Montgomery would have in Brooke).

He clearly made a poor choice when he named Cunningham to command the newly formed 8th Army. But what were his options? O'Connor was in an Italian POW camp. Percy Hobart, who had shaped the 7th Armored Division before the war, had been forced out of the Army in November 1939 over what was essentially a personality clash. Cunningham had run a successful campaign, even if its only real issues were logistic. It was certainly mobile, but it was in trucks not tanks. But perhaps it was the best, in the circumstances, Auchinleck could do. There is certainly no indication Dill had anything to do with the decision or raised any concerns about it. If Brooke, a much tougher character than Dill, was right perhaps Auchinleck had few options. Writing in March 1942 he told his diary "Half our Corps and divisional Commanders are totally unfit for their appointments, and yet if I were to sack them, I could find no better."[46] When Cunningham lost confidence in Crusader's prospects and Auchinleck relieved him, the replacement was however another flawed selection. Neil Ritchie, an infantryman, was, as noted before, junior to his corps commanders and had been primarily

46 Danchev and Todman, *War Diaries*, pp. 243-244. Entry for 31 March 1942. The following day Brooke noted that he was probably feeling "liverish" when he wrote it.

a staff officer, most recently Deputy Chief of the General Staff to Auchinleck in Cairo. His ability to grow into his job was stifled by Auchinleck's decision to remain at 8th Army headquarters for much of the rest of the Crusader offensive and thereafter to remain in close touch, visiting 8th Army often. Given the importance of the desert war this is not surprising, but it did mean that Ritchie never quite emerged from the staff officer role. He was always in Auchinleck's shadow. This in turn strengthened the position of the corps commanders – Norrie and Gott (who replaced Godwin-Austen), and the continuation of what was already a desert war tradition: command by committee and conference, which in turn would contribute to the Gazala defeat. Another personnel move Auchinleck made after Crusader would also become controversial. Lieutenant General Arthur Smith, the Chief of Staff in Cairo, was due to rotate out of that position. To succeed him Auchinleck chose Lieutenant General T.W. (Tom) Corbett, an Indian cavalryman currently commanding IV Indian Corps in Iraq. Corbett had spent the previous two years studying the training and employment of armor (an Indian armored division was, very slowly, taking shape in Iraq) and had been considered for the corps command in Burma that went to Slim. Corbett was certainly not the nonentity so brutally dismissed by Churchill as a "very small, agreeable man, of no personality and little experience."[47] Corbett's great fault in fact was he had had even less contact with the British Army than Auchinleck and no experience at all with anything as large and complex as GHQ Middle East. His shortcomings were soon evident. By the time the Gazala battle opened Brooke was expressing doubts about his suitability for the job. Auchinleck's mistake about Cunningham is understandable. Ritchie's appointment – and his subsequent overshadowing – less so. Corbett's selection was an error.

But it was not shaky staff work in Cairo or even the weaknesses of Ritchie, Norrie and Gott that was central to Auchinleck's problem. It was, as it had been since the Western Desert Force had first confronted the German army in March 1941, how the British Army fought and that was the most intractable of Auchinleck's problems. During the long series of exchanges between London and Cairo before the Gazala battles, Churchill, in the face of Auchinleck's refusal to come home, had taken advantage of the passage through Cairo en route to India of Lieutenant General Sir Archibald Nye, the Vice Chief of the Imperial General Staff, to cross examine both Auchinleck and others about the validity of Auchinleck's claims that he could not resume the offensive quickly. One of Nye's responses to London is particularly striking. Asked to explain in what way German armored formations were superior, Nye replied that, until recently, there had been a "failure to recognize the vital importance of the closest cooperation between tanks, artillery and infantry in the employment of armored formations."[48] This

47 Churchill's remarks on Corbett were recorded by Ian Jacob in the diary he kept at the time. Never published in full, it is held, with Jacob's other papers, in the Churchill Archive Center at Churchill College, Cambridge. The late Lieutenant General Sir Ian Jacob kindly allowed me access to it in the 1970s.

48 Mackenzie, *Eastern Epic*, p. 538. Connell does not refer to this quite important piece of information.

was a very accurate analysis – combined arms warfare was Rommel's secret – but there were a number of serious obstacles to rebuilding the 8th Army around it. There had to be buy in by its senior officers that it was a needed change, which would mean abandoning ideas about the use of tanks that had taken shape over the previous two decades – the intellectual legacy of the British Army's interwar "apostles of mobility." Then there had to be time for retraining – Nye had also pointed out that this had not been available. Finally, there had to be the right equipment. This too Nye noted but Auchinleck's desert army only began to get that in the Spring of 1942 when the first of the new more powerful 6 pounder anti-tank guns began to reach 8th Army, together with the American Grant tanks. And new weapons needed time to be mastered and integrated into tactical designs. Auchinleck never enjoyed any of these assets. The pressures of the situation he faced simply precluded it. His successor had more troops, better equipment and much more time to prepare. Churchill had balked at Auchinleck's proposed six-week delay; Montgomery's 8th Army did not launch its offensive for ten – although fighting a defensive battle in the interval. And, in any case, that battle more resembled an updated version of the Amiens battle from 1918 than any of the swirling armored clashes that had hitherto characterized the desert war: Montgomery however did set off the biggest of the controversies about Auchinleck's handling of 8th Army: it revolved around what his intentions were at the end of July fighting and what the connection was between those intentions and Montgomery's defensive success at the end of August.

And here we encounter the most controversial of Auchinleck's personnel choices: Major General Eric Dorman Smith. "Chink" Dorman Smith was one of the few British Army officers Auchinleck knew well before arriving in Cairo. When he had been Deputy Chief of the General Staff at Indian Army headquarters he met Dorman Smith, then the Director of Military Training there. On long early morning walks they came to know one another well and Dorman Smith served on the crucial Modernization Committee that Auchinleck chaired. When Auchinleck arrived in Cairo, Dorman Smith was serving as Commandant of the Middle East Staff College at Haifa in Palestine and the acquaintance was renewed. Wavell had drawn on Dorman Smith for advice and so did Auchinleck. This culminated in Dorman Smith becoming Deputy Chief of the General Staff in Cairo shortly before the Gazala battles opened. Dorman Smith was very bright with a sharp tongue to match his sharp mind. He had been promoted very fast. Both things had made him enemies, and the strong feelings he aroused tended to wash over on to his boss. In addition to complaining that Corbett was not up to his job as chief of staff, Brooke wondered in his diary whether Auchinleck was too influenced by Dorman Smith. When Auchinleck took over command of 8th Army, he took Dorman Smith with him as his chief of staff "in the field." The ill-defined relationship between Dorman Smith's responsibilities and Corbett's created confusion at a time when no additional complications were needed. But, above all, it produced one of the sharpest controversies about Auchinleck's intentions for the next battle when, at the end of the July fighting, 8th Army went over to the defensive to catch its breath before the next clash with Rommel. The argument was sparked by the claim Montgomery made in his tendentious *Memoirs* published in 1958 (and immediately confuted by Auchinleck) that 8th Army was planning to retire to the Nile Delta area when Rommel attacked, a plan Montgomery declared he immediately cancelled and then planned and conducted the successful defensive battle of Alam Halfa (30 August – 2 September) that stopped Rommel's last desert offensive.[49] The powerful counterattack to Montgomery's version (which really simply amplified what Churchill had written in *The Hinge of Fate* in 1950) came in the form of Corelli Barnett's *The Desert Generals*, published in 1960. A brilliant polemic, written with help from both Auchinleck and Dorman Smith, it argued that they left Montgomery the design for the Alam Halfa battle and that Montgomery plagiarized the plan for his first victory and then traduced its authors. Oceans of ink later it is clear that, of course, Montgomery's Alam Halfa battle resembled the forecasts and plans Auchinleck and Dorman Smith made for meeting the next attempt they were sure Rommel would make to breach the Alamein Line – the command of the 8th Army had changed not the geography of the Alamein position. More important, as the July fighting died down Auchinleck, Dorman Smith and 8th Army's corps commanders did a great deal of hard thinking about a future offensive of their own. Out of this came two miliary appreciations by Auchinleck, dated 1 and 2 August "which established the framework for the rest of the El Alamein campaign…[and] provides the final and conclusive proof that Montgomery's much-vaulted 'master plan' for 'his' battle of Alamein actually originated with Auchinleck and his corps commanders." The author of that assessment, Niall Barr, concludes "Every single element of Auchinleck's plan was later followed by Eighth Army under Montgomery's leadership."[50]

One final point that needs to be kept in mind about Auchinleck in Cairo – his considerable isolation. He does not seem to have been "clubbable." Because officers were not allowed to bring their wives with them when posted to the Middle East, Auchinleck left his wife in India (a separation that his official biographer identified as the beginning of the rift what would lead to the collapse of his marriage a few years later). He was not plugged into any British Army network and did not bring an Indian Army staff with him, despite the huge Indian Army contribution to the theatre.[51] Unlike Wavell, whose

49 Early "worst possible case" plans, drawn up in Cairo in early July, were still extant at GHQ in Cairo a month later. Rommel had been stopped, and the thinking of Auchinleck and Dorman Smith had moved on but somehow those plans remained to convince the new team that took over in Cairo in md-August that there was "defeatism" in the air under Auchinleck and this was reflected both in what Churchill wrote in the *Hinge of Fate* and what Montgomery claimed in his memoirs. Whether this confusion was due to Corbett's shortcomings or inadequate liaison between Auchinleck, Dorman Smith and Corbett is now impossible to say. Possibly both factors were in play, but the consequences bedeviled the history of Auchinleck's final weeks in command for a generation.

50 Niall Barr, *Pendulum of War: The Three Battles of El Alamein* (Woodstock, NY, 2005), pp. 188, 192. This forensic examination of the July-Noy. Battles around El Alamein is essential reading.

51 Auchinleck had several times pointed out to London how large the Indian contribution to Middle East Command was. In March 1942 he noted that there was 190,000 Indian troops in the Middle East. In early May he reminded Brooke that the 216,000 Indian soliders in the Middle East represented a quarter of his strength. Of the 14 divisions he controlled

tastes were quite eclectic, he had no large circle of acquaintances who could provide some relief from the demands of his almost unmanageably large job. There is no evidence that any of this affected his experience of command, but it might well have accentuated his dependence on certain ideas he had long formed, like his refusal to move before fully prepared, that lay at the root of so many of his clashes with Churchill and his ultimate removal.

As he flew back to India in mid-August 1942, Auchinleck must have assumed his career was at its close. But, in fact, its most challenging chapter was about to begin.

## The Twilight of the Raj

When Auchinleck left Cairo in August 1942, he may well have thought that his career was over. He had been removed as commander-in-chief of the major active theater in Britain's war against the European Axis. Then, offered the new Persia and Iraq Command – second tier but perhaps a major theatre in the near future – he turned that down as well despite being repeatedly urged to accept by the prime minster, who even gave him extra time to decide. Although his affections were deeply engaged with India, there was no slot for him to fill there. For some nine months he simply rested, occupied only by writing his official report on his tenure in the Middle East. But, as he rested and wrote, the course of the war was producing a situation that would bring him back to the center of events, not only in India's war but in the endgame of the Raj.

His successor in India, Wavell, had been Commander-in-Chief since mid-Summer, 1941. He was tired when he arrived in Delhi. He had in fact wanted to return to England on leave, but the prime minster refused, saying privately that he didn't want Wavell sitting in his club in London complaining (and, although this was left unsaid, becoming a focus for complaints about Churchill's management of the war). He was not an Indian Army officer and took over an army that he had little acquaintance with and that was in the midst of frenetic expansion geared entirely to the needs of the Middle East and doing so, moreover, in an equipment starved environment. In September 1941 he reminded London – again – of the most egregious case. India was raising an armored division but had not a single modern tank. Then Japan attacked and Churchill told Wavell to "look east", handing him responsibility for Burma and Malaya to which India Command would rush half trained units over the next two months. Then, at the first wartime summit, the Arcadia Conference in Washinton (Dec-Jan 1941-42), the Americans insisted on

six were Indian and in his Command as a whole he had the equivalent of 8.5 divisions of Indian Fighting units (plus large numbers of Indian support units). While British and Dominion formnations have received recognition – national official histories plus memoirs and secondary accounts – the huge Indian contribution is seldom noticed. Churchill virtually ignored it in his memoirs: the Indian official history is seldom consulted. The 4th, 8th and 10th Indian Divisions remained in the Mediterranean theatre until 1945. Their story is, finally being told in a forthcoming study by Daniel Marston.

a unified command in Southeast Asia to try to stem the Japanese onrush. And so was born the American-British-Dutch-Australian Command (ABDA). The Americans also nominated Wavell as its commander, a very dubious honor Churchill, nevertheless, felt constrained to accept. Devoid of resources, with little cohesion and with the initiative firmly in Japanese hands, ABDA was doomed at birth. By late February, Wavell was back in Delhi, facing a Japanese tide lapping at India's borders, with Churchill asking how soon he could launch a counter offensive.

The prime minster's eagerness for an offensive to retake Burma sprang almost entirely from American pressure. The roots of American enthusiasm for Generalissimo Chiang Kai Shek's government are beyond this essay but the fact became a major driver of policy in Britain's war against Japan. American Lend Lease supplies had reached China by a long road-rail link from Rangoon, christened the "Burma Road". Severed by the Japanese conquest of Burma, the Americans wanted it restored, which required the reconquest of Burma by the British. This issue dominated high level exchanges between London and Washington about Burma throughout the war.[52] It was not the strategy Churchill wanted to pursue but it was imposed on him by the pressures of alliance politics. The immediate result was the ill-fated First Arakan campaign launched at the end of 1942 – one partially trained, malaria ridden Indian division set out into some of the worst terrain and climate conditions Burma had to offer. Wavell's willingness to send troops he knew were not yet ready into battle was underpinned by a remarkable misperception about the Imperial Japanese Army. He had a "hunch" that they would not fight well on the defensive (he admitted, after the war, that he had underestimated the Japanese). The result was, when the Japanese counterattacked, a debacle as bad as anything that had happened in Malaya or Burma the preceding year but on a smaller scale. The Indian Army, expanded too quickly, had simply spread its cadre too thinly and switched its training emphasis from desert to jungle too slowly. But the shambolic end of the first Arakan offensive, masked to a large extent by the victorious conclusion of the North African campaign, (in which the 4th Indian Division played a significant role) was the final straw, as far as the prime minster was concerned. Never very enthusiastic about either Wavell or the Indian Army, Churchill set out to replace the one and marginalize the other. Wavell was summoned home for "consultations" which ended with his removal as Commander-in-Chief, India – and his elevation to Viceroy. A replacement for the incumbent Viceroy, Lord Linlithgow, a second-tier figure at best, whose tenure had been extended by wartime necessity, was overdue and no first rank figure in London wanted the job. So, as he had done when he shuttled Wavell from Cairo to Delhi, the prime minster solved a problem by sending Wavell, with a peerage, back to Delhi to tackle what was the most challenging civilian appointment in the British empire. That in turn meant a new commander in chief was needed. Leo Amery, the Secretary of State for

52 The complex Anglo-American arguments about strategy in the war against Japan are summarized in Raymond Callahan, *Burma 1942-45* (London, 1978) and at greater length in Christopher Thorne, *Allies of a Kind* (London, 1978).

India, had always hoped that Auchinleck would return to India and resume the appointment curtailed after six months by his move to Cairo. He lobbied vigorously, aided by the lack of any other likely candidate. Churchill, although he had removed Auchinleck from the Middle East command, clearly did not feel as skeptical about him as he did about Wavell. On his fifty-ninth birthday (and the one-year anniversary of Tobruk's surrender) Claude Auchinleck became, again, Commander-in-Chief, India.[53]

He was immediately confronted by a range of problems, all of which clamored for immediate attention. The most pressing was the obvious need to radically overhaul the preparation of the Indian Army for its war against Japan, preparation that the Arakan debacle had shown to be utterly inadequate. This had to be done while the prime minster, furious at the embarrassment of the defeat in the Arakan, planned to sideline the Indian Army, in his eyes too large and too unreliable, by creating a new command structure for the war against Japan that would employ a radically new, and unproven, approach to retaking Burma (thereby pleasing his exigent American allies). The Viceroyalty was in transition, and, in Bengal, a major famine was in progress. All in all, a much more difficult vista than even the one that had confronted him two years earlier when he arrived in Cairo. There he was confronted with a series of military problems; in Delhi in mid-1943 the problems were not only those posed by the war in Burma but those of alliance politics and the future of the Indian Army and, looming in the background, the great political question: the future of the Raj itself.

The issue of properly training the Indian Army to fight the Japanese was of course the first he tackled. At the root of the problem was open ended expansion with priority assigned to preparation for the Middle East. Simultaneous with Auchinleck's return as commander-in-chief, the Defence Committee of the War Cabinet in London ended that by setting a cap on the size of the Indian Army. The war in North Africa was over and the fears for the Northern Front gone, while Syria, Iraq and Persia were tranquil under the watchful eye of mostly Indian Army garrisons. For the first time since the collapse of France, the Indian Army had stability. Wavell, as he departed India for London, had appointed a committee, the Infantry Committee, to assess the problems of retraining the Indian Army. The need for a new training system had long been recognized. The few officers who had escaped from Singapore were used by Wavell to lecture in India Command on the problems of jungle combat. More importantly, after Slim withdrew Burcorps into Assam, he moved on to another corps command, XV Corps, where he set down his reflections on the problems of retraining the Indian Army and made a start doing just that. One of his divisional commanders during the retreat from Burma, Major General Bruce Scott, became Inspector of Infantry with oversight over training. But the

53 Auchinleck was back in India at the time of the "Quit India" protests in Aug-Sep 1942 (sometimes called the "Congress Revolt"). The Indian Army was heavily involved in its suppression, some 57 battalions being deployed to support – or replace – the police. Training cycles were seriously disrupted, with knock on consequences on the battlefield. Yet, curiously, there is no trace, either in Connell's official biography or in Auchinleck's correspondence that he offered any comment on it. In any case the Indian Army was umoved by the episode.

continuing churn due to expansion, and Scott's exhaustion after the retreat form Burma, combined to prevent much progress. But all the stars aligned as Auchinleck returned to the leadership pf the Indian Army. The decisions in London, although driven in part by worries about the political reliability of the now huge Indian Army, stabilized its force structure.[54] The recommendations of the Infantry Committee (on which Slim's chief of staff during the retreat from Burma served) paved the way for a radical restructuring of how the India Army was trained.[55] All this was in progress when Auchinleck returned. What he provided was the driving impetus to basically remake the Indian Army. Wavell had replaced Bruce Scott with Major General Reginald Savory as Inspector of Infantry in his last days as commander-in-chief, as part of his belated recognition that the Army he commanded needed upgrades if it was to meet the new challenges it faced. Auchinleck, who knew Savory well, raised the appointment to Director of Infantry thus giving Savory the authority to drive forward the changes set in motion by the Infantry Committee. The ideas that made the XIV Army the tremendous fighting machine it became were largely Slim's, via the Infantry Committee, but the machinery that took those ideas and turned them into the sort of rigorous training that produced the battalions that carried Slim to Rangoon was the work of Savory, powerfully supported by Auchinleck.[56] Slim would later write about what he called "the fundamentals of war – soldiers must be trained before they can fight, fed before they can march, and relived before they are worn out."[57] The first of these criteria, hitherto scanted in the rush to expand the Indian Army, was finally, adequately, met by what it is not too much to label a training revolution in the second half of 1943. The other large questions posed by the war in Burma – logistic support and troops' health – were also addressed by Auchinleck. Training, logistics, health and morale, which involved matters like leave and pay, are all unglamorous things to study but they were absolutely essential to victory. As all this was tackled in the background, in the foreground Auchinleck had to deal with the prime minster's urge for a resumption of the offensive, as well as the creation of the new command structure, South East Asia Command, that Churchill had devised to replace

54 It remains astounding that the Indian Army's stability during the "Quit India" upheaval did not lay to rest concerns in London about its loyalty but, on matters Indian, the prime minister was unteachable. The Chiefs of Staff, who might be thought to have rather more professional development, also noted that the capping of the Indian Army's size would make it safer against subversion. In fact, there were no major "loyalty"issues in the Indian Army during the entire course of the war.

55 The full story of how the Indian Army's training system changed during the war has been fully, and definitively, studied by Alan Jeffreys, *Approach to Battle: Training the Indian Army During the Second World War* (Solihull, UK, 2017). How that training revolution played out on the battlefield can be followed in Daniel Marston's *Phoenix from the Ashes: The Indian Army in the Burma Campaign* (Westport, RI, 2003).

56 A feedback loop, cycling back recent battlefield lessons into the training cycle, was the work of the Indian Army's Directorate of Military Training. For a full description of this process see Jeffreys op.cit.

57 Slim, *Defeat into Victory*, p. 164.

the "welter of lassitude and inefficiency" that he felt India and its army represented. And then there were the ideas of the wildly eccentric soldier who Churchill believed would deliver the victory in Burma he needed to satisfy his American allies.

When Auchinleck became Commander-in-Chief, India in June 1943, Churchill's ideas for a new command structure for the war against Japan were beginning to take shape. Finalized over the summer and at the Anglo-American Quadrant Conference at Quebec in August, South East Asia Command (SEAC) was activated in mid-November. Meanwhile, Auchinleck was responsible for the war in Burma and had to confront the prime minster with the controlling reality of that war: its logistics. In Assam, XIV Army (formed, under Slim's command, as part of the reorganization of the theater) was dangling at the end of a long, precarious supply line, made even worse by the 1943 monsoon. It had been unusually severe – roads (never very good) had been washed away, bridges destroyed, rail lines put out of action. Auchinleck had to point out that until the line of communication was functioning offensive action was impossible. It was, once again, not an answer the prime minster wanted. He had already noted in a minute to the British Chiefs of Staff that commanders in India "magnify their demands and the obstacles they have to overcome."[58] Churchill's blindness about logistics is curious. He had once understood quite clearly how important logistics was to campaigns in underdeveloped areas. He had taken part in the reconquest of the Sudan in 1898 and in the instant history he wrote, *The River War*, he devoted a chapter to the construction of the railroad which was crucial to that campaign's success. He certainly noted the importance of logistics to the campaigns of his great ancestor, the Duke of Marlborough, whose biography he had written in the 1930s. But the clamant pressure of alliance politics overrode other considerations. Even the monsoon and Churchill's itch for offensive action were not the sum total of the disruptions with which Auchinleck had to cope during the months before SEAC took over. There was Orde Wingate.

Britain has a rich history of eccentrics in uniform, but Wingate nonetheless stands out. A gunner, Wingate never practiced that military trade. Related to the late Victorian icon, General Sir Reginald Wingate, he served in the Sudan Defense Force, a small elite light infantry force, and then found his most powerful patron when posted to Britain's troubled Palestine Mandate where an Arab revolt, triggered by the growing numbers of Jewish settlers, was in progress. He discovered Zionism which henceforth commanded his total loyalty. He also ran an unconventional counter insurgency force, known as the "Special Night Squads" whose tactics skirted the boundaries of legality. The General Officer Commanding in Palestine at the time was Wavell who became a patron and protector. A few years later Wavell summoned Wingate to Cairo and gave him the job of organizing Ethiopian irregulars to complement the two-pronged offensive he was launching to eradicate Italy's ramshackle East Africa empire. Wingate enjoyed considerable success, albeit against demoralized Italian-led colonial levies. At the campaign's end, back in Cairo, sick and exhausted, minus Wavell's protection (he had left for India)

58 Churchill memo, 24 July 1943, quoted in Connell, p. 740.

and, as usual, at odds with nearly everybody – he tended to alienate regular officers – he attempted suicide. After his recovery he was posted to a very dead-end job in the UK from which Wavell again rescued him, summoning him to India, hoping to put his skills at irregular warfare to work against the Japanese in Burma. Given one British garrison battalion and one newly raised Gurkha battalion to work with, Wingate had carte blanche to work out his new "Long Range Penetration" (LRP) tactics. As the Arakan offensive stalled and then went into reverse, Wingate took his 77th Indian Infantry Brigade (popularly known as the "Chindits") into Burma on an air-supplied raid to disrupt Japanese communications. The Chindits remained behind Japanese lines for some two months, did some easily repairable damage, but finally cornered by the Japanese (far more formidable than the faltering Italian units in Ethiopia) had to break into smaller parties and make their way back to India. About a third of the force was lost; many of the survivors were unfit for further active service. Indian Army officers felt that he had badly mishandled his Gurkha unit. And, again, his patron was gone – Wavell had been called to London to receive his dismissal as Commander-in-Chief, India. That might have been the end of the Long Range Penetration. But in the absence of his patron, Wingate had remarkable luck (which Napoleon said was essential for a successful general). The Indian Army had had nothing but defeat at the hands of the Imperial Japanese Army – Malaya, Burma, and now the Arakan. Here was something that could at least be presented as a success and so the public relations officers were told to publicize it as such. The Delhi correspondent for the London *Daily Mail* coined the striking but meaningless phase "Clive of Burma". Simultaneously Wingate wrote up his report, had unauthorized copies printed before it was officially approved, and back channeled one to Leo Amery, Secretary of State for India – and, like Wingate, a "gentile Zionist." Amery passed it to Churchill. The result was explosive. It focused all of Churchill's anger at India Command, offered a way to bypass the Indian Army and the intractable logistic difficulties Auchinleck was, as in the Middle East, pointing out, and at the same time, it offered him a solution to the multiple problems the Burma campaign presented. Wingate and his unorthodox tactics could reclaim north Burma, opening the way for the Americans to restore an overland supply link to China, ending American doubts about British willingness to meet American goals in Burma, which in turn would ease alliance tensions, facilitating the attainment of policy objectives elsewhere – like the Mediterranean theater. Moreover, it would sideline the second-rate Indian Army, reducing its role to following up Wingate's LRP forces, mopping up and occupying reconquered territory. That, in turn, would allow reductions in a force swollen with unreliable troops, in the prime minster's view. What followed is well known. Churchill (whose first thought was to give Wingate command in Burma) ordered him home, dined with him in Downing Street and added him to the party he was taking to the Quadrant Conference in Quebec. On the voyage, Wingate produced a paper that proposed to reconquer Burma with a massively expanded LRP force. India Command would be turned into mass production machinery for LRP brigades, and the Indian Army would trail along behind cleaning up the aftermath of LRP victory. Churchill and Wingate found further common ground in their disdain for the Indian Army. Wingate referred to it as a system of "outdoor relief," that is, a welfare scheme. The prime minster adopted the phrase. In constructing his LRP army, Wingate wanted no Indian soldiers, only British and Gurkha units (he would later accept a West African brigade as well). Backed by Churchill, Wingate was a major success at Quadrant. The Americans were as impressed as the prime minster could have hoped for. The chief of staff of the US Army Air Force, General "Hap" Arnold even threw in a private air force for Wingate. All of this went with a rush, before Indian Army headquarters had been heard from. Wingate arrived in Quebec a substantive lieutenant colonel who had never commanded anything larger than a platoon in combat; he left an acting major general, given a corps size command and his own air force. It was a great success for Churchill and Wingate; the cost would be borne by Auchinleck and India Command.

In fact, Auchinleck's assessment had been very perceptive, had time been taken to consider it. About Wingate he noted that he had "exceptional power to inspire" his troops, but (and it was a very large "but") "the further he is removed from personal contact with the troops employed, for example, as corps commander, the less valuable he is likely to be."[59] In GHQ, India's official analysis of Wingate's plan Auchinleck made three very important points: first, LRP groups would not be trained and equipped to confront conventional all arms divisions (like those of the Imperial Japanese Army); therefore "main forces" divisions must be available to exploit any disruption the Chindits caused. Of course, any such divisions would have to be Indian Army, something neither Wingate or Churchill would acknowledge. Second, Wingate's plan for air supplied LRP formations required a massive increase in the number of air transport squadrons, which would in turn add a heavy additional burden on the already badly overloaded Assam line of communications, thus surfacing again the centrality of logistics which everyone at Quadrant seemed to have forgotten. Finally, the disruption caused by the creation of "Special Force" would be enormous. The 70th Division, one of only two British divisions in India, would have to be broken up; Indian divisions would also lose Gurkha units and every formation in India Command would be milked for technical specialists (especially signalers) and the high-quality officers Wingate insisted upon (British, not Indian, of course). But by the time this carefully considered response reached Quebec the die had been cast. Wingate was to command the largest "private army" of the war and spearhead a campaign to reconquer Burma, a campaign that would be conducted by the new SEAC Command headed by Rear Admiral Lord Louis Mountbatten, another of Churchill's personnel decisions about which opinions differed at the time (and since). Auchinleck was left to produce the army that, despite Churchill's prejudices, would ultimately win the war in Burma.[60]

59 Quoted in Connell, p. 744.

60 The 1944-45 campaigns of the XIV Army – and the career of Special Force – can be followed in Slim's brilliant memoir as well as Raymond Callahan and Daniel Marston, *The 1945 Burma Campaign and the Transformation of the British Indian Army* (Lawrence, KS, 2020) and Robert Lyman, *A War of Empires: Japan, India, Burma & Britain 1941-45* (London, 2021). An older account, Louis Allen, *Burma: The Longest War 1941-45* (London, 1984) is still of great value.

The establishment of SEAC marked the end of Auchinleck's involvement in command of active military operations but he still was commander-in-chief of an army approaching the two million mark, serving in Italy, garrisoning the Middle East from the Levant to the borders of the Raj itself and conducting the Burma campaign. In addition, there was the huge base that India had become, in whose operation the Indian Army was involved – and the Assam line of communications, one of the logistic miracles of the war.[61] Auchinleck was also guiding two important changes in the fundamental structure of the Indian Army, with important long-term consequences. When he had been, briefly, commander-in-chief in 1941 he had decreed "equal treatment" for officers, "regardless of color." This he now pushed forward hard. Indian officers became eligible to sit on court martials of British personnel and, finally (in 1945), pay differentials between British and Indian officers (based on the archaic distinction that British offers in India were serving "abroad" while Indian officers were serving "at home") were eliminated. Auchinleck, looking forward to a postwar in which India would become fully self-governing, told Wavell, now Viceroy, in December 1944 that he was working on the principle that the postwar Indian Army would be "officered entirely by Indian officers"[62] something that became official Government of India policy in October 1945. While this may seem now a decision taken rather late in the game it is well to remember that in 1944-45 no one anticipated just how rapidly the Raj would vanish. Indeed, as Auchinleck drafted his memo to Wavell at the end of 1944, the Indian Army stood on the brink of the sweeping victory that crowned the long Burma campaign and seemed a reassertion of the Raj.

In the "dry weather" campaigning season of 1945, Slim's XIV Army, buoyed by its victory in the 1944 Imphal-Kohima campaign, and reflecting the versatility and professionalism that the training revolution of 1943 had inculcated, conducted a master class in operational maneuver, pulverizing the Japanese Burma Area Army (i.e., army group), in one of the most dramatic and successful campaigns of the war. By the time Rangoon fell on 8 May, XIV Army – indeed SEAC's land forces – were overwhelmingly Indian. Ethnically British units were down to about 10% of that total – and were outnumbered by African units. But, shortly after Slim's multi-ethnic, polyglot imperial army crowned its long campaign with overwhelming success, one of the architects of that army, Claude Auchinleck, remarked, prophetically, that "every Indian officer worth his salt is today a nationalist."[63] The end of the war in Burma signaled not the reinvigoration of the Raj but the opening of its final act – the "transfer of power."

Three months after Rangoon fell to Slim, the Pacific war ended with dramatic suddenness with the nuclear explosions that consumed Hiroshima and Nagasaki. At

61 The history of the Assam line of communications is carefully studied in Graham Dunlop's *Military Economics, Culture and Logistics, 1942-1945* (London, 2019). Reading it makes "lassitude and inefficiency" seem quitye ill-informed as a commentary on what India Command was doing.

62 Daniel Marston, *The Indian Army and the End of the Raj* (Cambridge, 2016), p. 94. Esssential to understanding the end of the Raj.

63 Quoted in David Omissi, *The Sepoy and the Raj* (Basingstoke, UK, 1994), p. 242.

that point Auchinleck, with Indian Army units everywhere from Italy to Burma was faced with the need to bring a far flung army (much of it not under his operational control) home, demobilize it and put it on a peacetime footing, while structuring it to meet likely future demands This had to be done against dramatic changes in the political atmosphere in both Britain and India, which together would accelerate the move toward Indian independence. That, in turn, would raise the question of whether the British would, on departure, hand over to a single Indian state or separate Hindu and Muslim successor governments.

Churchill's wartime coalition ended shortly after Germany's surrender and the ensuing general election produced a Labour landslide. The new prime minster, Clement Attlee, had been a supporter of Indian independence since well before the war and had known Indian Congress Party leaders since that time. Sir Stafford Cripps, one of Labour's most powerful figures, had, as a member of Churchill's wartime government, carried to India during the 1942 crisis the offer of postwar Dominion status in return for immediate support for the war effort – an offer turned down by the Congress leadership, which was angling for immediate independence. There could be no doubt in 1945, in view not only of its past positions but of the multiple pressing issues at home – demobilization, reconstruction and national bankruptcy – and abroad – the looming Cold War and a growing crisis in Palestine – that the Attlee government would want to resolve the question of ending the Raj quickly. Equally, the Congress Party which had been in a virtual deep freeze since 1942, its leadership interned for the duration after its abortive "Quit India" uprising in 1942, was eager to assume power. By 1945 when politics revived the Congress leaders realized that a door hitherto closed in London by Churchill was now swinging open. Moreover, both sides now benefited from Churchill's remarkable quiescence on the issue over the next two years. He had delayed the passage of the 1935 Government of India Act by several years and closed down any further change during the war but in 1945-47 he was preoccupied by the emerging challenge of Russia (he gave his famous "Iron Curtain" speech at Fulton, Missouri in March 1946), the war memoirs he was assembling (the first volume appeared in 1948), and his interest in the emerging movement for European unity. He would criticize but there was a sense of resignation in his attitude. There was something almost elegiac in his remark to Wavell after the war's end: "keep a bit of India".[64]

Even if spared any Churchillian broadsides, London could still make problems for the Indian Army. Shortly before the war's end, to accommodate the American desire to focus on their impeding invasion of Japan, the British had agreed to extend SEAC's area of operational responsibility to the Netherlands East Indies and French Indochina. That meant, when Japan surrendered, "post hostilities tasks" – the disarming of the large Japanese forces there, the liberation and care of prisoners of war and the general maintenance of order pending the return of civil government – fell to SEAC. And the troops available for the task were Indian Army units. Powerful local nationalist groups strongly

64 Penderel Moon (ed.), *Wavell: The Viceroy's Journal* (London, 1973), p. 168.

opposed the return of Dutch and French colonial authority, however. The last campaigns of Slim's divisions were against the emerging Viet-Minh insurgency in Indochina and the large, determined nationalist forces in Java – a use of Indian troops to restore colonial authority that angered Indian nationalists. Auchinleck wrote to the Viceroy in November 1945 to complain of the "tendency of H.M.G. in London, the commanders on the spot, the Chiefs of Staff and the authorities in Burma, both military and civil, to regard Indian troops as available for use in any circumstances whatever and for any purpose whatever without taking into consideration national feelings in this country…"[65] This old impulse, to regard the Indian Army as a freely disposable imperial reserve, went back to its creation in the 18th century and remained a default setting even as London prepared to end the Raj. It appeared in other ways as well in this twilight of empire. At the conference held in Singapore in 1945 to discuss operations against Indonesian insurgents, Mountbatten asked that Indian troops be used as he didn't want British wives made widows since the war was over. A furious (and quite brave) staff officer asked if it was preferable for Indian wives to be widowed.[66] The Supreme Allied Commander's response was not noted. But the sense that the Indian Army would still in some way be available to support British strategic and foreign policy goals lingered in some British military and official minds until very late in the day.

Concern about overseas deployments was soon overshadowed however by the speed with which politics began to move in India. Auchinleck and GHQ India had the immediate task before them of demobilizing the huge wartime army while laying the foundations for a peacetime force that would be very different from the army of 1939. Auchinleck wanted to push on toward a truly national force by maintaining the new units raised from outside the family circle of the "martial races" (the term itself had been dropped during the war). He also wanted to push forward as rapidly as possible with the "nationalization" of the officer corps – the term "Indianization" had also been abandoned. Auchinleck appointed a committee to consider the future structures of the Indian Army. Known, from its chairman's name, as the Willcox committee, it reported that the Indian Army would need British officers for another twenty-five years, a recommendation Auchinleck ignored. He was very clear in his mind what was necessary: "we are to go," he told senior officers of the army, all still British, adding, "before we go it is our bounden duty to do all we can to ensure the continued well being and efficiency of our men and of the army…" He pointed out that this would mean some Indian officers would be promoted more rapidly than normal, but he pointedly added: "I will appoint no officer, British or Indian, to any post unless I am sure that he is properly fitted for it."[67]

The desire to hand over a fully functioning, high quality army was central to Auchinleck's policy. He intended to increase the number of Indian officers rapidly but not at the cost of lowering the quality of the Army. This put him increasingly at odds

65 Connell, p. 823.
66 Marston, *The Indian Army and the End of the Raj*, p. 193.
67 Connell, pp. 854-55.

with Indian politicians – a more politically attuned commander-in-chief might have moved faster but Auchinleck simply would not. For example, in one batch of wartime EICOs (Emergency Indian Communication Officers) only two of forty were selected for permanent commission. Nonetheless by the Spring of 1947, there were 8400 Indian officers to 11,500 British officers in the Indian Army and the plan was for nationalization to be complete by 1 July 1949. This transformation of the officer corps was done, as far as Auchinleck could manage, while keeping standards high. Indian officers of field grade rank were also pushed forward and there were generals-in-waiting by 1947. Although a few British officers remained at the top in both India and Pakistan for brief periods after independence it seems fair to say that Auchinleck pushed the change in the composition of the officer corps forward as fast as possible in the twenty-four months he had between VJ Day and 15 August 1947.

While the future of the Indian Army was being shaped in the background, the foreground was dominated by the issue of how to handle the officers of the Indian National Army (INA), a Japanese sponsored force recruited initially from Indian Army POWs and then from members of the large Indian community in Malaya. How to deal with the INA, which fell into British hands with the reconquest of Burma, became a highly politicized issue that pitted the Commander-in-Chief against the Congress Party.

How to treat former INA members was a very complicated matter. After screening some could simply be returned to their units (many had joined the INA to get out of Japanese POW camps and some hoped to desert back to British lines if given the chance – as some did). Others could be discharged. But Indian officers presented a special problem – they had broken their oaths and fought against the King Emperor. Moreover, a few had been responsible for the maltreatment of fellow POWs as they tried to persuade, or coerce, them into joining the INA. Clearly this could not be simply passed over – but nor in the atmosphere of 1945 in India could there be any question of the death penalty that military law would normally mandate. The Congress Party, seeing a political bonanza, championed the INA and a galaxy of Congress legal talent, including Gandhi's heir apparent, Jawaharlal Nehru, became defense counsel. Auchinleck, to underscore the importance of loyalty by soldiers, finally decided to put three INA officers on trial – a Hindu, a Muslim and a Sikh. He felt that not only was a fundamental principle for the future of the army at stake but that it was also necessary as a matter of keeping faith with those (a majority of Indian POWs) who, under severe pressure, had refused to join the INA. In long retrospect it is in fact difficult to see what other decision he could have taken. But unquestionably, it handed a public relations victory to the Congress Party (whose leading lights never seem to have grasped that Auchinleck was defending a principle of great importance to the functioning of the army they would soon inherit). The impact of the INA trials was further heightened by Auchinleck's choice of venue: the Red Fort at Delhi, freighted both with memories of both the glories of the Mughal Empire and the dark memories of 1857. The choice met Auchinleck's goal of avoiding any accusation of handling the trials in a secretive fashion. It also heightened the impact the trials had on public opinion, something that played into Congress Party hands. In the end, as was inevitable given the evidence, all three were found guilty. Military law stipulated in such cases death or transportation for life (i.e., confinement in a penal colony in the Andaman Islands in the Bay of Bengal). Auchinleck immediately commuted the sentence of transportation (death had never been an option) to cashiering from the army and forfeiture of pay and allowances. There were a handful of other trials before, in April 1946, Auchinleck cancelled further proceedings. He had done what he felt was absolutely necessary both to vindicate those who had remained loyal and to underscore the principle of loyalty crucial to the future of the army. Predictably his decisions have been sharply criticized but no one has yet explained what other course he could, at that moment, have taken.

Perhaps the most interesting document in his papers bearing on the INA trials is a long memorandum, about which his official biographer noted that he had "pondered the matter of the INA perhaps more seriously that any other issue in his life." Circulated to all senior officers of the Indian Army, in India and overseas, it started with a blunt statement: "Every Indian commissioned officer is a nationalist and rightly so…" Then turning to his fellow British officers of the Indian Army (many of whom had criticized his leniency) he pointed out that in criticizing it "they forget, if they ever knew, the great bitterness bred in the minds of many officers in the early days of 'Indianization' by the discrimination, often very real, exercised against them and discourteous, contemptuous treatment meted out to them by many British officers who should have known better." He then delivered a broadside against both the structure and spirit of pre-war policy: "…the early stages of "Indianization" from its inception to the beginning of the late war were badly mismanaged by the British Government of India, and this prepared the ground for disloyalty when the opportunity came. There is little doubt that Indianization was at its inception looked on as a political expedient which was bound to fail militarily. There is no doubt also that many senior British officers believed and even hoped that it would fail." He then took aim at the "eight units" scheme. "The policy of segregation of Indian officers in separate units, the differential treatment in respect of pay and terms of service as compared to the British officer, and the prejudice and lack of manners of some – by no means all – Bruitish officers and their wives, all went to produce a very deep and bitter feeling of racial discrimination…" he followed this very blunt statement about why pre-war Indian officers might well have become disaffected (which was also a list of things that, in two tours as commander-in-chief, he had changed) he put as bluntly as possible his goal in the INA trials, as in many other things: "The overriding object is to maintain that stability, reliability and efficiency of the Indian Army…"[68] In the Desert, amid disaster, he had said "I mean to win" – and did. In the last days of the Raj, he set out to hold together the army that had been his life.

By the time the INA trials wound down even bigger storm clouds had gathered. The last British attempt to broker a political solution that would preserve a united India had collapsed and the partition of the subcontinent became a real possibility, and, as it did,

68 Connell, pp. 813, 946-949. This whole memorandum, which Connell reproduced in an Appendix (pp. 945-954) deserves to be read in full.

unrest began to spread on a scale that would draw the army in, which would pose an even greater challenge than the INA trials.

The Attlee government, faced by a staggering array of problems, intended to remove India from its "to do" list quickly. A parliamentary delegation to investigate the state of Indian politics was quickly followed by a Cabinet level mission dominated by Sir Stafford Cripps, the Chancellor of the Exchequer. Cripps' contacts with Indian politics, which went back to the 1930s, had been largely with Congress Party figures. The plan that emerged, in May 1946 called the Cabinet Mission Plan, called for an Indian federation in which provinces would be autonomous with a "Center" responsible for matters of common concern (defense, foreign affairs and communications). The provinces would however be "grouped", two of the groupings consisting of Muslim majority areas in the northwest (Punjab, The North West Frontier Province, Sind and Baluchistan) and the east (Bengal and Assam). The third bloc would be made up of the remaining, Hindu majority, provinces. Individual provinces could opt out of their assigned grouping. An immediate Interim Government would be formed with no "official" (i.e., British) members and would shepherd British India to full dominion status. While it was the last British political initiative intended to preserve Indian unity, the provision for grouping indicated the impact on Indian politics of the Muslim League's demand for a separate Muslim Homeland, "Pakistan". As the shadow of partition began to affect not only politics but attitudes, "communal" hopes and fears began to intensify and riots began to break out in areas of high tension, i.e., areas where there were substantial mixed populations (Bengal and the Punjab, the Indian's Army's homeland, above all). For the next fifteen months, the background to Auchinleck's already complex job of demobilization, bringing home the large Indian Army formations overseas, pushing forward the nationalization of the officer corps and shaping the Army for a new era was to be anxiety over the possibility (and then certainty) of partition and the mounting pressure on the Army for peace-keeping as the normal mechanisms for maintaining order began, in key localities, to crumble.[69]

The machinery for the use of the army to bring "aid to the civil" when disorder exceeded what the police could manage was well understood and had been used time and again since 1919. The disastrous episode at Amritsar in the Punjab that year when serious overreaction by Brigadier Reginald Dyer had led to at least 400 civilian deaths produced a tightening of the regulations governing use of force by the military in such situations.[70] But the regulations, encapsulated in Indian Army Regulation D908 (which required sign off by a civil official before an officer could order troops to fire) presumed

69 The complex politics of the transfer of power in India are very well described in Yasmin Khan's *The Great Partition: The Making of India and Pakistan* (New Haven, CT, 2007). However, the Indian Army and Auchinleck are not much in evidence in its pages. For that one must turn to Daniel Marston's *The Indian Army and the End of the Raj*.

70 Slim wrote a (fictionalized) account of such a situation which was a conflation of several "aid to the civil" episodes in which, as a young officer, he had been involved. William Slim, *Unofficial History* (New York, 1962), pp. 73-98.

functioning civil administrations and police forces the army could support and that is what began to collapse in 1946-47. The Indian Civil Service – the legendary "steel framework" of the Raj – was faltering. British recruitment to it ended in 1939 and retirements were paused. By 1945 there were only some 400 British ICS officers left in the service, many, if not most, exhausted and looking toward the end of their Indian careers. The Indian ICS officers, now the majority, while maintaining the high standard of the service, would have been less than human if they had not begun to think about their situation under new masters. The problem faced by the police was far more stark – for the most part unarmed, more deeply embedded in their localities, they were much more susceptible to "communal" pressures as tension mounted. When summoned to "aid to the civil" duties, the army faced situations where the police had ceased to function – or become part of the problem – and the civil authorities were hesitant or ambivalent. At the same time the nature of the violence was changing. The mobs of yesteryear, not well organized and armed only with knives, clubs and whatever they could pick up, were dangerous but easier to handle than what had begun to appear. The country was flooded with ex-soldiers (some INA veterans) and weapons, some courtesy of the United States. There had been a large American presence in Assam and Bengal during the war – and mountains of US stores and weapons. As the Americans left, they were supposed to remove or destroy the depots. In many cases they did neither. As a result, in place of the unorganized mobs of the past, there were now well organized and armed groups. This was particularly true in the Punjab, whose mixed population was made up not only of Hindus and Muslims but Sikhs, whose homeland it was and where a Sikh kingdom had ruled barely a century before. Facing an uncertain future the Sikhs began to prepare to assert themselves, aided and abetted by the rulers of the quasi-sovereign Sikh princely states embedded in the Punjab who provided money, arms, advisors (they all had their own small armies) as well as safe havens in their territories. When facing this menacing situation, the Indian Army was also deprived of something that had always been available in the past – the assistance of available British Army units. The Attlee government, intent on liquidating the Raj as rapidly as possible, was anxious – as Mountbatten was in SEAC's post-hostilities engagements in the Netherlands East Indies – to avoid British casualties. London made clear that to avoid being seen as "taking sides," British troops were to stay on the sidelines except to protect British lives. As disorder mounted the Indian Army was faced with a near impossible task – maintain order, with weak or non-existent police and civil administrative support, amid increasingly murderous communal hostilities without becoming itself communal. The first major foreshadowing of what was to come was the "Great Calcutta Killing" in August 1946.

Still trying to make the Cabinet Mission plan work, Wavell was trying to assemble an interim government but by mid-summer there was political deadlock. The long-term consequences of the Congress Party's decisions, first to resign office in 1939 and then to mount the August 1942 "Quit India" revolt were that with Congress sidelined and its leadership in detention Muhammed Ali Jinnah's Muslim League, which remained in office and supported India's war effort, had a clear field, an opportunity of which they took full advantage. By 1945 the League was the dominant force in Muslim India and

Jinnah the "sole spokesman" for it. And "Pakistan" an aspiration in the 1930s that became the League's stated goal only in 1940, was Jinnah's inflexible demand. The Congress leadership seems not to have taken the League and its demands as seriously as they ought to have and were equally inflexible in their position that they represented *all* Indians (there were Muslims in the Congress hierarchy but the ruling trio – Gandhi, Nehru and Patel – were Hindu). And that therefore Britain must hand over a united India to them. Facing deadlock, Jinnah called for a "direct action" day to underscore the League's widespread support. The intent was ostensibly peaceful – strikes, marches, shop closures – but the reality was that in the feverish atmosphere of India, especially in an area of mixed population, violence was inevitable. Trouble began in Calcutta on the morning of 16 August. By the time it ended three days later some 4400 people were dead and 17,000 injured, with extensive property damage. The General Officer Commanding the Indian Army's Eastern Command, Lieutenant General Sir Francis Tuker (who had commanded with distinction the 4th Indian Division in North Africa and Italy) deployed British, Indian and Gurkha battalions to bring the situation under control. Auchinleck had, on the eve of the outbreak, noted that the Indian Army had, as yet, been little affected by the rising communal tensions and events bore him out. However, a very ominous sign had appeared as troops were deployed: "troops waiting to be called out…must not place full reliance on information provided by the police or by the civil authorities."[71] The doctrine of "minimum force" in aid to the civil depended on the civil administration and police, and their intelligence collection, to be functioning efficiently. Without that the army was very seriously handicapped, minimum force less likely. The Calcutta riots proved that Auchinleck's assessment of his Army's current state was correct but also forecast that keeping the peace was going to be increasingly problematic as the police and civil administration weakened. The communal ferocity displayed in Calcutta showed that civil war was a real possibility, and Auchinleck knew that civil war would take the Indian Army to the breaking point. As communal animosity deepened, increasingly violent eruptions happened throughout the ensuring months – in East Bengal, Bihar and United Provinces – and the army was repeatedly called in, and as repeatedly had to operate with reduced or absent civil administration and police support. In every case the army performed effectively. The 1/3 Madras Regiment, one of the non-martial races units whose revival Auchinleck had sponsored, a Hindu regiment, had even inflicted heavy casualties on Hindu mobs in defense of Muslim refugees, exceeding the Commander-in-Chief's expectations. But clearly there were limits. It was against this background that Wavell deployed his "Breakdown Plan," which was also to be his swansong.

71 Marston, op. cit., pp. 219-19. Marston's chapter on 1946 (pp. 200-238) is a careful analysis of how the Indian Army handles the crises and pressure of its last full year of existence. It needs to be emphasized that violent disorder was not the norm throughout the entire subcontinent. It was heavily concentrated in Bengal, Bihar, the United Provinces and, above all, in the Punjab – all areas where Hindu and Muslim populations were intermixed. And in the Punjab, of course, the large, militant Sikh community, determined to avoid Muslim domination, were an additional explosive charge.

Wavell was an exhausted man by the autumn of 1946. He had been under heavy strain since 1939, in the Middle East and then India. The deadlock between League and Congress, amid rising communal tension, spilling over into veritable communal pogroms convinced him that it was time to simply leave India. His Breakdown Plan proposed a staged withdrawal from southern and central India (where there had been no significant communal unrest), the vacated provinces being granted immediate independence. British authority would be maintained for a while longer in north India while a final effort was made to negotiate an agreed political settlement. If that failed, the withdrawal would resume, with the Raj exiting through Karachi. Auchinleck was not happy with the Breakdown Plan. He pointed out that the army had so far proven resistant to communalism and able to maintain order, but that Wavell's plan might very well set off a process of disintegration – south India was not the army's heartland; north India was. Wavell nonetheless took the plan to London late in 1946 and the Attlee cabinet balked at such a forthright admission of failure. The most powerful Cabinet member, Ernest Bevin, told the prime minster that Wavell was defeatist and needed to be replaced. The Viceroy returned to India without being told he was to go – although Attlee was already talking with his successor. Only in February 1947 was he told that he would be replaced by Rear Admiral Viscount Mountbatten of Burma who had returned to the Royal Navy since leaving SEAC.

Mountbatten was controversial during his lifetime and will doubtless remain so. General Sir Alan Brooke, the Chief of the Imperial General Staff 1941-46, was definitely not an admirer, telling his diary that no one had ever become a supreme commander with fewer credentials for the job. Energetic and ambitious, and a careful custodian of his image and reputation, he had as well the glamour of royal connections and was certainly a change from the tired Wavell. But, despite claiming he knew India and the Indian Army because he had commanded Indian troops in SEAC, in fact he knew little of either. SEAC headquarters had opened in Delhi but soon moved to Kandy in Ceylon (Sri Lanka) to separate itself from India Command. Slim and the overwhelmingly Indian XIV Army had won all of SEAC's victories and, as for understanding the Indian Army, he had to have explained to him, once Viceroy, that Indian Army battalions were not communally homogeneous – some were but most were mixed. That primer on a basic fact soon to be of immense importance was imparted by the only member of his staff with real knowledge of the Indian Army, General Lord Ismay, an Indian Army cavalryman and Churchill's wartime chief staff officer, who agreed to join Mountbatten's staff, foregoing a richly earned rest, because he felt "Dickie" would need strong staff support (Brooke had felt the same way in 1943 and gave Mountbatten the very competent Lieutenant General Sir Henry Pownall as his first chief of staff at SEAC).[72] Mountbatten arrived in India in March 1947 knowing that he would be the

72 Ismay's role in 1947 is curious. He was, as noted, an Indian Army officer (21st Cavalry) and the only one in Mountbatten's entourage. In his bland memoir – *The Memoirs of General Lord Ismay* (New York, 1960) he says little about his role – one chapter in a 467-page book. The fine

last Viceroy, with a target date for the final transfer of power of June 1948. That, which at least allowed slightly more than a year for planning and preparation, soon went by the board. After a round of meetings with political leaders, Mountbatten quickly decided that there was no way to preserve a united India and there would have to be partition – and that 15 August 1947 would be the target date. That announcement – made at a press conference in early June – gave Auchinleck some ten weeks to "reconstitute" (the word he preferred to partition) the Indian Army, while still maintaining order, handling demobilization and trying to accelerate the promotion of Indian officers without impairing quality. When partition had first become a topic, he had talked about 5-10 years. On the eve of Mountbatten's announcement Auchinleck and the army's senior officers thought at least a year was needed. They would get two months – at a moment when the weakening of the police and civil administration in the critical Punjab province accelerated into collapse, leaving the army as the only barrier to anarchy.

Mountbatten's arrival and rapid acceptance that partition was the only solution (as, at that point, it may well have been – the Attlee government certainly would never have accepted the prolongation of the Raj in order to try to preserve a united India) opened a chaotic final chapter for British rule in India. For Auchinleck, it was a last chapter in his career during which he was not only being asked to do the near impossible but to do it without the full support he had enjoyed from Wavell. As part of his drive to nationalize the army Auchinleck had in February 1946 chosen as his Private Secretary Lieutenant Colonel Shahid Hamid, a cavalryman and the first Indian officer to hold this key staff position.[73] Almost as soon as Mountbatten arrived, he told Auchinleck that he did not think it was appropriate for a Muslim officer to hold such a sensitive position. Auchinleck told the Viceroy that his staff choices were his affair and Hamid remained. In London, Montgomery had succeeded Brooke as Chief of the Imperial General Staff and soon a ruling arrived that would have cut Hamid

biography by John Kiszely, *General Hastings "Pug"Ismay: Soldier, Statesman, Diplomat* (London, 2024) fills in much more detail. Ismay had known Auchinleck since 1923. Despite the fact that he was, uniquely, in a position to do so, there is no evidence that he tried, during the war, to modify Churchill's wildly inaccurate view of the Indian Army. When Mountbatten, in effect, sacked Auchinleck, he sent a letter of sympathy but did nothing else. He seems to have become disenchanted with "Dickie" by that time but never voiced any criticism. In the end, it seems he had become more than a bit courtier as well as a fine staff officer.

73 Hamid joined the fledging Pakistani army in 1947, rising to the rank of Major General. His memoir, Shahid Hamid, *Disastrous Twilight: A Personal record of the Partition of India* (London, 1986) is a crucial source for Auchinleck's thoughts and activities in 1946-47. Auchinleck knew Hamid was a diarist and was collecting documents. He simply asked that Hamid not publish anything until after his death. Hamid and his family remained close to Auchinleck for years. It is not always clear in the published version what represents contemporary notation as opposed to later reflection and Hamid was clearly in Auchinleck's corner, but it is the closest approach we have to Auchinleck's own thinking during the crucial months preceding the transfer of power. There is an interesting account of Hamid in his granddaughter's family memoir: Mishal Husain, *Broken Threads* (London, 2024). Hamid's account of the last years of the Raj is an essential source.

out of the distribution list for particularly sensitive documents. Auchinleck simply reconfigured the paper flow, so Hamid continued to see what his (British) predecessors had seen. As CIGS Monty made two official visits to India. On both occasions he was very critical of Auchinleck, although not to his face. Hamid summed up Monty's behavior succinctly: "He hates anyone who has served in the Indian Army."[74] Even the emollient Ismay was disturbed by Montgomery's relentless criticism of Auchinleck, particularly as the CIGS knew so little of Indian realities. In the run up to independence and partition Auchinleck, who bore the immense burden of dividing the army while simultaneously needing it to remain effective and cohesive for the maintenance of such order as was possible as the Raj crumbled across North India, did so without firm support from either London or the Viceroy.

When the date for independence was moved from June 1948 to August 1947 and the concerns of the Commander-in-Chief and his senior officers were brushed aside with the order to just do it, the "reconstitution" plan produced required some units to be moved across the subcontinent so that they would be in India or Pakistan on 15 August. However most Indian Army battalions, were mixed containing "class companies", i.e., subunits drawn from different communities. To reconstitute such units, they had to be in effect broken up to send troops to their respective new nations. The same process was applied to the officer corps, with many officers reluctantly and tearfully leaving their regiments to move to their newly mandated homelands. The nationalization of the officer corps had perforce to be paused. The experienced British officers would be crucial during the transition period and the terms and conditions for their continued service had to be worked out, as did the future of the Gurkhas whose service in the Indian Army was governed by treaty arrangements with the client kingdom of Nepal. The complex discussions on this issue were only concluded on 7 August 1947, ensuring that the Gurkhas would soldier on in both the Indian and British armies. It was not only units that were involved. *All* the assets of the Indian Army, from armored vehicles to office wastebaskets had to be split up in 70-30 proportions with India getting the lion's share. Once divided, a great deal had then to be moved, in some cases across India. All the while disorder spread across northern India, requiring military intervention even as communal tensions began to be felt in the army itself.[75] Viewed in long retrospect it seems remarkable that the army kept functioning – a tribute to Auchinleck, his senior officers and the officer corps as a whole which did its job effectively to the end. Because it did, it is all too readily assumed by writers on the subject that their almost exclusive focus on the politics of partition is the correct lens through which to view the end of the Raj. But had Auchinleck's leadership faltered the bloodshed that accompanied the transfer of power would have been far worse.

74 Hamid, *Disastrous Highlight*, p. 1932. Interestingly Monty's brother Brian joined the Indian Army from Sandhurst and had a successful career, retiring as a colonel.

75 A good summary of the "aid to the civil" actions of the period – some of which amounted to battles, can be found in Marston, pp. 290-312.

On 14 August, Lieutenant General Sir Reginald Savory, the last Adjutant General of the Indian Army issued an order: "This is the last Indian Army Order.'[76] But, while a unitary India and a single army had dissolved, literally overnight, into two new Dominions (one of them in two parts) each with a piece of the old Indian Army, Auchinleck lingered on in a strange twilight as "Supreme Commander." In the partition plan, this position was to temporarily exist to oversee the last stages of the division of the army and its assets, as well as the shipping home of the remaining British army units in India. Additionally, Auchinleck supervised the rear guard of the old army – the Punjab Boundary Force (PBF).

Violent unrest and mounting death totals had increased in the Punjab throughout 1946. This only intensified once partition was decided on. This large, rich province has long been a place where Hindu, Muslim and Sikh were intermingled and the prospect of communal violence close to the surface. The task of drawing a boundary through it was entrusted to a commission which promptly deadlocked and so the line was drawn by its British chairman, Sir Cyril Radcliffe, a British barrister who had no prior experience of India and worked in virtual isolation in a cottage on the ground of the Viceregal mansion. Mountbatten (who may well have put his thumb on the scale in favor of India) delayed the release of the boundary award until after 15 August to avoid the quite predictable quantum leap in violence that it would occasion in the Punjab from marring the independence celebrations (and, perhaps, to ensure that coping with that violence would be the responsibility of the new dominions, not the departing Raj). The burden of controlling the situation, with the police and civil administration no longer functional, fell to the Punjab Boundary Force under Auchinleck's supervision. It was built around the 4th Indian Division and commanded by Major General "Pete" Rees. The division had a very impressive war record and Rees had been one of Slim's most dynamic divisional commanders, but it and he were set an impossible task: it was understrength – about 9000 strong on the eve of partition – and was trying to preserve order in a province the size of Germany, with 52,000 villages and a population of some 35 million. Millions of those were on the move – Sikhs and Hindus moving from West Punjab (awarded to Pakistan) to East Punjab and Muslims headed in the opposite direction. Armed bands preyed on the long, defenseless, refugee caravans. Refugee trains were often stopped and their passengers slaughtered. To this day there is no definitive casualty total, but it cannot have been far off a million at a minimum (and of course there were massacres elsewhere, especially in Bengal, a province similarly split). In the face of this Rees and

76 Connell, p. 898. Auchinleck thought Savory would have been an appropriate successor as Commander-in-Chief had the Raj continued. Savory kept a diary, now in the National Army Musuem among Savory's papers. It is a very usedful source for the mood among Auchinleck's senior staff in 1946-47. Savory noted that Auchinleck refused the peerage and other decorations Mountbatten offered because he wanted nothing that came at Mountbatten's hands. After retiring – he left India shortly after Auchinleck – he turned to history, writing *His Britannic Majesty's Army in Germany During the Seven Year's War* (Oxford, 1956). I would like to thank my colleague, Dr Alan Jeffreys, for providing me with copies of Savory's 1946-47 diaries.

the Boundary Force did what they could but inevitably it was akin to tackling a forest fire with a garden hose. Rees and his troops were accused of partisanship by both sides and the enormity of the task and the lack of political support from the new dominions led to the Force being stood down on 1 September. The units of the PBF had not been "reconstituted" and were therefore in many cases communally mixed. Although Auchinleck worried about the strain on the troops, good leadership from Rees down and army traditions kept it functioning.[77]

As the Punjab tragedy unfolded, Auchinleck was simultaneously dealing with the last stages of reconstitution and the division of assets. The former went smoothly, if sadly. There were affecting scenes as units were broken up to be distributed to the new dominions. The division of stores and equipment was more fraught. The pages of his Private Secretary's diary are full of complaints about the bad faith of India in denying Pakistan its fair share (set at 30%) of the Indian Army's assets. Lieutenant Colonel Hamid, at least, was convinced that the new Indian government was sure that Pakistan would quickly collapse and were anxious to encourage that process. Whether that is completely accurate, the result for Auchinleck was that Nehru's government became increasingly hostile to him, as he tried to see that Pakistan got its fair share. At length Mountbatten, now governor general of the new Indian dominion, and close to Nehru, wrote him a letter saying that it was time for him to leave. Read today there is slightly oleaginous air to his "Dear Claude" letter, which included a draft letter of resignation for Auchinleck to use and closed with the offer of a peerage, already approved by the King. Auchinleck brusquely refused the peerage. He agreed to resign and close his headquarters on 30 November. But before he went, he had one last service to perform – to prevent the two parts of the Army he had served in for 44 years from clashing on the battlefield.

Kashmir was a large province north of the Punjab, overwhelmingly Muslim but ruled by a Hindu dynasty. As he wrapped up the Raj, Mountbatten advised India's 562 princes that their treaties with the British Crown would terminate with the Raj and they should decide to which dominion they wished to adhere, taking due account of the facts of geography. Kashmir abutted both but its quite unimpressive ruler, Maharaja Hari Singh, dithered. While he did so, some 5000 Muslim tribesmen from Pakistan's Northwest Frontier Province began to cross into Kashmir to liberate their co-religionists. To what extent this incursion had official support or connivance from the Pakistan government, still organizing itself, was not clear then and remains obscure. Hari Singh suddenly came off the fence and chose accession to India. Nehru, now India's prime minster, ordered the Indian Army into Kashmir. The chief of staff of the Pakistan Army, Lieutenant General Sir Douglas Gracey (another XIV Army veteran) told Auchinleck that Jinnah, now governor general of Pakistan, had ordered the Pakistani army into Kashmir. Auchinleck promptly flew to Lahore, met Jinnah and warned him that if he did so, it would trigger a "stand down" order by him as Supreme Commander which would withdraw all British officers from both Dominion armies since the dominions would be at war with one

77 The PBF's story is well summarized in Marston, pp. 312-319.

another. At that moment both armies still had British commanders-in-chief (and British officers were still filling many other command and staff positions in both armies). Jinnah rescinded his order and war over Kashmir was, temporarily, postponed.

On 1 December 1947 Field Marshal Sir Claude Auchinleck left India. He had refused the peerage, despite urgings from Mountbatten; refused a grand farewell dinner; refused an honor guard at the airport. He was seen off by Lieutenant General Sir Arthur Smith, the Guardsman who had been his first chief of staff in Cairo and was his deputy supreme commander and Lieutenant General Sir Reginald Savory. They stood at the salute as the plane lifted off.

The remainder of Auchinleck's life was spent quietly. Like so many retired senior officers he joined some corporate boards but kept a low public profile. He did not write memoirs or give many interviews. He did, however, make his papers available to the writer John Connell who produced a massive biography, focused heavily on his time in Cairo in 1959.[78] When Montgomery published his tendentious memoirs, his misstatements about the situation of the 8th Army when he took over in August 1942 brought a letter from Auchinleck to the London *Times* correcting the record and ascribing Montgomery's errors to faulty memory.[79] A more potent counterattack on the Montgomery version, Corelli Barnett's *The Desert Generals*, published in 1960, benefitted from access to Auchinleck's papers as well as interviews he gave Barnett. Auchinleck also read and critiqued the manuscript before publication. Barnett's brilliant polemic was a major demolition charge set off under "Monty's" account and changed the tenor of the ongoing discussion of the desert campaigns. In 1967 Auchinleck left his first retirement home at Beccles in Suffolk for final retirement in Morocco. He died in Marrakesh on 23 May 1981 at 97. He had stipulated a private, quiet funeral.

How to assess his remarkable career? He was born into a strata of British society that provided the staff, civil and military, for empire. An army career was almost inevitable;

78 The Auchinleck Papers are now at rhe John Rylands Library at the University of Manchester.

79 There is one episode in the arguments over the desert campaign that is notable for what Auchinleck did not do. When Churchill published the fourth volume of his war memoirs, *The Hinge of Fate* (1950), Major General Eric Dorman Smith, by that time living in retirement in Ireland, having changed his name to Dorman O'Gowan, threatened legal action, claiming that Churchill's account of the command changes in Cairo in August 1942 libeled him. This touched off a considerable amount of anxiety – and preventative action – by Churchill (once again prime minister), his staff and his lawyers. The full, fascinating story can be followed in David Reynolds' *In Command of History* (London: 2005), pp. 356-359. In the end the matter was settled by Churchill's agreement, in return for Dorman O'Gowan dropping his action, to insert in future editions of the *Hinge of Fate* a footnote making clear that nothing in the text was intended to disparage Dorman O'Gowan. The interesting point in relation to Auchinleck is that, according to Reynolds, he had quietly made clear that, if the issue went to court, he would support his former "chief of staff in the field". Auchinleck's official biographer writing only s few years later was absolutely silent about this. But it is perhaps why Auchinleck was willing to provide so much help to Barnett – he was unwilling to quarrel openly with either Churchill or Montgomery but was determined to prevent their version of August 1942 from becoming orthodoxy. And, as in July 1942, he succeeded.

family economics made the Indian Army the obvious choice. The Indian Army's campaign in "Mespot" left a mark on him, as the Western Front did on Montgomery. It left with him the conviction that attacks should not take place unless they were properly organized and could be effectively supported – an attitude he voiced during the Narvik operations and that lay at the root of his cautious approach before Crusader and then in the late Spring of 1942 and finally when he was, briefly, responsible for Burma operations in 1943. It was at the root of his disagreements with Churchill. The tragedy for Auchinleck was that both he and the prime minster were right – from their perspectives. Auchinleck knew, before Crusader, that the 8th Army needed time to train and prepare; Churchill knew that for reasons of domestic morale and alliance politics, the British needed to show that they were capable of defeating Germans as well as Italians. And, in the event, Auchinleck defeated Rommel, the first British victory of the war over the German army. Eight months later he would do it again, taking over direct command of 8th Army at a moment when disaster loomed. "I mean to win," he said. And he did. Not in a tidy way but at that moment all that counted was stopping Rommel, and that he did. In long retrospect, arguments can be made about some of his choices – Cunningham, Ritchie, Dorman Smith – but given the problems he faced, he did an impressive job. His army, in terms of equipment, training and doctrine had serious limitations that he could not transcend. And he was in many ways an outsider to the British army into the bargain. It must also be remembered that his successor worked initially with a plan Auchinleck had already begun to develop and benefited from an infusion of new equipment, much of it of better quality, as well as heavy reinforcement – and never had to manage the swirling maneuver battles that had undone Cunningham and Ritchie.

But perhaps Auchinleck's most impressive achievements were in India. He joined the Indian Army just as the first shadows began to creep across the landscape of the Raj. He became the head of his service as the Indian Empire entered its twilight, even as it was called upon to produce a military effort greater even than that of 1914-1918. What he did in 1941 before being translated to Cairo laid the foundation for the immense growth of the Indian Army and the rapid improvement of the "nationalization" process. "Equal treatment regardless of color" was a revolutionary change. When he returned in 1943, he presided over another revolutionary change, this time in training and support that produced Slim's great XIV Army. He did not, of course, do it alone but he provided the leadership and drive that powered the whole process.

And, finally, his role in the "Transfer of Power". Again, it is possible to construct a bill of particulars with which to critique him, but one fact dwarfs them all: the Indian Army, under terrible strain as communal tensions mounted and then turned murderous, never broke – and it is good to remember that as bad as the violence of 1946-47 was it would have been orders of magnitude worse if the army had. And he did it in the face of first, a tired Viceroy, and then one whose support was never certain, and, in the end, lacking. Indian politicians of both parties, with little connection of their own to the army, and a deep suspicion of it, tirelessly accused him of favoring the other side. In fact, he did his best to see the two successor services were created as working institutions with an equitable division of assets (in this one respect he failed, through no fault of his own).

He left India a sad and disappointed man – he told Mountbatten that he would not accept a peerage for his role in a disaster. He never returned to India but did visit Pakistan, where his old regiment, 1st Punjab, was now part of the Pakistan Army. And Pakistan remembered him. In the military cantonment at Peshawar, once the base for the frontier wars of the Raj, there is a monument to him.

Claude Auchinleck had a remarkable career which culminated in playing an important role in the last great war the British Empire would ever fight and then in the dismantling of the central pillar of that empire. A final verdict on such a significant career, with numerous controversial episodes, is elusive. But it can be said of Auchinleck that he confronted some of the most trying situations any British officer of his generation would face and wrung from them as much success as was possible. And that certainly deserves to be remembered by History.

2

# The Last Sepoy General: Field Marshal William Slim

## Introduction

When he died in December, 1970, William Slim was a Field Marshal, a Viscount, former Governor General of Australia, former Chief of the Imperial General Staff, former Constable of Windsor Castle and a Knight of the Garter. To the members of the Burma Star Association – (British) veterans of the Fourteenth Army that he had shaped and led brilliantly to victory in the most complex and difficult campaign any British (or American) general conducted during World War II, he was "Uncle Bill," a beloved leader to whom they warmed not only because he had led them to total victory but because they sensed in him an empathy born of a background not unlike theirs.

But despite his eminence, and the heartfelt tributes his passing occasioned, Slim, and the campaign he carried to a victorious end, were already marginal to British memories of the war and became more so in the generation after his death. Winston Churchill was largely responsible for this, as he was for so much of how the war was perceived in Britain and the United States at the time, the war in Burma only interested Churchill as a factor in Anglo-American relations – the Americans wanted to reopen an overland link with China. Afterwards, when his massively influential memoirs were being assembled, he allotted minimal wordage to it. Indeed, so obvious was it that he had little interest in chronicling Fourteenth Army's campaign that members of the Burma Star association raised the matter with Slim, who raised it with Churchill, who had two brief chapters drafted by an assistant for inclusion in the final volume of his memoirs, *Triumph and Tragedy*.

But it was not only Churchill's neglect that pushed Slim and his army into a corner of Britain's historical memory (it never even merited that in American memoirs of the war). Slim came from the Indian Army, an organization crucial to British power east of Suez but always regarded with condescension by the regular British army – and, of course, after 1947, part of Britain's rapidly fading imperial era. By the time of Slim's death the Raj was viewed by many in Britain as a subject for embarrassment, or dismissive humor. Paul Scott's hugely influential "Raj Quartet" series of novels which began to appear in 1966 and were brilliantly adapted for television in 1984, certainly did not encourage nostalgia about the Indian Empire, its personnel or its institutions.

But even if history does not "repeat itself" there is definitely a cyclical quality to historical interest in major issues. Although there had always been a trickle of fine scholarly books on the subject, the largest exhibition ever mounted by Britain's National Portrait Gallery, "The Raj: Indian and the British 1600-1947" which ran in London for five months in 1990-91 may perhaps be taken as an indicator that a new, more nuanced, look at the Raj was beginning. The story of the Indian Army began to be more carefully examined as well, and a landmark in the study of the army Slim led was the appearance in 2003 of Daniel Marston's prize-winning *Phoenix from the Ashes: The Indian Army in the Burma Campaign*. Once attention focused on the Indian Army's remarkable transformation during World War II, Slim's achievement became manifest. This reevaluation culminated in an online poll on who was Britain's "greatest general" conducted by Britain's National Army Museum. It concluded with an all day symposium at the Museum in April 2011. At the end of the day, from a list of candidates that included Cromwell, Marlborough – and Montgomery – the final vote named Slim joint winner with Wellington, who had learned the general's trade in India, and who had been derided by Napoleon as a mere "sepoy general." Slim too was a "sepoy general, the last and greatest the Raj's Indian Army nurtured. Like Wellington, he won.

## Apprenticeship: 1891-1939

People like William Joseph Slim did not become army officers in the world he was born into on 6 August 1891. His father was a small businessman who failed in Bristol (where Slim was born) but achieved some marginal success in Birmingham. In the Neapolitan ice that was the social structure of late Victorian Britain families like Slim's were at the lower edges of the middle class (or the upper edge of the lower middle class) and their sons precluded from an army officer's career which required the family means necessary to pay the fees and expenses for attendance at the Royal Military College, Sandhurst, and, after commissioning, to provide a private allowance sufficient to meet the expenses incurred by officers who were not expected to live on their pay. Slim, fascinated by Britain's long military history as retailed in popular literature, came to want a military career very badly. But every door seemed firmly closed against him. He nevertheless never lost sight of his goal, showing quite early a trait that would serve him well in later decades ahead – skill in "working the system" that positioned him to grab fleeting opportunities. In Birmingham he finished his secondary education at King Edward's School – a "grammar school," a type of secondary school whose modest fees and high standards made them attractive to struggling, barely middle class families like Slim's. King Edward's, like many such schools, had an OTC (Officer Training Corps) in which Slim enrolled, keeping alive his dreams of an army career – if Britain ever got into a war that required army expansion, creating a need for more officers quickly. Such a war seemed far away however and when his time at King Edward's ended, further education was out of the question. Indeed his father's declining fortunes mandated that he quickly get a job – which he did, teaching in Birmingham's slums. His connection with the OTC had ended of course when he left King Edward's but Birmingham University, which he could not afford to attend, had an OTC unit. Somehow he continued an attachment to it. By the summer of 1914 – having moved from teaching to an engineering firm and then managing to wrangle an interview with a senior executive of Asiatic Petroleum, and landing a job with them he was getting ready to go overseas. Then the lights suddenly went out all over Europe. Slim immediately saw an opportunity to realize his dream. On 22 August 1914, Lance Corporal W. J. Slim of the Birmingham University OTC became Second Lieutenant W. J. Slim of the Royal Warwickshire Regiment. He had won his first battle.

Slim's next battle was nearly his last. His 9th battalion of the Royal Warwicks became part of 39 Brigade of 13th Division – a "new army" division made up of units formed from the enthusiastic volunteers who had flooded the recruiting stations in the war's opening months. Like all new army units, Slim's division was made up of incompetently trained soldiers commanded by raw officers like himself with only a sprinkling of regulars and many of those recalled from retirement with little relevant experience to impart (although keen on smart salutes as Slim discovered when he failed to render one). Most of Slim's subaltern contemporaries were destined for the Western Front where they would die: Slim's division however was ordered to the eastern Mediterranean where it would participate in an effort to reanimate the stalled Gallipoli campaign.

That campaign, conceived by the still amateurish machinery that directed the war in London, is remembered now primarily for the (temporary) blight it cast on Winston Churchill's career and, in Australia, as the heroic founding myth of Australian nationhood.[1] For Slim it was the starting point in a hard military education. The 13th Division was intended to participate in a major offensive to break the deadlock that had turned the tiny allied beachhead at Cape Helles on the tip of the Gallipoli peninsula into a miniature Ypres – with heat, swarms of flies and rampant dysentery thrown in. While waiting for the major push, Slim's battalion was put into the trenches at Helles in relief of an exhausted unit. In 15 days Slim's battalion had four officers (including its colonel) and 510 "other ranks" killed or wounded. It was a weary and much reduced battalion that was then committed to a role in the major offensive that was to break the Turkish hold on the peninsula.

That offensive had two prongs.[2] There was an amphibious assault at Suvla Bay and an attack mounted from the other small beachhead held by the British at Anzac Cove

1 The best recent account of Gallipol is Robin Prior's *Gallipoli: The End of the Myth* (New Haven, 2009). Hastings Ismay, an Indian cavalryman who became, 1940-45, Churchill's personal chief of staff in the prime minister's capacity as Minister of Defence wrote an interesting analysis of how the proposed Dardanelles/Gallipoli operation would have been handled by the machinery over which Churchill presided in World War II. It is a trenchant critique of the inchoate machinery that actually approved the operation in 1914/15. *The Memoirs of Lord Ismay* (New York, 1960), pp. 164-66.

2 The battle of Sari Bair is well covered by Prior, *Gallipoli*, pp. 169-189 (with excellent maps). The story of the 29th Indian Infantry Brigade, ignored in many accounts, has finally been

– so named from the Australian and New Zealand Army Corps that had seized it in April's initial landings and had since held it in conditions as bad if not worse than those at Cape Helles. Overall command at Anzac was held by Lieutenant General William Birdwood, an Indian Army officer who was a protégé of Field Marshal Lord Kitchener, the Secretary of State for War and the dominant voice in military policy making in London in 1914-15. Slim's battalion was part of a force – a mixture of army, and Anzac units plus the 29 Indian Infantry Brigade (the most professional of Birdwood's units) – that was to attack at night, uphill, over a nightmarishly tangled and inadequately mapped landscape, in the face of determined, entrenched defenders.

The attackers were aiming at the crest line of the range of hills that were the central spine of the peninsula. Success would turn the Turkish defenses at Cape Helles and give the British a dominating position, swinging the campaign decisively in their favor. Such was the hope, but the design of the attack, shaped by the constraints of terrain, was not a recipe for success to begin with, while complex night operations, difficult enough for experienced troops and veteran staffs, were far beyond the capacity of the troops (except for the Indian Army units) Birdwood had.

The result, after several days of chaotic, desperate fighting, was complete defeat. Slim's battalion was scattered by the difficult terrain as it tried to move uphill in the darkness. He found himself commanding his company since every other officer had become a casualty (by the time the offensive, known as the battle of Sari Bair, ended on 10 August every officer of the Warwicks had been killed or wounded). On the night of 7/8 August Slim's much diminished company made contact with Major Cecil Allanson whose 1/6th Gurkhas (of 29 Indian Brigade) had gotten close to one of the objectives, Hill Q. Agreeing with Allanson that they would jointly attack the summit at dawn, Slim was trying to position his men for the attack when he was shot through the lung, the bullet then smashing his shoulder. His batman, subsequently killed, got him to an under-equipped dressing station where the linen wrapping from his solar topee (steel helmets were not yet in general use) was used to bandage him. There followed an agonizing downhill stretcher trip to the beach, evacuation on a barge that at first could not find a ship with room for more casualties, then, finally, a hospital ship on which, sedated, he returned to Britain expected by the attending doctor to die on the way. A Royal Army Medical Corps doctor who saw him on arrival recommended surgery to wire together the bits of the shattered shoulder, which would leave him with a largely useless arm,

told in Peter Stanley's excellent *Die in Battle, Do Not Despair: The Indians on Gallipoli, 1915* (London, 2015). pp. 192-216 give a detailed examination of the battle of Sari Bair. Slim's official biographer, Ronald Lewin, covered Slim at Gallipoli: *Slim: The Standard Bearer* (London, 1976), pp. 17-27. Lewin's biography, which won the W. H. Smith Literary Award, was written shortly after Slim's death. Lewin was able not only to use Slim's papers but to interview and correspond with many of Slim's army contemporaries who themselves left neither memoirs nor papers. Lewin's own papers (now deposited, together with Slim's, in the Churchill Archive Center at Churchill College, Cambridge) therefore contain a great deal of material that would otherwise have been lost to history.

adding "You're finished with soldiering for good."[3] Slim was rescued from despair by a young doctor, a recent recruit from civilian life (and more aware of recent advances in treatment) who advised him quietly to refuse surgery and opt for newer treatment methods. Slowly he regained use of the shoulder and arm and by September 1915 an army medical board pronounced him, rather confusingly, permanently disabled but fit to return to active service in three months. He was posted to the 12th Battalion of the Warwicks, a holding unit for replacements awaiting posting to battalions on active service. He had become an officer against the odds, survived a near fatal wound (and the RAMC doctors). Now he set his sights on a return to active service, and the exchange of his temporary commission for a permanent one.

An officer in a holding battalion had fairly light duties, which allowed Slim to begin what became a lifelong habit – writing about his experiences. That would produce the clear, accessible style found in *Defeat Into Victory*, his classic memoir, never out of print since it first appeared in 1956. He also found a way around the major barrier that stood between him and a permanent commission – his total lack of "private means." Established in 1795, the West India Regiment was perhaps the least attractive unit on the army list, its normal peacetime duties on assorted Caribbean islands as well as British Honduras (now Belize) and British Guiana (now Guyana) being accomplished by heat, boredom, disease and professional stultification. But it was cheap – as Slim told a fellow subaltern, it attracted those who were broke. Moreover it was rapidly expanding for overseas service and officers were needed. Slim became one of them on 1 July 1916. It is more than doubtful that he ever intended to soldier in Trinidad or Barbados. A regular commission however positioned him to transfer into another regiment, if he could find one he could afford. In the meantime, there was the problem of returning to active service. This he solved in a characteristic way – opportunism allied to skill in making the system serve him.

Holding battalions produced replacement drafts for the regiment's active service units. These drafts were accompanied by a conducting officer who, having delivered his charges, returned to the holding battalion. When a draft was due to leave for Slim's old unit, the 9th, currently serving in the 13th Division in Mesopotamia (now Iraq), Slim arranged to be the conducting officer. But his draft delivered, he did not return to Britain. Instead, in September 1916 he emerged as a temporary Captain with the 9th Royal Warwicks. Clearly, somehow, he had outflanked "permanently disabled" and maneuvered himself back onto active service. The RAMC was the first, but far from the last, to discover how hard it was to keep Slim from his objective.

The 1914-18 Mesopotamian campaign, now almost forgotten (although we live daily with its long-term consequences) was begun by the Government of India and depended throughout on the Indian Army. The Raj had long handled Britain's relations with the Persian Gulf and its pre-war plans in the event of hostilities with the Ottoman Empire had included the dispatch of a force, designated Indian Expeditionary Force D, to Basra at the head of the Gulf to protect British interests in the area, the most important being

3 Lewin, *Slim*, 26.

the terminals from which the Anglo-Persian Oil Company (largely owned by the British government) shipped the output, vial to the Royal Navy, of its south Persian outfields. Then a classic case of "mission creep" set in. Institutional and personal ambitions and the hope for prestige enhancing – and easy – victories over the Turks led to steadily expanding goals culminating in a decision to drive on Baghdad with one weak Indian division whose logistics were very precarious while medical arrangements were nearly invisible. Overreach led straight to disaster. Stopped short of Baghdad by stiffening Turkish resistance, driven back to its base at Kut-al-Amara on the Tigris River and besieged there, the 6th Indian Division surrendered in April, 1916.

It was an article of faith among all British policymakers – civil and military – that prestige was the oxygen of their eastern empire. The surrender at Kut therefore to be erased by victory. The War Office in London took over direction of the campaign from Indian Army headquarters in Delhi (although India continued to provide nearly all the troops plus most of the logistic support). The command structure in both Mesopotamia and in India was shaken up, and a new commander appointed to what was now called the Mesopotamian Expeditionary Force.

Lieutenant General Stanley Maude was a Guardsman (who however learned Urdu to communicate with his Indian troops) and an excellent administrator who set about overhauling the MEF completely. He had barely taken command when Slim reached the theater. Once again with his old division and battalion, now command his former company, he had a front row seat as Maude carried out his own exercise in turning defeat into victory. Some years later, in one of the articles he wrote during the interwar years, under the pen name Anthony Mills, Slim said this about his time with the MEF: "To watch an army recovering its morale is enthralling: to feel the process working within oneself is an unforgettable experience."[4] That judgment foreshadowed, with almost uncanny precision, what he would do twenty five years later, with Fourteenth Army. Slim entered Baghdad with Maude's army in February, 1917. He was still far from completely well. He was spitting blood and "chunks of lung," the incompletely healed lung irritated by the sand and grit-saturated air of Mesopotamia. The advance continued after Baghdad's fall, even through "Mespot" was by now very much a secondary theater, rather like the Italian theater after D-Day. And like the retreating Germans in Italy, the increasingly threadbare Ottoman army proved to be tough and tenacious defenders.[5] On 29 March 1917, in an attack on a Turkish rear guard position on the Tigris, north of Baghdad, Slim was again wounded in an action that cost the 9th Royal Warwicks a third of its strength (and won for Slim a Military Cross, an award created in 1914 to recognize

4 Field Marshal Viscount Slim, *Unofficial History* (New York, 1962), 42. The best general account of the 1914-18 campaign in "Mespot" is by A. J. Barker, *The Bastard War: The Mesopotamian Campaign, 1914-1918* (New York, 1967); there is a good recent study of the Kut debacle, by Nikolas Gardner, *The Siege of Kut-al-Amara: At War in Mesopotamia, 1915-1916.* (Bloomington, IN, 2014)

5 The first three chapters of *Unofficial History*, based on articles Slim wrote in the 1930s recount episodes from Slim's service in Mesopotamia.

gallantry under fire by junior officers). Evacuated along the now smoothly operating casualty treatment system's communications line to a base hospital, Slim's wound, although serious, did not seem to pose any threat to his career. However trouble loomed for him because, as a British Army officer his wounding (and award recommendation) was reported to the War Office in London, which, upon consulting his file, suddenly became aware that a "permanently disabled" officer supposedly tucked away safely with the Royal Warwicks holding battalion at Bovington in Dorset was instead very gallantly commanding a company fighting on the Tigris and getting himself seriously wounded – again. A demand for an explanation was issued and the hospital authorities in MEF, who knew a bureaucratic mare's nest when they saw one, quickly disembarrassed themselves of Slim, packing him off on a hospital ship to Bombay, thereby making him India Command's problem. It proved to be the decisive moment for his military future.

Slim of course had encountered the Indian Army before – first on the slopes of Hill Q and then in Mespot where most of MEF was Indian Army. Now, after recovery at Simla, the summer capital of the Raj in the Himalayan foothills, he was drawn into its headquarters. Temporary Captain W. S. Slim, West India Regiment, was posted to Indian Army headquarters in November 1917. We do not know how this came about but Slim is unlikely to have left matters to chance. No more was heard from the War Office, presumably satisfied that a third grade staff appointment in Delhi was an appropriate posting for an officer "permanently disabled." In November 1918, now a temporary Major, he was moved up to a second grade staff appointment. But the end of the war immediately raised the question of his future.

The West India Regiment was a professional dead end. The Indian Army however was not – and was a place where its largely middle class British officer corps could live on their (reasonably generous) salaries without recourse to "private means." Slim had had time to assess its possibilities for himself, as well as time to make a strongly positive impression, attested by excellent annual reports. Slim applied for a transfer in January 1919, endorsed by the Commander-in-Chief, India, General Sir Charles Monro. The India Office in London, the final authority, agreed grudgingly – they were refusing transfers at the time (large numbers of temporary officers were seeking permanent commissions as the huge wartime British army shrank). However, said the India Office, the transfer should be as a Lieutenant, not a Captain. (Economizing? Bureaucratic score settling? Impossible now to say.) Monro however, citing Slim's good service, stood his ground and it was as a Captain that Slim was "gazetted" to the 1st Battalion, 6th Gurkha Rifles on 27 March 1920. He would remain with the Raj's Indian Army for the rest of its existence.[6]

The regimental home of the 6th Gurkha Rifles was Abbottabad (now in Pakistan), named for James Abbott of the East India Company's Bengal Army, one of the

6 For readers not familiar with the Indian Army of the British Raj, the best introduction remains Philip Mason's *A Matter of Honour: An Account of the Indian Army, its officers and men* (London, 1974). Mason belonged to the last generation of British administrators in India and his account is in places both defensive and nostalgic. No more recent book has however covered the entire story with Mason's narrative skill.

legendary figures in the establishment of the Company's authority in the Punjab and on the Northwest Frontier. The regiment itself began as the East India Company's Cuttack Legion in 1817, then became a paramilitary gendarmerie, raised to police India's Northeast Frontier in Assam. Originally a mixed Sikh and Gurkha unit, it then morphed into the all Gurkha 42nd Assam Light Infantry and finally, upon moving to Abbotabad, the 6th Gurkha Rifles. By the time Slim joined the 6th, the Gurkha Brigade (actually ten two battalion regiments, equivalent to two divisions) was regarded, not least by its officers, as the Indian Army's elite, the equivalent of the Brigade of Guards in the British Army – the gold standard of Indian soldiering. It was this tightly knit military family that would provide a large number of Slim's subordinates in Burma two decades on. Slim was a regimental soldier for five years and, in addition to routine garrison life, experienced both of the duties that were central to the life of the Indian Army in the interwar years: frontier campaigning and "aid to the civil."

From the time the East India Company's conquest of the Sikh kingdom in the Punjab brought the Raj up against India's mountainous northwestern frontier and the ferocious tribesmen who lived there, the problem of "the Frontier" had preoccupied the Indian Army. Controlling the Pathan (now commonly called Pashtun) tribesmen was the immediate problem, but, as the eastern frontiers of Czarist Russia crept remorselessly closer to those of the inchoate Afghan state, an even greater problem loomed. Russian influence in Afghanistan might precipitate a major frontier war – or, in the worst case scenario – Cossacks might clatter through the Khyber Pass. For three quarters of a century before Slim arrived at Abbotabad, every Indian Army unit had spent much of its time on the frontier, about one year in three. An impressive body of doctrine had evolved to guide both training and operations there. Frontier warfare was low intensity warfare but no less lethal for that – the tribesmen pounced on the slightest loss of focus and alertness, the smallest tactical misstep. The frontier taught hard lessons, especially about the need for rigorous training. Slim, already a combat veteran, went through this graduate course in small unit action and left a description of it that would be hard to better.[7]

Frontier combat, however testing, was comparatively straightforward. Far otherwise was the Indian Army's second major commitment, "aid to the civil," i.e., supporting the civilian authorities in situations where unrest had become riot and outrun the capacity of the (mostly unarmed) police force to contain. Such situations became frequent during the interwar years as both the incidence of political agitation increased, and aroused by that, "communal" (i.e., Hindu- Muslim) clashes became more frequent. And there hung over any such troop deployments the memory of Amritsar where, in response to serious rioting troops were deployed in April 1919.

7 Slim, *Unofficial History*, 102-123. This essay, entitled "Student's Interlude," can be supplemented by the numerous descriptions of Frontier warfare in John Masters's minor classic, *Bugles and a Tiger* (London, 1956). Masters, who served in the 4th Gurkha Rifles, became, in retirement, a talented historical novelist. The best scholarly treatment of the Indian Army on the frontier is T. R. Moreman, *The Army in India and the Development of Frontier Warfare, 1849-1947.* (London, 1998)

In a severe overreaction to the situation – to put it no higher – Brigadier Reginald Dyer, commanding the troops, opened fire on a crowd in a public park, killing at least 379 people and wounding some 1,000 more. Although Amritsar was not at all typical of how the Indian Army handled such situations – and despite the fact that Dyer was criticized by a subsequent inquiry, removed from command and retired, and his actions subsequently condemned by Parliament (and denounced in a brilliant speech by Winston Churchill), Amritsar was a decisive event in the decline of the Raj. Gandhi decided the British could not be trusted and launched his first great protest against British rule and "Amritsar" hovered over the Raj for the remaining 28 years of its life. Indian Army officers were very conscious of the career marring – or terminating – possibilities of any "aid to the civil" duty, should they make a decision, subsequently judged to have been incorrect. Since the officers concerned were usually junior – "aid to the civil" usually resulting in the employment of troops in small detachments – the pressures were even greater.

Most important of all for Indian Army units involved in such duties was the intense stress placed upon the sepoys, often asked to confront their co-religionists. The only unrest in the Army's ranks during the interwar years in fact took place at Peshawar, capital of the Northwest Frontier Province in 1930 when several platoons of the Royal Garwhal Rifles, having endured a day of brickbats and bottles from a mob against whom they were not allowed to retaliate, refused to deploy for a second day of similar duty. All in all, deployment in support of civil authority presented challenges and pitfalls that must have made Frontier duty seem comparatively simple. This too Slim experienced, and described in an illuminating essay that, while perhaps a trifle too good humored, nevertheless catches the chaotic and ambiguous situations young officers often faced and the burden of responsibility that frequently fell to them.[8]

Regimental service, frontier fighting and aid to the civil were episodes in a career whose trend was now steadily upward. Slim served as adjutant of his battalion (a crucial step in a soldier's career); his annual reports were all good (although one colonel did

8 Slim, *Unofficial History*, 75-98. This essay, entitled "Aid to the Civil" carries a note by Slim telling the reader that it describes not one incident, but three, conflated into one narrative. Slim also, in his introduction, addresses the question of "tone" – whether he has treated "too lightly" episodes which were "grim and terrible" (vii-viii). He pleads guilty but claims that humor in bad situations has been one of the historic strengths of British soldiers. And, in the essay he describes the troops committed as British even though in any "aid to the civil" duties, he would certainly have commanded Gurkhas. Perhaps, writing for British readers he decided using British characters would work best. (The Raj authorities preferred to use British or Gurkha troops in such situations, thinking they would be perceived as neutral in their sympathies by Indian crowds, a perhaps erroneous assumption.) The disaffection among the Royal Garwhal Rifles at Peshawar in 1930 is dealt with by Philip Mason, *A Matter of Honour: A History of the Indian Army, Its Officers and Men* (London, 1974), 451-53. There are good, scholarly studies of the problems of using the Indian Army in an "aid to the civil" role: Nick Lloyd, "The Indian Army and Civil Disorder: 1919- 1922," and Rob Johnson, "The Indian Army and Internal Security: 1919-1946" in Kaushik Roy (ed.), *The Indian Army in the Two World Wars* (Leiden, 2012), 335-390.

note that he rode well "for an infantryman," an interesting example of the hippophilia that was one of the hallmarks of interwar British officers). In 1926 he married Aileen Robertson, a Scots clergyman's daughter and in the same year entered the Indian Army Staff College at Quetta.

There also he made an impression. One fellow student was sure he would end his career as Commander-in-Chief.[9] From his time at Quetta comes another story which signposts Slim's evolving approach to battle. Told by a member of the Directing Staff that his solution to a problem set was akin to using a pile driver to crush a walnut, Slim replied "Sir, have you ever seen a walnut that has been crushed by a pile driver?"[10] Slim's sense, that forcing the enemy to retreat was good, annihilating him even better, would play out dramatically on the battlefields of Burma in 1944-45. So would something else that he first encountered at Quetta. One instructor, with whom he became close, was Percy Hobart, a British officer from the Royal Tank Corps.

Hobart's ideas on mobility and the use of armor – and the sort of army mobile warfare required – clearly lodged in Slim's brain to bear fruit later. Slim left Quetta at the top of his class with an "A" grading and glowing recommendations, including the Commandant's "…he is an interesting man to have dealings with," a remarkable example of understatement.[11]

Slim did not return to regimental duty for a decade after leaving the staff college. First came a posting to Indian Army headquarters in Delhi, where he spent four years. One of his initiatives there produced some trouble for him. He was interested in the possibilities of air supply for troops in the field (which would be the lifeblood of Fourteenth Army in 1944-45) and approached his opposite number at Air Headquarters, India, to suggest a collaborative endeavor. Relations between the RAF and the older services were icy at best and when Slim's initiative was reported to the Air Officer Commanding, India, that worthy promptly placed an agitated call to the Commander-in-Chief, India, complaining of a violation of his turf. The result was that Slim was personally dressed down by the C in C. It made no difference to the glowing reports he received however (and investigations into supply dropping, especially appropriate packaging and the development of cheaper parachutes than the standard silk model quietly continued). Staff duties in India were followed by a posting back to Britain to fill the Indian Army slot on the directing staff of the British Army's staff college at Camberley. Once again he made a strong impression – after Camberley he was chosen to attend the Imperial Defence College in

9 That prophecy could have come true. On the eve of Indian independence, Nehru told the last Viceroy, Mountbatten, that he wanted Slim as independent India's first commander-in-chief. Slim, seeing the job as replete with thorny political issues, declined. Lewin, *Slim*, 260.

10 The story comes from Brigadier Michael Roberts, a fellow Gurkha officer (10th Gurkhas). Roberts Papers, MRBS 1/4, Churchill Archive Center, Churchill College Cambridge. Roberts would later be part of the team that produced the Cabinet Office Official History of the war in Burma and would also act as Slim's research assistant both on *Defeat Into Victory* and *Unofficial History*.

11 Lewin, *Slim*, 48.

London where rising officers from all the services, and senior civil servants, spent a year in a graduate studies atmosphere, considering the large problems of strategy.

These years "at home" were important to Slim in several ways. The Indian Army had always been a thing apart – distance, a focus on India's unique challenges and British Army snobbery had always kept its officers largely isolated from the British Army. Slim got an opportunity to meet – and impress – many who held, or would soon rise to, senior positions in that Army. He also got the leisure to develop further his skills, pursued since the dark days after Gallipoli, as a writer. There was a strong incentive to do so. Indian service, civil or military, was well compensated, which made it possible for men with little or nothing in the way of private income to serve there, living on their salaries. However when posted "home" many Indian allowances were either curtailed or stopped. For Slim, with a wife and two children the resulting loss of £400 per annum was a very serious matter. He now began to write not for pleasure but out of financial necessity. The articles he placed with newspapers and periodicals (under the pseudonym "Anthony Mills") using an old school friend as agent – serving officers did not write light articles – brought in needed cash and, when later collected in *Unofficial History*, constituted something of an autobiography. But while time in Britain gave Slim a wide acquaintance with the British Army, and made him an accomplished writer of light essays, it posed a major problem in addition to the gaping hole it tore in his finances: a threat to his promotion prospects and therefore to his future in the Army. By the time Slim's year at the IDC was over, he was a 47-year-old Major and had been away from regimental service for over a decade. Promotion in the Indian Army had historically been slow and the golden opinions Slim had garnered at Quetta and Camberley (including a strong recommendation from General Lord Gort, VC, the Camberley commandant, for promotion to lieutenant colonel) would be of no avail unless the 1938 Promotion Board made him a colonel. It did but by only one vote – the "no" voters were cast on the grounds of age. The deciding vote was cast by General Sir John Coleridge of the 8th Gurkhas. Slim returned to India in 1938, a lieutenant colonel – he would not see Britain again for seven years. He took command of the 2nd Battalion, 7th Gurkha Rifles then stationed at Shillong in Assam – a province he would get to know very well in coming years. He did not however remain long with the 2nd/7th. In the Spring of 1939 he became commandant of the Indian Senior Officers School at Belgaum (which he himself had passed through only a year before prior to assuming command of the 2nd/7th). The appointment carried with it (local) Brigadier's rank. On 3 September 1939 Neville Chamberlain declared Britain at war with Germany; the Viceroy and Governor General of India, Victor Alexander John Hope, 2nd Marquees of Linlithgow, promptly told the Indian Empire that the King Emperor's declaration of war meant India, too, was at war.

Only the German invasion of Belgium in 1914 allowed Slim to become an officer, now a second German decision opened another door for him. In the face of considerable odds he had become an officer, survived Hill Q, gotten himself a regular commission in the Indian Army and squeaked by a promotion board that could have ended his career. Now he would have the chance to prove the truth of the assessment made by chief of the general staff in India who wrote on his 1932 annual report "By reason of his special qualities… in the interests of the Service, [he] is worthy of special attention."[12]

## Command

The outbreak of war saved Slim from what would have otherwise almost certainly have been retirement in a few years on grounds of age. He quickly began to lobby for an active command – commandant at Belgaum he regarded a dead end. By the end of September he had a brigade, 10th Indian Infantry Brigade, made up of three Indian battalions. Since Indian Army modernization had barely begun, preparing for the Middle East, as part of the 5th Indian Division, was particularly challenging. The brigade was to be motorized but had, as yet, no trucks. None of the sepoys could drive – most had never had any dealings with motor vehicles at all. There were no mechanics. Slim began training for motorization using horsed transport to simulate motor vehicles, while garages in the vicinity were scoured for possible driving instructors (as was the local civilian community). Trucks finally appeared in March 1940. The 10th Indian Brigade was originally destined for Iraq, as part of an operation christened "Sabine" to guarantee the security of the Iraqi and south Persian oilfields but it was abruptly shifted to the Sudan in August, 1940, as part of a design to eliminate Italy's East African empire (comprising what are now Eritrea, Ethiopia and most of Somalia). This would eliminate any threat to the shipping lanes through the Red Sea which were the lifeline of Britain's Middle East theater (and, by removing the designation "combat zone" from the area made it possible for American shipping to deliver supplies to Egypt, easing the mounting strain on British shipping). The offensive would have two prongs: one, mounted from Kenya, driving north into Italian Somaliland and the second, based in the Sudan, moving east, into Ethiopia. Slim's brigade would open the attack from the Sudan, the first major British ground offensive of the war, in fact. It went very badly.

Major General Lewis Heath's division was short a brigade and to bring it up to strength, three British battalions – the peacetime garrison of the Sudan – were added to it. Two of Heath's brigades lost an Indian battalion and got a British replacement. The two spare Indian battalions were then combined with the remaining British battalion to produce the third brigade. The drawback was that, over Slim's protests, a tightly knit unit that had trained together was disrupted on the eve of going into its first action.

The position Slim's brigade was to attack in November 1940, was Gallabat perched on the Sudan-Ethiopia frontier. It comprised two linked, fortified centers, strongly garrisoned. Slim planned on a two part operation to deal with each in turn. The first half was successful and one Italian position was taken. Then the Italians counter-attacked. Slim's small armored contingent was stopped by mines and terrain, while his air cover, obsolescent Gladiator biplane fighters, was brushed aside and Italian bombers hit his

12 Ibid., p. 53.

positions hard. The Essex, fresh from undemanding garrison duties, retired in panic, which communicated itself to transport drivers, also new to air attack, who also began to pull out. Endeavoring to halt the rout, Slim actually knocked down the Essex' colonel (a breach of army regulations). Matters were gotten under control but the Essex had to be pulled out of the line. The question now was: could the attack be revived? Slim at first thought so but he was down to his two reliable Indian battalions and the commanding officer of one of them, the Royal Garwhal Rifles – who would do the attacking – and his artillery commander counseled against it (both would serve with Slim eighteen months later on the retreat from Burma). Slim consolidated his partial gains and accepted defeat in his first battle.

Gallabat had major consequences for the development of Slim's generalship. Years later, he reflected on it in an essay entitled revealingly, "Counsel of Fears." Long after it had been nearly forgotten (the British official historians gave it a paragraph), Slim not only wrote but published a quite detailed account of the Gallabat battle. He makes clear that as he approached his first major battle he was "angry," because he had lost his Punjabi battalion, "tough, quick- moving, well-commanded" because of a "policy decision made in far-off Whitehall." (Churchill was adamant that the traditional inclusion of a British battalion in any Indian brigade be maintained.) He also includes a vivid and unsparing description of the rout of the Essex, who he clearly never wanted. He does not mention knocking down their commanding officer, much less then sacking him. He does however say this about his effort to stem the panic: he confronted parties of bolting soldiers "one party with an officer who angered me very much." An indirect reference perhaps to the Essex colonel? But the most interesting sentence in the essay is the one assessing his own decision not to renew the attack the following day (which his key subordinates all strongly supported): "When two courses of action were open to me I had not chosen, as a good commander should, the bolder. I had taken counsel of my fears." It was not a mistake he would ever make again. Gallabat, and his analysis of his failure, was clearly a crucial moment in the development of his generalship.[13]

He did not remain long in East Africa after Gallabat. His staff car was caught in the open by Italian fighters and in the strafing attack he was hit in the posterior by three bullets as he dove for safety. The wounds were serious and painful, but not life threatening. Slim did endure, however for the second time, a long painful journey back to a

13 Slim's account of Gallabat is in *Unofficial History* (New York, 1959), pp. 125-148. Churchill, whose view of the Indian Army, was, and remained, deeply condescending and suspicious, was a firm believer in the post-Mutiny rule that every Indian Army brigade had to include a British battalion both to set an example of good soldiering for the sepoys, and, in the last analysis, to ensure their loyalty. That belief, like nearly all of Churchill's thoughts on India, was totally out of date. All Indian brigades became increasingly common as the Indian Army steadily grew while the British Army experienced a growing, and ultimately insolvable, manpower problem. The fighting quality and reliability of Indian units were unaffected by this change. (Slim made a point in his essay on Gallabat of the fact that the Essex' battalion, rebuilt after their debacle, later had a fine record of service. He was nearly always generous in judgment.)

base hospital (air evacuation of casualties as yet not available). Returned to India for convalescence, he was briefly attached to Army Headquarters, then named Brigadier General Staff (BGS) to Lieutenant General Edward Quinan, who was about to take command of an expeditionary force preparing to move into Iraq (a problem Slim had been studying during his brief time at Army Headquarters). But Slim was not destined to become a staff officer. The vanguard of Quinan's force was the 10th Indian Division, commanded by Major General W. A. K. Fraser, was already disembarking at Basra.

Fraser suddenly asked to be relieved because "he no longer had the confidence of his subordinate commanders." The Commander-in-Chief, India, General Sir Claude Auchinleck named Slim on 15 May 1941 to replace him, citing Slim's "energy, determination and force of character." Slim now had what he later described as one of the best appointments in the army – divisional command. Over the coming months Slim would demonstrate what a quarter century of soldiering, capped by the experience of Gallabat, had taught him.[14]

Iraq was a British creation, its final form settled by Winston Churchill, then Colonial Secretary, at a conference in Cairo in 1921. British control, lightly masked by a League of Nations mandate, continued until 1932 when Iraq became independent and a member of the League of Nations. That independence was qualified however. As part of the imperial air route to India, the RAF maintained two large bases – Habbaniya west of Baghdad and Shaiba near Basra – and Britain was linked to Iraq by a mutual defense treaty that gave Britain the right to move troops across Iraq if necessary. Britain also equipped the Iraqi army and the British ambassador in Baghdad remained a key figure in Iraqi politics. Iraq had been conquered in 1914-18 by a largely Indian Army force and any force transiting Iraq would be drawn largely from India. At the outbreak of war India already had a plan in case intervention in Iraq became necessary. Iraqi nationalists had grown increasingly anti-British as the 1930s wore on, an attitude strengthened by German and Italian propaganda and further sharpened by British policy in Palestine, seen in the Arab world as favoring the Zionists. All this culminated in April 1941 in a coup in Baghdad led by a nationalist politician named Rashid Ali al Gailani and backed by four Iraqi officers, the "Golden Square." The pro-British Regent (and the British ambassador) fled and Sir Archibald Wavell, the British Commander-in-Chief, Middle East, with his hands full with the German attack on Greece and Rommel in Egypt's Western Desert, asked India to handle the problem. London concurred. At Karachi, the 20th Indian Infantry Brigade was already loaded and ready to sail for Malaya. It was redirected to Basra, together with 10th Indian Division headquarters. Theoretically, the British were obliged to ask Iraqi permission before landing troops but since the request coincided with the arrival of 20th Indian Brigade's convoy at Basra and the landing at

14 The relief of Fraser is slightly mysterious. Ronald Lewin, *Slim: The Standard Bearer* (London, 1976) simply says he fell ill. Robert Lyman, in his excellent *Slim, Master of War* (London, 2004), p. 5, cites a contemporary note from Auchinleck to the Viceroy, from which the phrase quoted in the text comes. What lay behind it all now seems irrecoverable. Whatever it was, the Fates seem to have decided to give Slim a break.

Shaiba of half a battalion of British troops air-lifted from India, the Iraqis had no time to object. With Shaiba safe, Basra secured by two Gurkha battalions and another of Sikhs, and 10th Indian Division building up to full strength, Slim entered the scene.

The RAF station at Habbaniya was under siege, conducted with almost comic opera ineffectuality by the Iraqi army. Slim was ordered to push north, up the road to Baghdad and Habbaniya as part of a relief effort (another very scratch force was making its way across the desert from Palestine as the second prong of the relief operation). There was little opposition from the Iraqi army – the demolitions blown in the bunds (levees) along the Euphrates, which caused extensive flooding did more to hold up Slim's division. One of the officers of the 2/4th Gurkha Rifles was outraged to learn that the Iraqis had equipment not available in India. Britain had supplied up to date equipment (as required by the Anglo-Iraqi Treaty) to the Iraqis, while the Indian Army, much of whose reserves of equipment had been shipped back to Britain to help fill the gaping holes left by the abandonment of nearly everything on the Dunkirk beaches, went without. "Even Mr. Churchill came to learn," he wrote later, that "[the Indian Army] was of more value to our cause than the Arab conscripts now busily supporting the Golden Square..."[15] Slim's division entered Baghdad – his second visit to the city – but Habbaniya had already been relieved, and the advance of the desert column from Palestine had forced the Iraqis to seek an armistice. Slim's division continued north to occupy Mosul (whose airport had, briefly, hosted the Luftwaffe's brief foray in support of the Golden Square). The campaign however was over, although the Indian Army would occupy Iraq for the balance of the war.[16]

If Iraq did not pose much of a test of generalship, another campaign loomed in which Slim would have greater scope for his growing skills. Vichy controlled Syria had provided staging posts for the Luftwaffe's brief and ineffectual attempt to support the Golden Square. With the Germans now in control of Greece and Crete, London decided that to leave Syria in hostile Vichy hands was too much of a risk. Wavell was ordered to take control of Syria and, very reluctantly, opened yet another campaign on a shoestring. As two columns drove into Lebanon and Syria from Palestine, Lieutenant General Sir Edward Quinan's Iraq Command, the new headquarters set up to oversee the occupation

15 John Masters, *The Road Past Mandalay* (New York, paper ed., 1961) p. 17. In view of Churchill's attitude toward the make up of Indian Army units, it is worth noting that the division's three brigades – 20th, 21st and 25th Indian Infantry Brigades – were made up entirely of Indian battalions.

16 The political and strategic background to what was, in effect, the Indian Army's reconquest of Iraq are in Geoffrey Warner's *Iraq and Syria 1941* (London, 1974). A brief military narrative is in the British official history, Major General I. S. O. Playfair, et. al., pp. 177-197. A much more detailed account can be found in the Indian official history: Dharm Pal, *The Campaigns in Western Asia* (New Delhi, 1957). This volume, a product of the Combined Inter-Services Historical Section, India and Pakistan, was part of a lengthy series produced under the general editorship of Bisheshwar Prasad, one of the few successful collaborative efforts between India and Pakistan, perhaps because when it was carried out the senior officers in both countries had common roots in the undivided army of the Raj.

of that country, was ordered to send a third column up the Euphrates to outflank the French facing the main British (actually mostly Australian and Indian) attack from the south. Transferred from Iraq Command to Lieutenant General Sir Henry Maitland Wilson's Palestine based force, Slim was ordered to take Deir-es- zor, a hundred miles up the Euphrates, where the only bridge in the 500 miles between Habbaniya and the Turkish frontier spanned the river. The brief campaign that followed showed how far Slim had come since Gallabat.

The problems Slim faced were a rehearsal for later experiences. The French had a fairly large force in Syria – some 25,000 regulars with about 90 tanks (most committed to stopping Wilson's drive on Beirut and Damascus). They also had an equal number of French officered local troops. More important for Slim, committed to an advance across desert terrain devoid of cover, little air support was available to him – a mere eight fighters, four Hurricanes and four obsolete Gladiators, biplanes dating from the early 1930s flowed by inexperienced pilots. His logistics were also precarious – which was to be his situation until 1945. Because there were not enough trucks, most of Iraq Command had to be grounded to give his 21st Indian Infantry Brigade the mobility and logistic support needed. Moreover, fuel had to be trucked up in flimsy cans many of which burst in transit due to the rough going. Because rifles were in short supply in India the drivers of "second line transport" drawn from the Royal Indian Army Service Corps or the Indian Army Ordinance Corps were in addition to being recent, incompletely trained recruits, unarmed. The open desert across which they drove, often inexpertly (few Indian Army recruits were mechanically literate when they enlisted), was infested with raiders, the most notorious being the band led by Fawzi Qaqukji, who had plied his trade in Palestine during the 1936-39 Arab Revolt against the British Mandate. Now funded by both the Vichy authorities and the German representative in Syria, Dr. Rudolph Rahn, he found a very soft target in the unescorted supply trucks and their defenseless drivers. Slim had a very good eye for talent which served him well throughout his career. He found an answer to his logistic problem in Lieutenant Colonel A. H. "Alf" Snelling, eventually to become Fourteenth Army's logistic wiz and who he pinched from a Line of Communications Area command. While Snelling rounded up every conceivable form of transport, including local rivercraft and village donkeys, Slim ran a brief counter-insurgency campaign, finding escorts for supply convoys and raiding villages that supplied the hostile bands with information, recruits – and storage for their loot. At length Brigadier C. J. Weld's 21st Indian Brigade was ready (just) to jump off, accompanied by an Indian cavalry unit "mounted" in armored cars that were not only true museum pieces but terribly vulnerable because their armament could not be used in an anti-aircraft role.

The Syrian border post at Abu Kemal was undefended but as 21 Brigade rumbled onwards towards Deir-es-zor, the Vichy air force, more modern aircraft with more experienced pilots began to bomb the columns. Despite this however, 21 Brigade closed up on Deir-es, defended by French officered Syrian units. Slim's plan was to push two Gurkha battalions straight up the Deir-es-zor road, which ran along the Euphrates, while his third battalion, accompanied by the antediluvian armored cars, swung wide into the desert, regained the road north of Deir-es-zor and attacked from an unexpected, and, it was hoped, undefended direction. The plan put into execution on the night of 30 June almost immediately came unstuck. Scattered and disoriented by sandstorms, out of radio contact with Weld because of atmospheric interference caused by the storms, its fuel almost exhausted by driving in low gear through soft sand (averaging seven miles a gallon), the outflanking column was well short of its objectives the next day. Weld recalled it, concerned that its low fuel state might leave it stranded in the desert, immobile and vulnerable if it continued its wide sweep. He proposed therefore to alter the plan to suit the amount of fuel left, sending the outflanking column on a shorter hook that would bring it against Deir-es-zor from the west, rather than the north. It was, in view of the fuel situation, the orthodox solution. "Then I remembered Gallabat, eight months before," Slim recalled, "when I had taken counsel of my fears and missed by chance. This time I would not. I would listen to my hopes rather than my fears. I would take the risk." Ordering Snelling to find more fuel even if it left every other 10th Indian Division unit immobile and to get it to him by the evening of 2 July, he told Weld to drain every possible drop out of every 21 Brigade vehicle not in the outflanking column. He would send them forward again aiming for the road north of Deir. If they got there, they would have barely ten miles of "going" in their tanks. Snelling came through. Ordering loads dumped regardless of what was being carried, he got the transport needed and then immobilizing vehicles all the way back to Baghdad, he collected the fuel. At 0415 on 3 July the column set out. By noon Deir was in Slim's hands, the French local troops stripping off their uniforms and melting into the civilian population. Slim lunched in the Vichy commandant's quarters off food prepared for the vanished occupant. He had also acquired eighty new trucks, a great deal of fuel and enough rifles to arm his Transport Company drivers. His generalship henceforth would be characterized by boldness (and a dependence on improvisatory logistics). In a report on the lessons of the brief campaign, Slim wrote of the tactical advantages that flowed from boldness and acceptance of risk: "Commanders must be prepared to show initiative and act without waiting for orders from above." That lesson is central to the essay he later wrote on the Syrian campaign, unsurprisingly entitled "It Pays to be Bold" (in *Unofficial History* it follows the chapter on Gallabat). Slim had been to the Indian Staff College, taught at the British Army equivalent and attended the Imperial Defence College. But his military education was completed by first, Gallabat, and then his experience with 10th Indian Division.[17]

17 Slim wrote a report on the capture of Deir-ez-zor which the Indian official history reprinted in full: Pal, pp. 527-530. Slim clearly used this in writing his own account of the battle, which appears in *Unofficial History*, pp. 149-175. The quotation in the text is pp. 163-64. "Second line transport" were the truck companies that hauled supplies from a base to the point, close to the front, where the supplies were handed over to the fighting units. There is another personal account of the Iraq, Syrian and Persian campaigns by John Masters (4th Gurkha Rifles) *The Road Past Mandalay*, pp. 2-64. Masters also left a very perceptive pen portrait of Slim's impact on the officers of the 10th Indian Division when he assumed command (pp. 30-32). Playfair and Pal give detailed descriptions of the shoestring campaigns in Syria and Persia.

After the conclusion of the Syrian campaign, Slim and his division became responsible for northern Iraq. But quiet garrison work did not last long. In August 1941, London (in cooperation with its new Prussian ally) decided to occupy Persia (now Iran). The Shah had proved reluctant to consent to the removal of the large numbers of German and Italian personnel living and working there and with Persia's heightened importance as a transit corridor for aid to Russia, the danger they posed, as a potential fifth column, seemed too great to ignore. Slim commanded an improvised force – a scratch armored brigade, not all of whose units actually had tanks, plus four Gurkha battalions – that entered Persia from northern Iraq, while other Indian units, based in the Basra area, took control of Abadan and the South Persian oilfields and refineries. There was little opposition, the large but not very enthusiastic Persian army very quickly ceasing resistance. Slim chronicled this part of his story in two essays that later appeared in *Unofficial History*. Trickier to deal with than the Shah's army was a Kurdish tribal revolt, contained without too much difficulty (Slim rated the Kurds as formidable, if less so than the Pathan tribesmen he had faced on the North West Frontier). More difficult than either the Shah's soldiers or the Kurds were the Russians who had moved into the country from the north. His light-hearted account of his contacts with the Red Army does not completely conceal his anxiety about keeping the Russians out of the sphere assigned to British occupation and oversight. He records ordering the colonel of the 2/7 Gurkhas, once his battalion machine gun officer when he had briefly commanded the unit in Assam on the eve of war, to get to an appropriate blocking position no matter how many trucks were written off in the process or Gurkhas knocked out in road accidents. In the event all went off smoothly and the greatest hazard turned out to be to his liver as he worked his way through repeated vodka soaked social encounters with Russian officers. After their Persian interlude Slim and his division reverted to training for a possible encounter with an opponent infinitely more formidable than the Iraqis, Vichy officered Syrians or Persians encountered so far. If the Red Army collapsed, as seemed to many (including the Joint Intelligence Committee in London) quite probable, the German army coming through the Caucasus or Turkey might be their next opponent – in Slim's very apt simile, 10th Indian would be the orange flung in the path of the oncoming steamroller. But he was not destined to fight the Germans. By early March 1942 his divisional headquarters was at the RAF station at Habbaniyah. Quinan's Iraq Force had by that time become the Tenth Army and under it a corps headquarters, IV Indian Corps, controlled the 8th Indian Division and Slim's 10th Division (by this point holding the Middle East, from the Mediterranean to the borders of the Raj depended entirely on the Indian Army). Quinan called Slim early in March to tell him he was to be in Delhi in three days for a "new job." More than that Slim did not know as the flying boat that would take him to India lifted off Lake Habbaniyah.[18]

18 The 10th Indian remained in Iraq then moved westward, fighting in the Desert War against Rommel and finishing its war in Italy. Its odyssey is a fair picture of how the Indian Army supported Britain's war across the globe.

## Note: The Indian Army and the Middle East[19]

The Indian Army had always been crucial to both the establishment and maintenance of the British position in the Middle East. In 1801 Company troops were part of the force that mopped up the French army occupying Egypt. When Britain intervened in Egypt in 1882, establishing its "veiled protectorate" Indian units were again deployed, two brigades taking part in the shattering victory over the Egyptian army at Tell-el-Kebir in September 1882. Indian units deployed to Egypt at the beginning of World War I and thereafter played a role in the Palestine campaign (providing most of the troops in that theater by 1918). Of course the Mesopotamian campaign was almost exclusively Indian Army. Pre-1939 plans called for the deployment of Indian forces to Egypt again, and the 4th Indian Division formed there in 1939, followed by the 5th Indian Division. The Indian Army played as noted a major role in the destruction of Italy's East African empire. The 4th Indian would also spend its war in the Desert, the Middle East and Italy. India had a plan for intervention in Iraq if needed that played out as already described.

But it was only after the brief Iraqi, Syrian and Palestinian campaigns concluded that the Indian Army commitment to Middle East ballooned. Those campaigns overlapped the launching of Hitler's attack on Russia. Attention in London, Cairo and New Delhi turned immediately to a potential "northern front" for the Middle East theater. The intelligence assessment in London was that the Soviet Union would not last long and that by autumn the Germans might be threading their way through the Caucasus or, alternatively, driving through Anatolia, the Turks presumably cowed by the Wehrmacht's destruction of the Red Army. General Sir Claude Auchinleck, who took over as Middle East Commander in June 1941, was an Indian Army officer and came from the job of Commander in Chief, India. He was very sensitive to the Raj's historic fear of any threat to its sphere overland from the north. Although the threat would not be German rather than Russian, dispositions were quickly made to confront it, should the worst happen. A new 9th Army commanded by Lt. Gen. Sir Henry Maitland Wilson, was established in Syria, to base with the Turks and prepare to face a German thrust through Anatolia. Wilson's troops were a shifting mixture of Australian, New

19 While the brief campaigns in Iraq, Syria and Persia have been adequately covered, Paiforce and Tenth Army have vanished into a historical black hole. An official publication *Paiforce: The Story of Persia and Iraq Command, 1941-1946* (London, 1948), anonymously authored, is well written but clearly aimed at a general readership. The British official theater history, Major General I. S. O. Playfair, et. al., *The Mediterranean and Middle East, Vol. III, British Fortunes reach their Lowest Ebb* (London, 1960), gave it an appendix (pp. 424-26). The India official history Dharma Pal, *The Campaigns in Western Asia* (New Delhi, 1957) provides the fullest treatment (pp. 359- 461).

By late 1942 American units, with vastly greater resources, began to assume the major role in running what they christened "the Persian Corridor" route to Russia. But Indian units continued to both provide internal security and much logistic support until the war's end. The last Indian units left in 1947.

Zealand, British and Indian units, either recuperating from, or preparing to depart for, the campaign against Rommel in the Western Desert. Farther east, Sir Edward Quinan's command, officially known as "British Troops in Iraq" (despite the fact that most were Indian) became Tenth Army in January, 1942. Operational control of Tenth Army rested with Middle East Command in Cairo – a clumsy arrangement that had Auchinleck looking simultaneously west and north. Auchinleck himself suggested in July 1942 a separate command, covering Iraq and Persia. When, the following month, Churchill descended on Cairo bent on restructuring the Middle East command to focus it exclusively on beating Rommel (and giving him the victory he desperately needed), Auchinleck's proposal took concrete shape as "Paiforce" (Persia and Iraq Force). Auchinleck relieved by Churchill in Cairo was offered the new command but declined (it would, in effect, have been a demotion). Wilson was thereupon moved from 9th Army to Baghdad to command Paiforce, a job he held until he himself moved to Cairo as Middle East Commander-in-Chief in February 1943. By that time however the German threat from the north had evaporated with the Russian counteroffensive at Stalingrad and Paiforce became a backwater for the remainder of the war.

From its beginning however, as British Troops in Iraq, then Tenth Army, the force committed to holding the northern front in Iraq and Persia was overwhelmingly Indian Army. When Tenth Army came into being, it comprised three Indian divisions (6th, 8th and Slim's 10th) plus an Indian armored brigade (lacking tanks) and a brigade of the British 50th Division. This force grew as the German 1942 summer offensive drove deep into the Caucasus. By September 1942, Quinan had two corps headquarters, three Indian infantry divisions, an Indian armored division (still largely without tanks) and an Indian motor brigade. A British armored brigade and two divisions destined for the Middle East were also available. A Polish division (made up of prisoners released from Russian camps and being equipped by the British) was taking shape.

This was a very substantial force and a heavy commitment for the Indian Army. It was also Tenth Army's apogee. After Stalingrad, it was run down. One Indian Infantry Division, the 5th, went back to India, eventually to join Slim's Fourteenth Army. The 6th and 8th followed the 4th and 10th westward to continue their war in Italy. The armored division, never fully equipped, would eventually be disbanded and its component formations used elsewhere.

Behind the fighting formations there was a huge influx from India of base, line of communications, construction, water transport and port operating units, as the Basra Shaiba area became not only the base for Tenth Army and the rest of Paiforce but also for the huge Anglo- American project to feed Lend Lease supplies over an upgraded road-rail network north through Persia, to Russia. Unglamorous, this massive logistical effort nonetheless played an important role in allied strategy.

In his massive history of the war Churchill never spared a line for this Indian contribution to maintaining British control of the Middle East and to the construction of an enormous logistical support base there to sustain both the imperial war effort and the Anglo-American commitment to aid Russia.

## Burma: The Long Retreat[20]

When Slim's flying boat touched down on a lake outside Gwalior, he had no idea what his next assignment would be. A long train journey brought him to Delhi but not to any more information about his next posting. He did discover that he was to accompany the chief of staff of the Indian Army, Lieutenant General Edwin Morris, to Burma. After a slow journey by air, Slim and Morris reached Burma's summer capital, the hill station of Maymo, east of Mandalay, and met with the recently appointed commander of the forces in Burma, General Sir Harold Alexander. Still none the wiser about his own future, Slim returned to India, having at least had a good opportunity to access how grim the situation was for Burma's defenders – as well as to begin to fear that this "familiarization tour" was the prelude to a staff assignment, a prospect he regarded with dread since he did not feel staff-work was his strong point. Finally, in Calcutta, he was summoned to a meeting with the Commander-in-Chief, India, General Sir Archibald Wavell. In a sitting groom at Government House, the vast, gloomy (and, Slim feared, unsanitary) residence of the Governor of Bengal, he was told by the famously monosyllabic Wavell that he was to return to Burma to take command of a corps being formed there, adding that he should leave as soon as possible. Slim would spend the next three years fighting in Burma, transforming himself from a relatively unknown Indian Army major general into the iconic "Uncle Bill," commander of the "Forgotten Army." Yet there was a great deal of serendipity in that appointment.

No one had ever considered Burma at risk and the provision for its defense in December 1941 reflected that. An officer on his last posting before retirement was GOC (General Officer Commanding). There was the grandly named Burma Army whose only unit was the 1st Burma Division made up of recently raised, incompetently trained, badly equipped Burma Rifles units

20 Slim left his own account of the Burma campaign in *Defeat Into Victory* (London, 1956). It is essential reading. Slim's official biography by Ronald Lewin, *Slim: The Standard Bearer* (London, 1976) is much better than the average authorized life. Lewin drew on interviews with many of Slim's contemporaries who themselves wrote nothing. Lewin's papers are in the Churchill Archive Center, Churchill College, Cambridge. Louis Allen, *Burma: The Longest War, 1941-1945* is an excellent study by a former XIV Army intelligence officer whose command of Japanese enabled him to tell the story from both sides of the battle lines. Raymond Callahan, *Burma, 1942-1945* (London, 1978) concentrates on theater strategy and alliance politics. Robert Lyman's *Slim, Master of War: Burma and the Birth of Modern Warfare* (London, 2004) is a perceptive analysis by a professional soldier turned historian. For those wishing to plunge further into the weeds, there are two official histories: S. W. Kirby, et. al., *The War Against Japan*, 5 vols. (London, HMSO, 1957-1969) is the most accessible. The three volumes produced by the Combined Inter Services Historical Section, India & Pakistan – Bisheshwar Prasad (ed.), *The Retreat from Burma, 1941-42* (Calcutta, 1954-1959) are hard going but have a mass of tactical detail. Slim's papers are also at the Churchill Archive Center. They are rather surprisingly sparse – some papers however remain in family hands.

whose hastily commissioned British officers (most drawn from the British business community in Burma) were as unready for war as the men they led. The division had virtually none of the supporting arms and services that make a division a coherent fighting force.[21] The one bright spot was that it included an Indian infantry brigade but the Indian Army's breakneck expansion over the previous eighteen months meant that its battalions had a very high percentage of new recruits as well. On the eve of war, the 16th Indian Infantry Brigade arrived to become Burma Army's reserve. It had been hastily thrown together and had never trained as a unit. "Milking" – the detachment of trained soldiers to form the cadre of newly raised units – had reduced two of its three battalions to half their regular strength – a deficiency met by adding 300 new recruits to each, in one case three hours before the battalion entrained for its port of embarkation. During that train trip, the brigade signals units joined.

Once in Burma, as its commander dryly remarked, "the disadvantage of no one knowing the Burmese language was realised" but no interpreters were available.[22] Once the Japanese attacked the 17th Indian Infantry Division was quickly added to Burma's defenders. However it had been recently raised, its battalions were also made up of new recruits, inexperienced NCOs and newly commissioned officers. It was not considered ready for combat without considerable additional training. Moreover, two of its three brigades were almost immediately sent to Singapore, so only the headquarters and one brigade actually reached Burma. The 17th Indian had one more handicap – its commander, Major General J. G. Smyth, V. C., was a very sick man. He had persuaded the medical authorities in India (perhaps aided by the weight of that V. C.) that he was fit enough for service. His one brigade division was brought up to strength by adding the unready 16th and pulling out of India yet another half trained brigade from another newly raised Indian division. The 17th Indian never had an opportunity to do any training as a division.

Burma's defenses were therefore far less impressive than they looked on paper. The command structure in Burma was as muddled as the state of the new Indian brigades. Burma answered not to India Command but to Far East Command in Singapore, which largely ignored it. When Japan attacked, London handed it back to India (where it had always logically belonged) with the not very helpful prime ministerial injunction to "look

21 The pre-war Burma Rifles were recruited largely from the non-Burmese hill tribes – Karens, Kachins, Chins – who live in the horseshoe of mountains that rim the plains where the Burmese predominated. Burmese feelings about the Raj were tepid at best. Realizing this Burmese had not even been enlisted, the British preferring the reliable hill tribesmen who saw them as protectors. In 1939 only 472 of the 3,669 rank and file of the "Burmese" units were ethnic Burmese. The policy changed with the decision to expand the Burma Rifles but the new units, in addition to lacking equipment, training and experienced officers, were often deficient as well in commitment. Hence the high rate of desertion once 1st Burma Division was committed to combat against the highly motivated Imperial Japanese Army.

22 Kirby II, pp 440-41, App 2 "The State of Training of Brigades Forming 17th Indian Infantry Division in December 1941." This hair-raising document details how utterly unprepared the division was for combat. Brigadier J. K. Jones' remark quoted is at p. 441.

east." Wavell made a quick trip to Rangoon and promptly removed the GOC but then replaced him with Lieutenant General Thomas Hutton, his Chief of the General Staff in India. Hutton was primarily a staff officer and had not held a field command since his 1914-18 service on the Western Front.

Moreover, like Wavell, Hutton was a British Army officer and all his principal subordinates came from the Indian Army (even Burma Rifles officers had, prior to wartime expansion, been Indian Army officers serving four year attachments). Wavell told Hutton to hold Rangoon.

Hutton told Smyth to hold the Japanese on one of the river lines east of the city. Smyth, ill and under relentless Japanese pressure, knew that was an unrealistic expectation for his largely new troops but retreated as slowly as he could (which was still too fast for Hutton). Finally, at the Sittang, the last river barrier before Rangoon, the combination of Smyth's debility, Japanese aggressiveness and the "fog of war," produced disaster. The bridge over the Sittang was blown with two thirds of Smyth's division on the wrong side. In the aftermath, 17th Indian Division mustered only 41% of its established strength – and rifles for only a third of that number. This was the point at which Slim entered the picture.

Wavell, shortly after cleaning house in Rangoon, had become the first supreme allied commander of the war. As head of the "American-British-Dutch-Australian" command (ABDA) he was responsible for everything from Burma to Australia. With headquarters in Java, poor communications and disaster everywhere he looked, he had little time and less ability to affect matters in Burma. That job fell to his acting replacement in India, General Sir Alan Hartley. As the 17th Indian Division fell back, Hartley and the Viceroy, Lord Linlithgow, decided a more inspirational commander than Hutton was needed (which argues they had no real understanding of either the situation on the ground in Burma or the state of the 17th Indian – an odd failing in Hartley's case, since he was an Indian Army officer). The decision of Hutton's replacement was made in London, where Churchill and Alan Brooke, the newly appointed Chief of the Imperial General Staff, settled on a general with abundant charisma – General Sir Harold Alexander, whose courage and unflappability were legend. Hutton went back to his real métier as Alexander's chief of staff. However, "Alex" was from the Irish Guards and the army in Burma was heavily Indian. It was therefore decided to create a corps headquarters, Burma Corps ("Burcorps") under an Indian Army general. The two names suggested to Brooke were Lieutenant General Thomas Corbett, commanding IV Indian Corps in Iraq and Major General W. J. Slim, commanding 10th Indian Division in that corps. Brooke's influential deputy, Lieutenant General Archibald Nye, the Vice Chief of the Imperial General Staff, spotted Slim's name. Nye had known Slim from the time when they both had been instructors at Camberley. Nye supplied the nudge that led to Slim's meeting with Wavell in the cavernous gloom of Government House in Calcutta.

Slim became an acting lieutenant general and a corps commander in the worst conceivable circumstances. Burcorps was a hastily cobbled together expedient in an impossible situation. He was to take command of the disintegrating 1st Burma Division (its Burmese troops had been deserting from the campaign's opening days; only the ethnically distinct hill tribesmen remained with their units) and the nearly shattered 17th Indian Division in a situation where reinforcement was impossible, air cover nonexistent, supplies scant and irreplaceable, civil government collapsing, and the local population at best indifferent and often hostile.[23] His opponents held every card. One of his few assets, besides his own physical and mental resilience, was his principal subordinates. What was left of the 1st Burma Division was commanded by J. Bruce Scott from the 6th Gurkha Rifles. 17th Indian was now in the hands of D. T. "Punch" Cowan (in the aftermath of the Sittang, Wavell had sacked Smyth, reduced him in rank and forcibly retired him). Cowan also came from the 6th Gurkhas. Slim and his two division commanders came from the same regimental family and had known one another for years. It was an invaluable asset in a precarious situation (and a foreshadowing of the outsize role Gurkha Rifles officers would play in the Burma campaign). His corps BGS (Brigadier General Staff – the corps chief of staff) H. L. "Taffy" Davies and his corps artillery commander, Brigadier G. de V. "Welcher" Welshman, had both been with him in East Africa. Slim also had the 7th Armoured Brigade. Veterans of the desert war against the Italians and then Rommel, the brigade had been rushed into Rangoon just before its evacuation. In addition to its mobile firepower, the brigade was a veteran presence and had its own signals – crucial because Burcorps hastily thrown together headquarters had a weak signals component (and few maps!).

It was fortunate for Slim that he had the armoured brigade and a dependable team of subordinates because he had very little else to be cheerful about. It was not even certain exactly where Burcorps was retiring to. On 18 April, Wavell told Alexander that if forced to retire from Burma (a certainty by that point) some of his troops should fall back into China, which had contributed the equivalent of two weak divisions to Burma's defense. Alexander was reluctant to send troops into China and Slim adamant that none of his units would end their retreat stranded in the famine stricken province of Yunnan. Finally on 23 April, Wavell accepted reality and ordered Burcorps to fall back into India's northeastern frontier province of Assam. This episode however introduces the final complication Slim had to deal with: the China factor, which would hover over the Burma campaign until its end.

The Roosevelt administration was strongly committed to the support of the Chinese Nationalist government and its leader, Chiang Kai-Shek – indeed U.S. support for China had been a major factor in the steadily worsening of Japanese-American relations that

23 Burcorps' retreat was conducted amid the chaos of a failing civil administration and the massive flight of Burma's large Indian population, seen by Burmese nationalists as collaborators of the Raj. This dimension of the campaign is well covered in Christopher Bayly and Tim Harper, *Forgotten Armies: The Fall of British Asia, 1941-1945* (London, 2004) and Michael D. Leigh's *The Evacuation of Civilians from Burma: Analysing the 1942 Colonial Disaster* (London, 2014). Slim said little in *Defeat Into Victory* about either the refugee problem or the disintegration of the civil administration. Both however vastly complicated his task: roads were clogged with terrified, hungry, often diseased crowds of civilians, while railroads, telephone lines, indeed any aspect of civil government was rapidly vanishing.

culminated in the Pearl Harbor attack. When the Lend-Lease bill passed in March 1941, China immediately became a recipient of American supplies, which reached the Chinese via the port of Rangoon and a long rail and road link – the "Burma Road" – ending at Kunming in China's southwestern Yunnan province. When Japan attacked Chiang quickly offered two Chinese "armies" to aid in the defense of his Burmese lifeline. Wavell was cool to the idea, feeling the British Empire should not be defended by foreigners. Chinese "armies" were far less than they seemed. A Chinese division was about the size of a British (or Indian) brigade. A three division "army" was therefore equivalent to a weak western division. Furthermore, Chinese formations had none of the supporting arms and services that gave a division is cohesion and much of its punch (in some units not even all the troops had rifles). They were therefore dependent on the British for supplies – which the British did not have. This, and the progressive collapse of the civil administration, led to the Chinese living off the countryside in the manner of pre-modern armies. However, in seeking limit to the Chinese presence in Burma, Wavell had reckoned without alliance politics. Churchill, in Washington for the first wartime Anglo-American summit (the Arcadia Conference) soon discovered that, as he later told Wavell, he had to learn, and remember, a new priority: "China." Two Chinese armies moved into eastern Burma, and with them came their nominal American commander, Lieutenant General Joseph W. Stilwell, a toxic Anglophobe who would bedevil the British until 1944.

The Chinese operated in a separate area – the Sittang valley – from Burcorps, which retired up the Irrawaddy valley to the west. Most of the burden dealing with Stilwell and the Chinese fell on Alexander whose tact and charm must have been sorely tried. Since Slim and Stilwell were corps commanders under Alexander, Slim saw enough of Stilwell to take his measure. He respected Stilwell's abilities as a fighting soldier and his skill in coaxing real effort out of his nominal, balky, Chinese subordinates (who double checked his every order with their own high command and sometimes had to be bribed to attack). He also noted that Stilwell was a very different man in private conversation than he was when he had an American audience.

Stilwell, in turn, seems to have felt more positively about Slim about other "limey" generals – perhaps because Slim with his lower middle class background and grammar school education didn't trigger Stilwell's antipathies the way most British senior officers did. Perhaps also because Slim was so clearly no one to trifle with.

During the retreat however Slim had relatively little to do with Stilwell and the Chinese. He had his hand full shepherding Burcorps out of one precarious situation after another. 1st Burma Division dwindled away – by the end of the retreat it was an Indian division in all but name. The 17th Indian, now under the dynamic Cowan and heavily Gurkha in composition had pulled itself together and, attenuated as it was, fought well through the balance of the retreat which, after Mandalay was abandoned, took Burcorps northwest towards the Irrawaddy's great tributary, the Chindwin. Across the river lay Assam, where an army of laborers gathered by the Assam Tea Planters Association from its workforce was hacking out a road from the Chindwin to Imphal where, Burcorps hoped, lay safety, supplies, and rest. Its retreat was nearly intercepted at one point and it was then forced to fight a stiff rearguard action as it was ferried across the Chindwin, leaving behind its artillery, tanks, and trucks which could not be gotten across the bridgeless river. Burcorps and its exhausted commander reached Imphal in early May 1942, in a dead heat with the monsoon that would have hopelessly bogged their withdrawal. As Slim observed, they looked like scarecrows but still behaved like soldiers.

Years later, that retreat – the longest in British military history, and, in fact, one of the longest on record – must have been very much on Slim's mind when he penned these lines about generalship:

> He [the general] is short of sleep, he is tired, he is probably wet, his nose is running and his sodden map is flapping about in his hands. Before him stand, in a rather forlorn group, some of his staff, a couple of subordinate commanders convinced that whatever eventuates they will have the dirty work to do, and most embarrassing of all, an ally or two, oozing suspicion. If the military situation is bad – and the odds are it will be – they will just stand looking at him, their eyes all asking the same mute question "what do we do now?" …They want an answer and they want it now …He knows and they know that unless something pretty brisk and decisive is done quickly neither he nor they will be here in a week's time.[24]

The retreat of Burcorps had provided plenty of opportunities for Slim to show his leadership skills, his physical and mental toughness, and to be brisk and decisive in extricating his command from situations where dithering would mean destruction. For the sort of offensive inclinations he had shown at Deir-es-Zor there had been no opportunities, but Slim was already pondering what he had learned, the lessons he would apply when the chance came to redeem defeat with victory. But first he had to survive, professionally, that defeat.

Generals who have lost battles very often find their careers at an end – either pushed into retirement (like "Jackie" Smyth) or relegated to second tier commands. Slim however would survive – a tribute to the reputation he had built before Burcorps, and the acknowledged hopelessness of the situation he faced. By the time he assumed command, Rangoon had fallen, the RAF had vanished from Burmese skies, and his two divisions were in tatters. He did very well to extricate Burcorps. In addition, overall responsibility for the campaign lay with Alexander whose own legend, buttressed by Churchill's admiration, meant that defeat in Burma would not blot his record – and "Alex" approved of Slim. It is easy to note all this in retrospect but at the time what must have been in the foreground for Slim was the reception he met with when he reached Imphal.

The northeast frontier of British India – the province of Assam – had never been thought to be at risk. When suddenly it was, frantic improvisation was the order of the day. No road linked India and Burma – the sea offered an easier and cheaper highway. Wavell had ordered the road extended from Imphal in Assam to the Burmese border on the Chindwin River but there were no engineering resources to spare. So, as noted above, a hastily gathered army of civilian laborers from the tea estates hacked out a

24 This essay is in the Slim Papers 5/2/2, Churchill Archive Center.

rough track. Imphal itself was linked by a nominally all-weather road to Dimapur on the narrow gauge railroad that ran up the Brahmaputra River valley. This precarious line of communications was never intended to support anything but the local economy. Now in the late Spring of 1942, Imphal was host to a corps headquarters and the newly raised 23rd Indian Infantry Division (whose commander, Major General Reginald Savory, would play a critical role in the wartime history of the Indian Army). Then the remnants of Burcorps were added (and of course thousands of mostly Indian refugees from Burma were also reaching Imphal). The precarious logistic situation at Imphal meant that the rest, recuperation, and rehabilitation that Slim and his troops hoped for was simply not possible. While, in the circumstances, the Spartan conditions that greeted Burcorps were generally unavoidable, nothing excuses the attitude exhibited by the IV Corps commander, Lieutenant General Noel Irwin.

Irwin was a British rather than an Indian Army officer. He had a distinguished record as a young officer in World War I. He also had a short temper and was moreover from the Essex Regiment. The Essex Colonel Slim had sacked at Gallabat was a personal friend. Affronted regimental pride (and perhaps as well long standing British Army disdain for the Indian Army) colored Irwin's attitude to Burcorps and its commander. Irwin met Slim's concern about the conditions his exhausted men faced (they even had to build their own "brashas" – bamboo huts – to shelter from the monsoon) by making clear that he thought Burma had been lost because both the troops and their commander were inferior soldiers. Slim protested, in a tense meeting, that Irwin was wrong about what had happened in Burma, adding (with considerable restraint) that Irwin's attitude was "rude." The response could not have been more quintessentially blimpish: "I can't be rude – I'm senior."[25]

Burcorps was dissolved with Cowan's 17th Indian remaining in IV Corps (where he, and it, would serve until 1945). I Burma Division, a mere wraith by the time it reached Imphal, would eventually be reformed in India as the 39th Indian Infantry Division. Slim, now without a command, went on much needed leave (and must have wondered, in view of Irwin's reception, what his future was likely to be). As he left Imphal, his men cheered him.

Slim's future was brighter than his reception by Irwin might have indicated. When he returned from leave, he became commander of XV Corps, with headquarters at the historic Barrackpore cantonment near Calcutta, a military station that dated back to the early days of the East India Company's army. After an interval of planning the defense of the exposed coasts of Bengal and Ornissa, Slim and his corps headquarters migrated to Ranchi in the inland province of Bihar. Here Slim began to turn the "lessons learned" from his experience with Burcorps into a doctrine and training regimen for his corps that would become a template for the military renaissance that, in a remarkably short time, transformed the badly beaten Indian Army of 1941- 42 into the great XIV Army of 1944-45.[26]

25 This story is told in Slim's official biography: Lewin, *Slim*, p. 105. It has never been confuted.
26 The reconfiguration of the Indian Army thinking to meet the challenges of its new war began almost immediately. Some officers were ordered back to India from Malaya in order to see

When Indian Army expansion began in 1940 speed and numbers were what counted. To simplify training, the army focused on the Middle East, then taken as the likely destination of the burgeoning force. This in turn meant mechanized and motorized units, which in turn meant masses of vehicles. The army's intelligence school set up shop in Karachi, the army's port of embarkation for the Middle East, and focused its attention on the German and Italian armies.

The problems of jungle warfare and the nature of the Imperial Japanese Army were not ignored but were very much a residuary legatee where the army's time and attention were concerned.[27]

The result first in Malaya and then in Burma was the commitment of raw troops under inexperienced officers to combat in conditions where such training as they had received was largely irrelevant while the masses of vehicles, clogging the few roads, were an invitation to the Japanese to use their favorite tactic: swing around the road bound Indian units, put a roadblock behind them, cutting their communications and forcing them to reverse field and fight their way out. Even if successful, the loss of men and vehicles produced disorganization further weakening already outmatched units. It was this state of affairs Slim set himself to change.

The analysis was easy – implementing the reforms that analysis called for much harder, especially since many changes required action well above Slim's pay grade. But at Ranchi, the remaking of the Indian Army got seriously underway. The first thing Slim assessed was himself. He regretted not being able to wrestle initiative from the Japanese: "When in doubt as to two courses of action, a general should choose the bolder." There again the echoes of Gallant and Deir-es-Zor, although here Slim may have been too hard on himself – given the situation in March 1942, he had no effective way of taking the offensive.[28] "Defeat is bitter," he continued, "…the commander has failed in *his* duty

that "lessons learned" were transmitted; others escaped. Circulation of their information began immediately. Burcorps brought out of Burma a great deal of hard-won knowledge. Savory, commanding the new 23rd Indian Infantry Division at Imphal drew on that in training his troops. The equally new 14th Indian Infantry Division formed its own school of jungle warfare. What was lacking in 1942 was not awareness of the urgency of retraining for the new war but the imposition from above of a systematic army-wide policy to accomplish it. That would come in 1943.

27 The Directorate of Military Training had issued pamphlets and guidance memoranda on "forest warfare." How much attention was paid to them in an atmosphere of frantic scramble to ready units for the Middle East is an open question. In 1938 Slim, then commanding the 2/7th Gurkha Rifles at Shillong in Assam, had taken the Japanese as his battalion's notional enemy. He drew on the Assam Rifles, a paramilitary unit made up of Gurkhas, which patrolled Assam's wild, jungle clad hills, to provide jungle fighting instructions to his men.

28 Shortly after taking over Burcorps, Slim was ordered by Alexander to attack the Japanese on his front. Slim used 7 Armoured Brigade, supported by a brigade-sized infantry force. The Japanese promptly cut the road behind the attackers who, reversing course, had to fight their way home, suffering considerable losses. Burcorps, even with the veteran armored brigade, simply wasn't capable of offensive operations against the Japanese. Slim, *Defeat Into Victory*, pp. 44-77 describes the episode.

if he has not won victory – for that *is* his duty." Clearly Slim experienced, at least briefly, a moment of soul-searching depression, but he surmounted it, telling himself, "shake off these regrets… remember only the lessons to be learnt from defeat – they are more than from victory."[29] Slim summarized those lessons in a training memorandum to guide XV Corps. They boiled down to this: well trained, physically fit troops, who patrolled relentlessly, refused to panic at Japanese encircling tactics but regarded them as opportunities to encircle the Japanese in turn and who relentlessly pressed to seize and hold the initiative.[30] Slim saw well trained infantry – as he said, able to "go anywhere, and do anything, go on doing it and do it on very little" – as the bedrock of the Army.[31] And that in the end is what he got.

Ironically, the process that turned what Slim did at Ranchi into the new Indian Army norm and finally into his magnificent XIV Army was set in motion, inadvertently, by Noel Irwin.

XV Corps reported to Eastern Army. In midsummer 1942, that command became vacant. Irwin handed over IV Corps to Geoffrey Scoones (a Gurkha Rifles officer) and, doubtless to the great relief of Cowan and Savory, moved up to army command. Almost his first action was to evict XV Corps from Barrackpore, sending Slim to Ranchi. At the moment Irwin took over, Slim was working with the 14th Indian Division on a plan for an offensive in the Arakan, the costal province of Burma that abutted Bengal. Normally, an army has one or more corps headquarters between itself and its divisions, but Irwin was a micromanager who decided to dispense with XV Corps and direct the offensive himself (his low opinion of Slim doubtless reinforced his decision). In addition to Irwin's need for control, leading to a poor command structure, the decision to launch an offensive into the Arakan at all is an illustration of the strategic muddle that surrounded the war in Burma until 1945. If left to decide on their own, Churchill and the British Chiefs of Staff would undoubtedly have stood on the defensive on the Indo-Burmese frontier until such time as an amphibious counterattack could be launched to

29 Slim, *Defeat Into Victory*, p. 121.

30 Slim, *Defeat Into Victory*, pp. 142-43. It is interesting that at Ranchi, Slim had under his command, at one time or another, three divisions which would later play a major role in XIV Army's victories. Major General Frank Messervy's 7th Indian, Major General Harold Briggs' 5th Indian, and Major General Douglas Gracey's 20th Indian. Briggs ("Briggo") had compiled a distinguished record in the desert fighting against the Rommel. Slim thought he was one of the best divisional commanders he knew. Messervy, who Slim knew from East Africa, later also commanded a division in the desert and would command a corps in XIV Army. Gracey, another Gurkha Rifles officer, commanded his division with distinction throughout the war. Messervy was the first commander in chief of Pakistan's army, succeeded in that position by Gracey. Briggs commanded in Burma during its uneasy transition to independence. Slim, by then CIGS, persuaded him out of retirement to direct the counterinsurgency campaign in Malaya, where he laid the foundation for Britain's victory. Slim was fortunate in his subordinates.

31 Slim, *Defeat Into Victory*, p. 539. In this passage, Slim was writing specifically about his Indian Divisions.

Gurkha soldiers in a trench at Gallipoli. On 9 August 1915, the Gurkhas temporarily stormed the highest point on the peninsula at Sari Bair ridge. Slim served in a supporting role with 9th Battalion, Royal Warwickshire Regiment. He was very impressed by the Gurkha regiments, particularly the 1/6th Gurkha Rifles whom he subsequently joined. (National Army Museum 1976-05-52-11)

General William Slim as GOC in Chief, 14th Army. He is standing beside the 14th Army formation badge which he designed, but was only adopted after an open competition. The red and black represented the colours of the British and Indian Armies and the sword pointing downwards against heraldic convention, because Slim knew the 14th Army would have to reconquer Burma from the north. The hilt formed the 'S' for Slim and on the handle was the army's title in morse code. (National Army Museum 1951-02-10-2)

Field Marshal Viscount Slim on his 75th birthday, oil on canvas by Leonard Boden, 1967. (National Army Museum 1967-05-79)

retake Rangoon and cut off the Japanese forces in Burma as the British had been when Rangoon fell in March 1942. An overland campaign held few attractions. But an assault from the sea seemed very far away in mid-1942. The British had lost naval command of the Bay of Bengal months before and seemed unlikely to have the resources to regain it again any time soon.

However Britain's powerful and exigent American ally was unwilling to await the distant day when British seapower reappeared. China was important in American strategic calculations. The Americans also saw China's war with Japan as a compelling saga of a brave people fighting for freedom. To support this fight Washington had poured Lend-Lease supplies into China via Rangoon and the Burma Road. Severed by the Japanese, the Americans wanted an overland link restored (meanwhile they put together an airlift over the "Hump" – the mountains on the Burma- China border – that kept a trickle of supplies flowing). Churchill understood that alliance politics made an effort to meet American expectations if necessary. Wavell, again Commander- in-Chief, India, knew that with direct assault on Rangoon ruled out and offensive action from Imphal impossible for logistic reasons (IV Corps were on half rations because of the inadequacy of the line of communications) only an overland advance into the Arakan remained. And so the Indian Army's first offensive against the Imperial Japanese Army took shape: a crawl down the Arakan's Mayu peninsula where a short amphibious hop to Akyab Island would be possible. On Akyab airbases could be built to cover an assault on Rangoon – someday. Wavell knew the 14th Indian Division was new, raw – and riddled with malaria. But he also – remarkably – underestimated the Japanese and knew something had to be done. And so, Irwin, setting aside the only senior British officer in India who had actually faced the Japanese in battle, started Major General Wilfred Lloyd's 14th Indian Division into the Arakan. It was a series of bad decisions by Wavell and Irwin (as well as Churchill) that sowed the seeds of disaster.

By New Year's 1943 Lloyd's advance had been stalled just short of the tip of the Maya peninsula, and the strait separating it from Akyab. The Japanese were dug in, holding a line of well constructed, ferociously defended bunkers – a defensive tactic with which the Indian Army would become all too familiar in the years ahead. Lloyd's raw troops could not crack the Japanese line. Wavell, under pressure from London, would not accept failure. Irwin, conscious of Wavell's gaze, pushed more raw Indian brigades into the Arakan until Lloyd's divisional headquarters was trying to manage the infantry strength of an army corps, an unmanageable situation. Meanwhile Slim, who during his brief time at Barrackpore had worked out a much different offensive scheme, one that eschewed frontal attacks in favor of the same kind of outflanking moves the Japanese had used against him in Burma, sat on the sidelines at Ranchi.

Irwin did send Slim in mid March on a brief visit to Lloyd's headquarters. Slim asked Irwin (since Lloyd was trying to manage a much larger force than a divisional headquarters should or could) whether he was now proposing to bring in XV Corps headquarters. No, said Irwin. So Slim returned to Ranchi – only to be pulled off a train before dawn two weeks later and told XV Corps was moving to the Arakan where a Japanese counter offensive had begun using the same infiltration and outflanking tactics that had worked so well for them in Malaya and Burma in 1941-42 – and achieving the same level of success against inexperienced Indian troops – "a rather unwilling band of raw lives," as one of Slim's liaison officers characterized Lloyd's force. However, Irwin ruled, Slim was not to bring his entire headquarters, only the operational side – Irwin preferred to keep control of the administrative (i.e. logistical) aspect of the campaign. Furthermore Slim and his headquarters were not to deploy to the battle zone but to remain in readiness at Chittagong, the base area for the Arakan operations. Finally, when it was much too late, Slim was allowed to take over and tidy up the wreckage. Irwin wanted a position held during the impending monsoon which Slim regarded as unsustainable. Slim persuaded Irwin that it was necessary to pull 14th Division back to a position both tactically sounder and logistically sustainable once the monsoon made movement next to impossible.

Irwin's next move was almost predictable. Having carefully involved Slim in the Arakan fiasco just enough to make it seem like a plausible decision, Irwin sacked Slim, by telegram.

Once again Slim's career seemed to have run aground. Once again appearances were deceiving. In far off London, Churchill was furious with the Arakan defeat – it embarrassed him in front of his American allies, already very skeptical of British willingness and ability to reopen their way to China. Sarcastically he minuted that only the small scale of the operations prevented the Arakan defeat from being a full-scale public relations disaster. He then summoned Wavell – for whom his enthusiasm was muted at the best of times – home for "consultations." Wavell would return but not in a military role. As he exited, Wavell, who must have suspected his time as commander-in-chief was nearly over, took two important decisions: he ordered Alan Hartley, once again deputizing for him, to set up an Infantry Committee to study the whole issue of how to revitalize the Indian Army's key arm. And he sacked Noel Irwin – Wavell knew who had run the Arakan offensive, and he knew what it was like to be handed an impossible job.

Irwin received his dismissal notice while visiting Scoones' IV Corps headquarters at Imphal. Scoones' Brigadier General Staff, Ouvry Roberts, who had been Slim's GSO I (divisional chief of staff) with 10th Indian in Iraq, witnessed the moment and later recounted it to Slim's official biographer. Irwin sat down and sent Slim a brief message: "You're not sacked, I am."[32]

And so Slim remained XV Corps commander and his full headquarters began to plan a renewal of the Arakan offensive. The 5th and 7th Indian Divisions moved into the Arakan, joining Major General Cyril Lomax's 26th Indian Infantry Division which had replaced the exhausted 14th (destined to be converted to a training division). But while XV Corps planned there was taking place a radical overhaul of both the command structure for the Burma campaign and the way the Indian Army was trained. The former gave Slim the central role in the campaign and the latter the instrument with which to do it.

Churchill had long been dissatisfied with India Command and its army (which he distrusted). Indeed the whole Raj aroused his ire – "a welter of lassitude and inefficiency,"

32 Lewin, *Slim*, p. 124.

he called it. All this was vented at Wavell who he took with him to the May Anglo-American summit in Washington, the "Trident" Conference, complaining during the entire voyage on the *Queen Mary* about the Indian Army's failings going back to the 1857 mutiny in the Company's Bengal Army. At Trident, Churchill began to discuss a new integrated theater command on the lines of the one over which Eisenhower presided in the Mediterranean. Slowly over the following months it would take shape as South East Asia Command (SEAC) which would take over the war in Burma from India Command (which would, however, continue to train and supply troops and logistic support). Churchill toyed with several possibilities for Supreme Commander, setting finally on Lord Louis Mountbatten, a naval officer, then Chief of Combined Operations with the rank of Commodore. Mountbatten's talent was modest at best but he had charm, charisma, and royal connections. He was given a trio of service commanders and the mission of both opening the road to China and crafting a maritime/amphibious strategy to strike across the Bay of Bengal aiming ultimately at retaking Singapore and, Churchill hoped, restoring imperial prestige in Asia. The core purpose of SEAC however was its role in alliance politics – assuring the now dominant Americans that the British took seriously the task of clearing north Burma to make possible a new overland link with China.

To further this purpose, Churchill brought Orde Wingate to the next Anglo-American summit at Quebec in September. Wingate, a British Army gunner, was a Wavell protégé.

Wavell had first noticed him in Palestine during the 1936-39 Arab Revolt against the British Mandate. Wavell was the GOC there in 1937-38; Wingate was running a counterinsurgency program against Arab irregulars. Wavell later employed him to lead Ethiopian guerillas against the Italians in 1940-41, and brought him to India in 1942, hoping to use him against the Japanese. Wingate was given a brigade to train in his "Long Range Penetration" (LRP) tactics. Wavell then allowed him to mount a raid into Burma that had few concrete results but, coinciding with the debacle in the Arakan, could at least be presented as a victory – an opportunity that public relations officers in India seized with both hands. Highly placed patrons (Wingate collected them) brought him to the prime minister's attention at a moment when Churchill's disdain for the Raj and its army was at its peak. The results were startling. Wingate was ordered back to London. Churchill, after a dinner conversation at 10 Downing Street decided to take Wingate (who disliked the Indian Army as much as he did) to the impending Anglo-American summit at Quebec (the "Quadrant" conference). There he presented him and LRP to the Americans as the key to the problems of reconquering north Burma. Wingate was good at selling his ideas. FDR and his Chiefs of Staff were duly impressed. Wingate left Quebec a major general, promised a vastly expanded LRP force (the infantry equivalent of an army corps), a private air force (courtesy of the Americans), and a commitment to make his operations the centerpiece of the 1944 campaign in Burma. This remarkable sequence of events, while a coup for the prime minister in alliance politics, laid up no end of problems for SEAC, the Indian Army, and Slim.

But all that lay in the future. In the foreground were a series of command changes in India consequent of SEAC's creation, one of which transformed Slim's prospects.

The biggest was Claude Auchinleck's return as Commander-in-Chief, India. Although Churchill was no admirer of the Indian Army, he had met Auchinleck when he was, briefly, in the U.K. in 1940. The Auk's conduct in the field during the doomed Norwegian campaign and then in Britain at Southern Command (the potential invasion front) impressed the prime minister. Auchinleck became Commander-in-Chief, India, in 1941 but Churchill moved him to Cairo when he finally lost confidence in Wavell (sending Wavell to India). When Auchinleck in turned failed to defeat Rommel, Churchill sacked him in August 1942 – but did not completely write him off.[33] Now, after nearly a year unemployed, Churchill sent him back to Delhi. He would remain commander-in-chief until the end of the Raj and the division of its army in 1947 – the last, and greatest, "Jangi Lat Sahib" in the army's history. (Wavell would return to India as Viceroy, no first rank British political figure being willing to accept the job.) SEAC's creation meant more new appointments. General Sir George Giffard, intended as Irwin's replacement at Eastern Army, moved up to be Mountbatten's land forces commander presiding over the newly created 11th Army Group. That vacated Eastern Army. That command was retitled XIV Army and Slim was summoned from XV Corps headquarters at Chittagong to lead it. Flying immediately to Calcutta, he found himself, only recently facing dismissal, in a car bound again for Barrackpore, now his new headquarters. Looking at the army commander's flag on the bonnet, Slim "wondered where I was really going."[34]

## Burma: The Turning Tide

The vehicle in which Slim would make his journey was the Indian Army. XIV Army is always described as "British," but that is somewhat misleading as far as its composition is concerned. In the entire course of Britain's war against Japan, only three complete British divisions fought "east of Suez." The 18th landed at Singapore in time to swell the total losses when the city fell a few weeks later. The 70th Division moved to India from the Middle East and was briefly part of Slim's XV Corps at Ranchi. Slim thought it well trained and led but it never had a chance to fight as a division, being broken up in late 1943 to become part of Wingate's "Special Force." The 2nd Division arrived in India just in time to have one of its brigades chewed up in the last stages of the Arakan operations. Thereafter, it was pulled out of the Burma campaign to train in India for the amphibious operations SEAC hoped to launch. It would not however take part in one, joining XIV Army in March 1944 – the only complete British division to fight in Slim's army. Of course there were numerous other British units. Ever since Indian Army reorganization after the "Great Sepoy Mutiny" of 1857, every Indian brigade was supposed to have a British battalion. Thus an Indian division would be one-third British. But in the face of

33 I have explored the Wavell-Auchinleck switch and the Auk's subsequent period as Commander-in-Chief, Middle East in *Churchill and His Generals*. (Lawrence, KS, 2007)

34 Slim, *Defeat Into Victory*, p. 167.

the multiple demands on Britain's limited manpower pool this was decreasingly the case. Moreover as manpower stringency became intense in 1943-45, British battalions serving in XIV Army were at the end of the line for replacements and chronically understrength. By 1945, nearly 70% of XIV Army was Indian or Gurkha – and most of the rest were African. If Britain had to fight a war in Burma, as alliance politics demanded, it was the Indian Army that would wage it.

As noted above, there had been early moves in 1942-43 at reorienting and retraining that army for its new role but as yet these were initiatives by individual commanders – most notably Slim at XV Corps – rather than a systemic army-wide effort. Bruce Scott, who had commanded the foredoomed 1st Burma Division, had become the Army's Inspector of Infantry. He was however a very tired man and moreover could do little in the face of the perpetual churn in the army due to open-ended expansion. In mid 1943 however, just before Slim took over XIV Army, everything began to change.

Open-ended expansion had long been recognized as the root of the Army's problems. In May 1943, the War Cabinet in London accepted the recommendation of Leo Amery, Secretary of State for India and Burma, to put an end to it, capping the Indian Army at thirteen infantry and two armored divisions.[35] It helped that Churchill was absent – at sea on his way to the Trident conference, complaining to Wavell about the Indian Army's failings. (The business-like Clement Atlee was a better War Cabinet chair when Indian matters were on the agenda, since Churchill seldom was helpful when the Raj was under discussion.) The following month Auchinleck returned as commander-in-chief and the Infantry Committee, appointed by Wavell as he exited, made its report. Chaired by the deputy chief of staff at army headquarters, one of its key members was "Taffy" Davies who had been Slim's chief of staff at Burcorps. The committee's report, not surprisingly, drew the conclusions Slim had drawn as he reflected on Burcorps' experience. Training had to be harder and more realistic, oriented to meeting the Japanese in the jungle and defeating them and it. It also had to be longer, moving from basic to unit training, then progressing through training divisions to reinforcement camps where newly learned skills were constantly reinforced. To standardize training, incorporating "lessons learned" and "best practices," the Directorate of Military Training updated – indeed rewrote – its 1940 manual on "Forest Warfare." The September 1943 edition, nicknamed "The Jungle Book," became the trainers' bible – and a feedback loop was developed to keep it up to date with new lessons being learned at the front.

Auchinleck put his powerful impetus behind all this. He also focused responsibility for the whole process in the Inspector of Infantry, upgrading the office to Director and summoning Reginald Savory from divisional command in IV Corps to Delhi to provide

35 The Indian armored divisions never fought as divisions being repeatedly amalgamated, and then, ultimately, in 1943, disbanded, their brigades distributed to other formations. At one time, as many as five armored divisions had been proposed. The great problem with organizing divisional size Indian armored units was, initially, lack of equipment and British technical personnel and then the fact that Burma tank brigades for infantry support, not divisions for independent maneuver, were needed.

the drive and energy that would see that the new dispensation took root, army-wide. Auchinleck also tackled issues like improved leave and better rations – all the small issues so important to morale. At the same time the medical services were turning the corner in the battle against malaria. When Slim arrived in Barrackpore to assume command of XIV Army, the makeover of the Indian Army had begun. Supported by Auchinleck and Savory, he saw that the pace never slackened. The Army that the Japanese had beaten with such ease in Malaya, Burma, and, most recently, in the Arakan, was being reshaped with remarkable speed. It was a change the Japanese missed. The Army they expected to confront was gone – and its replacement would destroy them.[36]

But the remarkably fast turnaround of the Indian Army was yet incomplete – new doctrine, revamped training, better morale – all were important changes, but the new Indian Army had yet to face the test of battle. The Japanese were about to supply that. There had been a change in both the Japanese command structure and outlook in 1943. The very aggressive Lieutenant General Mutaguchi Renya took over the Fifteenth Army and reassessed the defensive posture the Japanese had assumed in Burma after they overran it. Wingate's raid had done next to no damage but opened Mutaguchi's eyes to the fact that the wild country between Assam and the Burmese plains was not by itself an adequate defense. Mutaguchi had commanded a division in Malaya and had a very low opinion of British and Indian soldiers. If they could cross the jungle clad border mountains, the unconquerable warriors of the IJA could easily do so, preemptively seizing the British base area at Imphal and foreclosing any future British attack. Mutaguchi's layers of superiors all the way back to Imperial General Headquarters in Tokyo concurred – with the tide of war now running strongly against them, the Japanese public would be cheered by a (cheap) victory. And so the die was cast – the 1943-44 dry season would see Japanese offensives along the length of the Indo-Burma frontier: first a preliminary attack in the Arakan to draw in and tie down British reserves, then a massive assault on Imphal by Fifteenth Army's three divisions – and of course a vast haul of booty in the

36 Three excellent books track and explain this transformation: Daniel Marston's prize-winning *Phoenix from the Ashes: The Indian Army in the Burma Campaign* (Westport, CT, 2003), Alan Jeffreys' *Approach to Battle: Training the Indian Army During the Second World War* (London, 2017), and Tim Moreman's *The Jungle, the Japanese, and the British Commonwealth Armies at War* (London, 2005) between them thoroughly examine changes in the doctrine, training, and battlefield performance of the Indian Army that underlay Slim's great victories.

One other great change deserves mention: the officer corps of the Indian Army was becoming Indian. When in 1917 the British government committed itself to Dominion status for India, it also committed to King's commissions (full officer status) for Indians in the Raj's army (previously the highest an Indian could rise was to be a VCO, a Viceroy Commissioned Officer, an intermediate category between Indian NCOs and British officers, exercising some officer functions but without the status of full officers. Indian troops saluted VCOs; British troops did not). "Indianization" proceeded slowly during the interwar years for a variety of reasons, not all of them creditable. Open-ended Indian Army expansion changed matters dramatically. There was no way to find enough British officers as the army hit the million mark by the end of 1941 on its way to 2 million. Auchinleck was a strong supporter of Indianization, which of course would make Indian independence inevitable.

form of British supply dumps in the Imphal plain (in Malaya the Japanese had christened these windfalls "Churchill supplies"). Slim's new army was about to have a field test.[37]

The Japanese attack in the Arakan opened on 4 February. A brigade-sized force penetrated a gap in 7th Indian Division's front – frontages in Burma were so big and the vegetation so dense that there were always gaps to be exploited – overran and dispersed 7th Indian's headquarters and headed for the supply depot at Sinzweya which supported the 7th and the other front line division, 5th Indian. For two years this had been a formula for a Japanese victory and an Indian Army debacle. But both 5th and 7th Indian had very experienced commanders, Harold Briggs and Frank Messervy (who survived the loss of his headquarters as he had a similar episode in the desert war). Even more important, they had had months to absorb the new training and doctrine of XIV Army. Briggs immediately sent the talented Brigadier Geoffrey Evans (who had just arrived and had to be told where Sinzweya was) to organize the defense of the supply dump. Evans quickly improvised a force out of miscellaneous infantry and rear area troops, backed by some gunners and two squadrons of tanks, in what became known as the "Admin Box." Messervy reached the box and using the armored units' radios reassumed command of 7th Indian. The Japanese hurled themselves at the box – and were stopped cold.

When Slim assumed command of XIV Army, he made it policy that any unit cut off by Japanese encircling tactics were not to retreat but to stand fast. Sustained by air supply, they would form the anvil against which the Japanese would be crushed. And the Arakan battle played out to Slim's design. Evans' scratch force held their perimeter (Slim had insisted that even rear area troops be fit and combat trained – a mandate validated by the defenders of the Admin Box). And the Japanese discovered they were up against what became one of the most vital weapons in XIV Army's arsenal: the American-built Douglas DC3, known to the British as the Dakota.

Air supply was an idea that went back almost to the birth of airpower. Slim, as noted above, had worked on the issue when a staff officer at Indian Army headquarters a decade before and Wingate's air-supported raid had helped refine techniques. Slim's principal logistician, "Alf" Snelling ("Grocer Alf"), now a major general, had built the ground support organization necessary, designing parachutes made of jute when a shortage of parachute silk developed. The story of the XIV Army is intertwined with the Dakota.

37 There was one other element in Mutaguchi's plan: the Indian National Army (INA). Originally formed by IJA intelligence officers from the masses of Indian POWs taken at Singapore, it was thought of by the Japanese largely as a propaganda asset. In 1943, Subhas Chandra Bose, a charismatic Bengali radical who had escaped house arrest in India and fled to Berlin early in the war, arrived at Singapore, repatriated by the Germans via U-boat. Bose took over the INA and made it the army of his government in exile, recognized by the Japanese. Bose convinced Mutaguchi that if his "army" appeared on Indian soil, the Indian Army would defect to him, causing the collapse of the Raj. It was, of course, fantasy. Bose's two "divisions" were brigade-sized, under-equipped, and poorly trained (most were recruits from Malaya's large Indian population). The IJA despised soldiers who surrendered and had little enthusiasm for the INA, whatever Mutaguchi might feel. A complete failure in the end, its survivors became porters for the Japanese by the campaign's end.

Most of the Dakota squadrons in the theater belonged to the American Hump airlift organization, the British having decided in 1940 to forego manufacturing transport aircraft in favor of fighters and bombers, while drawing on American production for transports. This made XIV Army heavily dependent for air supply on the Americans and the politics of Dakota availability a major preoccupation for Slim. But in the Arakan enough were available to underpin Slim's design.

Over the next five weeks, the Dakotas showered down 714 tons of everything from ammunition to razor blades. Slim brought up his reserves to crush the Japanese on the anvil of the 5th and 7th Indian divisions. He later told the official historians that he used massive force because he wanted XIV Army's first battle to be an overwhelming victory – "have you ever seen a walnut that has been crushed by a pile driver?" He had expected the IJA's manic commitment to offense to aid him. Hitherto the Japanese had won quickly; when they could not they had no tactical answer beyond doubling down, hurling attack after attack at Evans' defenses, which, like the old British square, did not buckle. The Japanese attacking force lost 5,000 of its 8,000 men – and doubtless more bodies lay undiscovered in the jungle. For the first time the Indian Army had won a clear-cut victory over the IJA and they would never lose again.

As the Arakan battle wound down and Slim's old XV Corps prepared to resume the offensive there was a much bigger battle opened on XIV Army's Central Front in Assam.[38] The Arakan battle showed that XIV Army could not be beaten in a defensive battle. The next battle would be a much more severe test. Mutaguchi planned to envelop the Imphal plain, XIV Army's base area for the central front, a sprawling complex of dumps, camps, and hospitals occupying the only large flat space between the Brahmaputra valley to the north and the plains of north Burma to the east. His 33rd Division would strike at Imphal from the south, cutting off and destroying on its way the 17th Indian Division, deployed some 160 miles south of Imphal. His 15th Division with most of his armor and artillery attacking from the southeast would do the same to 20th Indian, operating in the Kabaw Valley well in advance of the Imphal plain. Finally, his 31st Division would strike across the wild and jungle-covered Naga hills, aiming at Kohima, a small supply depot astride the only road that linked Imphal to Dimapur, a vast base area, sprawling for a dozen miles along the Brahmaputra valley railway, which linked XIV Army to the rest of India. With Kohima in its hands, XIV Army would be cut off, while his other divisions would have shattered two of IV Corps' three Indian divisions. The rest would be mopping up and tallying the haul of "Churchill supplies." So far the official plan. Privately Mutaguchi hoped to move on Dimapur and once in the Brahmaputra valley to unleash Bose and his INA to bring down the Raj. His plan was based on logistic recklessness (a common IJA failing). His divisions carried supplies

38 In addition to the sources on the Burma campaign mentioned in fn. 1, Robert Lyman's *Japan's Last Bid for Victory* (London, 2011) is an excellent account of Mutaguchi's defeat by XIV Army. My own *Triumph at Imphal-Kohima* (Lawrence, KS, 2017) covers the battle in more detail than is possible here.

for three weeks. After that "Churchill supplies" would sustain them. There was no fall-back plan (unless Mutaguchi's decision, based on reading about Genghis Khan, to drive herds of cattle and goats with his divisions as mobile meals, qualifies as one). His first chief of staff pointed out the logistic precariousness of the operation. Mutaguchi fired him. His successor did not question the plan. The incomparable Japanese warrior spirit, Mutaguchi reckoned, would sweep all before it. The British and their Indian hirelings were contemptible soldiers – Imphal would fall in time to be an April birthday present for the emperor. The greatest weakness in Mutaguchi's plan, however, was not in fact logistic but his failure to notice what had happened in the Arakan and to realize that the army he had swept aside with such ease in Malaya no longer existed.

When Slim took over as army commander in the autumn of 1943, Scoones and his corps had already had over a year of both small scale campaigning and large scale logistic infrastructure construction behind them. Even though numerous question marks hung over future plans for the theater, the assumption was that IV Corps would be required to advance to and eventually across the Chindwin. To support that advance communications had to be drastically improved. Scoones' two divisions began a slow forward movement on two separate axes of advance, spooling out behind them newly made roads and the armies of civilian labor whose pick and shovel work supplemented that of the troops themselves (mechanical equipment for road building or anything else was rare in the XIV Army). Having rebuilt itself and recuperated from its Burcorps experience (after reaching Imphal, 25% of the division was found to be suffering from malaria), Cowan's 17th Indian Division started down the Manipur River valley, south of Imphal, aiming for Tiddim and Kalewa on the Chindwin, nearly two hundred miles away. It simultaneously reconfigured itself into an Indian Light Division, trading its vast tail of vehicles (it had been originally intended for the Middle East) for mules and jeeps.[39]

Douglas Gracey's 20th Indian Division, yet to see any significant combat, moved southeast into the Kabaw Valley, aiming ultimately for the Chindwin as well. Scoones' third division, 23rd Indian, now commanded by Ouvry Roberts (who had been on Slim's 10th Indian Division staff in Iraq) was Scoones' reserve. IV Corps had some of the advantages Slim had had in Burcorps. Scoones, Cowan and Gracey were all Gurkha Rifles officers; Roberts, who was British Army, had a great deal of experience with the Indian Army. As all of Scoones' divisions inched forward, they were increasingly

39 The line of communications to Assam was very precarious in 1942. Never intended to support anything but the tea industry, it had to be quickly and dramatically upgraded to support not only IV Corps at Imphal but Stilwell's Chinese-American force at Ledo and the American Hump airlift to China, which operated mostly from newly built airfields in Assam. Slim's campaigns in 1943-45 depended on the successful improvement of the Assam line of communications, a task whose successful completion is a remarkable story in itself. Graham Dunlop's *Military Economics, Culture and Logistics in the Burma Campaign, 1942-45* (London, 2009) is the only major study of the subject. Although U.S. Army railway operating troops played an important role from March 1944, the success in improving the Assam line of communications was very largely the work of the Raj machine – civil and military – that Churchill dismissed as a "welter of lassitude and inefficiency."

involved in small scale actions with the Japanese (who were also edging forward in preparation for Mutaguchi's offensive) – platoon, company, and battalion engagements that, along with the new XIV Army training norms, sharpened fighting skills and increased the troops' confidence. By the time Slim took over, IV Corps was a far better fighting force than it had been a year earlier.

It was clear by early 1944 that the Japanese were planning to attack on the Central Front. "Sigint" information, the thickening up of the Japanese presence on the Chindwin and more aggressive patrolling by them, especially in 17th Indian's sector – all portended a forward move – and it was hard to miss the growing herds of cattle and goats gathering near the Chindwin. In response, Slim and Scoones recast their plans for a continued forward movement. On the Central Front, as in the Arakan, Slim planned to turn the invariable and relentless Japanese commitment to the offensive, their belief that attack solved all problems, against them. He would pull his advanced divisions back to the "gates" to the Imphal plain – the point where the roads debouched onto it – and make a stand there where, backed by the firepower of his artillery, armor and tactical airpower, the Japanese, invariably attacking, would be shredded. Then XIV Army could take the offensive. It was, as the Arakan operations had shown, a sound concept but putting it into execution in Assam was several orders of magnitude more complicated.

First, the armies of laborers working behind Cowan and Gracey (60,000 or more, Slim estimated) had to be pulled out and the laboriously constructed roads prepared for demolition; then the whole sprawling layout of depots, dumps, and workshops on the plain had to be reorganized, concentrating them in defended "boxes" and sending surplus personnel back to India. The crucial all weather airfields on the plain had also to be enclosed in defenses – supply by Dakota being crucial to his design – and, finally and most important of all, the timing of Cowan and Gracey's withdrawal had to be just right: too soon and morale would drop if ground laboriously acquired was given up without a fight; too late and the Japanese Fifteenth Army might destroy Slim's XIV Army in detail. And it was over the timing of Cowan's withdrawal that the whole plan nearly came apart.

Slim's final plan, worked out with Scoones, called for Cowan and Gracey to begin their pullback once it was certain that the Japanese offensive had begun. Scoones decided that the trigger for ordering the withdrawal would be the crossing of the Chindwin by a battalion strength Japanese force. However the Japanese again sprang a surprise. By the time the Japanese attack opened a whole regiment (equivalent to a British brigade) was already across the Chindwin, behind Cowan and poised to cut off 17th Indian Division.

Slim would later, rather disarmingly, admit in his memoirs that battles he fought seldom went according to plan. The Arakan battle had opened with the Japanese securing tactical surprise. It happened again on the Central Front. The Japanese put a roadblock across Cowan's line of withdrawal before Cowan's division began its retreat. (Scoones' IV Corps headquarters were not quick enough in appreciating the developing situation and issuing retirement orders.) The rest of the Japanese 33rd with most of Fifteenth Army's armor, artillery and motor transport, moved against Gracey's division, reaching for his left flank. Meanwhile the entire Japanese 31st Division struck across the

Naga Hills towards Kohima, seeking to block the road to Dimapur, severing IV Corps' communications (XIV Army had estimated since November 1943 that a brigade-size force was the most that the Japanese could maintain across that jungle covered, mountainous, roadless terrain). While IV Corps was not outnumbered significantly by the Japanese, the need to protect so many points of entry to the Imphal plain meant that it was possible the Japanese could obtain a decisive edge at some point and sweep into the plain, seizing the vital airfields, which were Slim's answer to Japanese encirclement tactics – especially if the Japanese were able to tip the odds in their favor by destroying Cowan's division.

Slim said in his memoirs that his mistakes were redeemed by his army (the closest he came to blaming Scoones was to write that Scoones was trying to manage too much and that he ought to have kept the authority to order 17th Indian Division's withdrawal in his own hands). It was in the unexpected opening of the battle that the seachange in the Indian Army became utterly clear. Cowan's division, largely Gurkha with only one British battalion, turned itself around and started back up the road – 16,000 men, 2,500 vehicles, and 3,500 mules. The Japanese were still excellent at emplacing blocks and still held them tenaciously, but 17th Indian simply punched its way through them reaching the plain in good order, leaving a thoroughly demolished road behind them. Cowan had ordered all surplus stores destroyed before the withdrawal began – an order which worried units that remembered Burcorps' retreat. But, as in the Arakan, the Dakotas came, dropping supplies onto the constricted drop zones available in the mountainous terrain through which the road snaked. Gracey's 20th Division also withdrew in good order, sidestepping or clearing blocks that infiltrating Japanese had placed across their line of retreat. As Cowan's division reached and then blocked the southern entrance to the plain while Gracey sealed the Shenam pass, the eastern gate, it was already clear that Fifteenth Army's core assumption was wrong. The Indian Army of 1941-42 was gone; its replacement could not be outfought. The Japanese could still move cross country rapidly, reach their opponent's road communications, block them and die in defense of those blocks. But the results were now very different. The Dakotas always came and the fighting power of Slim's well-supplied formations was so much greater that the blocks could not be held. The commander of the Japanese 33rd Division, Lieutenant General Yanagida Kenzo, drew the correct conclusion. By the time he reached the southern gate of the plain in early April, his division had taken heavy casualties and was well behind schedule. Provisioned for three weeks only, there had been no haul of Churchill supplies and his logistic situation was tightening. Ahead stood the unbeaten 17th Indian, with its artillery, armor, and tactical air support. Yanagida told Mutaguchi that the operations had failed and recommended that he withdraw to a position that could be supplied and held during the monsoon, now only weeks away. Mutaguchi fired him.

The same story repeated itself on the north side of the plain. IV Corps' 23rd Division under Ouvry Roberts covered the northeast gate to the plain but two of its three brigades were pulled south to push down the Tiddim Road and link up with the withdrawing 17th Division. But the right wing of the Japanese 15th Division was lapping around Gracey's left, aiming for the northeastern gate, where a recently made road entered the plain. This momentarily open back door was also slammed in the face of the Japanese when the 50th Indian Parachute Brigade – the only one in the Indian Army and put at Scoones' disposal by Slim – was inserted into the gap left by Roberts' departing brigades. Its heroic stand at Sangshak blunted the Japanese thrust and bought time for the arrival of the leading brigades of Briggs' reinforcing 5th Division, airlifted from the Arakan, to deplane and seal the last of the gates to the plain. Mutaguchi's design rested on his ability to rapidly capture British supply dumps. He had failed by early April. His refusal to admit that would prolong the battle for three more months, and destroy Fifteenth Army.

Slim, in contrast, once his reborn army had taken positions sealing off the Imphal plain and fatally disrupting Mutaguchi's plans knew that, although hard fighting lay ahead, he now held the winning cards in his hands: he would let the almost mindless Japanese commitment to the offensive expose them to the massive firepower XIV Army could develop – however, the approaches to the plain would become a killing ground. Slim's problems tactically were simpler than those he faced from the byzantine command structures within which XIV Army was embedded.

The key element in his plan was the Dakota. It had been crucial to the "Admin Box" victory and would be even more so to the unfolding struggle around Imphal which was several orders of magnitude larger and sprawled over a much larger battlefield (it was 160 miles from Imphal to Cowan's position at the beginning of the battle; another 160 from Imphal to the major supply hub at Dimapur). The monsoon was barely a month away. Air supply would be vital to sustaining XIV Army once concentrated in the plain. Slim was clear that the two all-weather fields had to be held at all costs and the sprawl of camps, depots, and workshops on the plain had been reorganized and concentrated into defensive boxes that protected them. Slim's problem was that most of the Dakotas on which he depended were not directly controlled by the British.[40]

They were USAAF squadrons supporting the American airlift of supplies to China. The U.S. Joint Chiefs of Staff had vested control in Stilwell who wore multiple hats and could always evade issues by switching from one to the other. Moreover Stilwell spent most of his time at his headquarters in northeastern Assam where his Northern Combat Area Command (NCAC) – two American trained, equipped and advised Chinese divisions – was inching its way forward covering the U.S. Army road builders constructing the "Stilwell Road" from Ledo south to the point where (someday) it would tie into the old Burma Road. Since SEAC headquarters was in Delhi, and preparing to move to Kandy in Ceylon (Sri Lanka) liaison was far from easy. Mountbatten had asked for the right to draw on airlift squadrons in an emergency and been refused by Washington.[41] The Americans did concede however that Mountbatten could deal with Stilwell's deputy,

40 There were only three RAF Dakota squadrons available in the theater.

41 At the November 1943 Sextant conference in Cairo, Roosevelt and Churchill agreed that Mountbatten could, on his own, shift 1,100 tons of carrying capacity *per month* from the airlift to support combat operations in Burma. In the three month Imphal battle, 18,800 tons of supplies were flown into Imphal – which was far from the only supply commitment the Dakotas had to meet.

Major General Dan Sultan, who was based in Delhi, and, more important, worked smoothly with the British. Mountbatten's not inconsiderable contribution to the victory Slim won, was to win the battle for enough Dakotas to make it possible. In a complex tangle of negotiations involving SEAC, London and Washington, enough were found from the airlift or borrowed from the better endowed Mediterranean theater to sustain XIV Army throughout the three month battle, but Slim fought the battle conscious that adequate air supply capacity for his army was a week to week juggling operation, and subject to the vagaries of alliance politics.

The importance of the Dakotas was underlined when Mutaguchi's third division, the 31st, striking across the Naga Hills (whose name belies their 8,000 foot peaks) cut the Dimapur road at Kohima, a small town that was both a civil administrative centre and a small military depot. The weight of the Japanese thrust at Kohima came as a surprise – XIV Army had assumed that a regiment (equivalent to a British brigade) was the most that could be supplied across the Naga Hills. The usual Japanese disregard for logistic reality might have given them a brief tactical advantage and possession of Kohima, the responsibility for whose defense had been tossed back and forth between several headquarters with resultant delay in completing its defenses.[42] Kohima was saved by two things: the stubborn defense of two outposts by the newly raised Assam Regiment (one of the Indian Army's new, non-martial races regiments) which, like Sangshak, bought time, at a high price. Then, at the last minute, with enough reinforcements arriving to secure Dimapur, a British battalion, the 4th Royal West Kents, was rushed into Kohima where it provided the core of a very miscellaneous garrison (similar to that which had held the Admin Box). The ten day siege of Kohima has an epic quality which doubtless accounts for the intense concentration of subsequent writers on it, almost to the exclusion of the much larger, more complex, and far more momentous, battle around the Imphal plain.[43] The Japanese 31st Division broke its teeth on Kohima's defenders but remained dug in across the Dimapur-Imphal road, the clearing of which was now the task of Lieutenant General Montagu Stopford's XXXIII Corps, arriving from India by air and rail.

42 Originally the responsibility of Scoones' IV Corps, Slim shifted control of Kohima to 202 Line of Communications Area based at Dimapur with orders to hold Kohima, and, above all Dimapur, at all costs. Considering the latter his prime responsibility, Major General R. P. L. Rankin pulled back units screening Kohima to guard the sprawling depot. Then the arriving XXXIII Corps commander, Lieutenant General Montagu Stopford took control – but left Kohima under Rankin's (non-operational) headquarters. The only way to make sense of all of this is to assume that everyone had their eyes on IV Corps' struggle and underestimated the weight of the oncoming Japanese attack. See Raymond Callahan, *Triumph at Imphal-Kohima*, pp. 92-95 for a detailed discussion of this point.

43 The most recent account is Fergal Keene's *Road of Bones: The Siege of Kohima, 1944* (London, 2010). The most carefully detailed is Leslie Edwards, *Kohima: The Furthest Battle* (Stroud, UK, 2009). The traditional focus on Kohima by British writers may also be due to the fact that a British battalion played a crucial role there – the sprawling Imphal battle was largely an Indian Army affair.

Slim's fundamental design had proven sound. The Japanese had been held at the gates to the Imphal plain; Dimapur was secure, and by holding Kohima its British and Indian defenders had given XXXIII Corps a somewhat less difficult task. On 10 April Slim ordered his divisions to take the offensive. He knew that the IJA's offensive ethos – and refusal to yield a yard of ground when on the defensive – would keep its units fixed in place, attacking when they could or dying where they stood, as his now confident infantry, backed by artillery, armor, and air power, decimated them. The ensuing three month struggle was basically an exercise in attrition. IV Corps at Imphal and XXXIII Corps driving south towards it imposed punishing levels of loss on Japanese units that were ill supplied, increasingly riddled with illness and denied by their military ethos and dysfunctional command structure any tactical flexibility. One Japanese regimental commander sent a battalion, down to twenty men, into a counterattack on a 17th Indian Division unit, "reinforcing" them with his headquarters clerks. They were promptly annihilated. While the Japanese command culture played into Slim's hands, his own posed continual problems. Mountbatten, so helpful over the Dakotas, caused considerable difficulty in other directions. As noted above, Slim's immediate (and very supportive) superior, the 11th Army Group commander, General Sir George Giffard, was not only superior to Mountbatten in rank, but so repelled by "Dickie's" style that he could not bring himself to work easily with him.

Mountbatten, in turn, sniped at Giffard continually and, in May, had his chief of staff, Lieutenant General Sir Henry Pownall, tell Giffard he was to be replaced (although this did not happen until October). Moreover, Mountbatten seems to have had a shaky grasp of Slim's overall plan (although Giffard certainly understood it well enough). The job of IV Corps was *not* to fight its way out of the Imphal plain. It was the anvil, XXXIII Corps, driving south, was the hammer (or pile driver). When anxiety was expressed in London about how long IV Corps could hold the plain, dependent solely on Dakotas, it was reflected in waspish notes from Mountbatten to Giffard asking when he could launch an offensive by IV Corps to meet XXXIII Corps, which Giffard knew was not Slim's plan. It also produced a bizarre suggestion to Slim, almost certainly from Mountbatten's headquarters, that an armored column be rushed down the road from Dimapur, escorting supply trucks on the model of the supply convoys the Royal Navy had fought through to Malta – or tried to. It is hard to believe the author of this gem had ever looked at a large scale map – or taken note of how little actually ever reached Malta, for that matter.

Throughout Slim maintained his aim – and his calm. Imphal, he said, would be relieved by the third week of June (the actual date was 21 June).

In addition to worry over Dakotas, the Mountbatten-Giffard quarrel and exhortations to act Nelsonic, Slim had the problem of Stilwell. When SEAC was created, the justification for an army group command was that Giffard would supervise, not only Slim's XIV Army but Stilwell's NCAC. Stilwell however disliked Giffard on sight and refused to accept orders from him. Since sacking Stilwell was out of the question, there was no option but to accept Stilwell's offer to take orders from Slim – but only until his advance reached Kamaing, a town of no particular significance on the way to

Myitkyina, the objective toward which his Chinese divisions were creeping. Supervising the Imphal-Kohima struggle, as well as his old XV Corps operations in the Arakan, Slim had little time to spare for Stilwell, whose advance was being efficiently slowed by a single Japanese division. Fortunately Stilwell's operation had little direct bearing on Slim's fight. Stilwell got what he wanted – freedom from British supervision. He later told Slim smugly that he had never disobeyed an order from him. Slim's answer was that he only gave orders he knew Stilwell would obey.

While "Vinegar Joe's" private war was largely irrelevant to Slim as he conducted his battle, it was far otherwise with Orde Wingate. At Quadrant he had been given a corps size force with no real thought given to the impact of this on either India Command or XIV Army.

Assembling Special Force necessitated braking up the 70th British Division, which had been part of Slim's XV Corps and Ranchi. He later said that this well trained formation would have paid far greater dividends fighting as an intact division under XIV Army. Several other units were broken up as well and four Gurkha battalions transferred to Special Force. Wingate would not take Indian units but accepted Gurkhas (Gurkha officers felt he had badly mishandled the one Gurkha unit that had been on his first raid). As Special Force organized itself however what Wingate proposed to do became less and less relevant to the situation taking shape on the Assam front. Wingate had been intended to spearhead a general advance by XIV Army, Stilwell's NCAC and, theoretically, a Chinese force from Yunnan (Yokeforce). These converging thrusts would push the Japanese out of north Burma, clearing the way for Stilwell's road and fulfilling American desiderata for the Burma campaign. But by the time Special Force was ready to take the field, the picture had changed dramatically. XIV Army was shifting to a defensive stance; Yokeforce, impressive on paper but never much more than a bargaining chip for Chiang, was unlikely to move soon. There remained NCAC, its Chinese divisions moving slowly forward, an advance Slim understood that Wingate's primary mission was to accelerate. As circumstances changed around him, Wingate's ideas and proposals became more sweeping, doubtless in an attempt to keep Special Force, and its commander, central to theater strategy. A clash with Slim was almost inevitable. Slim later said that it was hard to cooperate with someone who saw matters only from his own point of view. Wingate had a single-mindedness, he later wrote, that came close to fanaticism. His success at Quadrant – and Churchill's permission to contact 10 Downing Street directly if he felt there was an attempt to obstruct his plans – encouraged him to ride roughshod over anyone he believed was not supporting him as wholeheartedly as he required. Then he came up against Slim.

Slim had met Wingate in East Africa and discussed with him Wingate's evolving ideas on "long range penetration." He was dubious that concepts derived from success against the ill- led and demoralized Italian forces there (and amid a supportive population) would be as effective against the much tougher Japanese – and among a population of ambiguous loyalties. As Wingate's ideas expanded, he began to envision "strongholds" – defended airheads that would be the base from which his LRP "columns" would sortie forth to disrupt enemy communications.

His strongholds however would require garrisons, and he tried to lay claim to the 26th Indian Infantry Division (Slim's army reserve) – apparently Indian troops were acceptable for static duties. When he was denied, he reminded Slim of his right to communicate directly with Churchill. Slim simply pushed a message pad across his desk and told Wingate to go compose his message. Wingate withdrew, without the message pad, and made no further claim on the 26th Indian. (He eventually accepted Nigerian battalions for his strongholds.) That was not the only time when Slim had to call his bluff. During the planning for "Operation Thursday," Special Forces' incursion into Burma, a dispute arose over the rate at which two of his brigades would be flown into Burma. This came down to the availability of Dakotas. Slim could only increase the rate of Wingate's build up by shutting down all other air supply operations – he had 81st West African Division, part of XV Corps' renewed push in the Arakan, on air supply as was lonely Fort Hertz in the extreme north of Burma (which the British held onto in 1942) and Fort White, in the Chin Hills south of Imphal, a center from which the Chin Hills tribes were rallied against the Japanese. This Slim declined to do. Wingate then refused to accept the draft order Slim had composed embodying his decisions. The rest is best told in Slim's own words:

> I gave him an unsigned copy of the draft, told him to take it away, sleep on it that night, and come back at ten o'clock the next morning, when I would give him the same order signed. I told him I had never had a subordinate officer refuse and order but if one did, I knew what to do… next day… I rather expected trouble, but… I passed the signed order across to him, and, with a slightly wry smile, he accepted it without comment.[44]

Wingate thus discovered what others, going back to the RAMC doctors in 1915 had learned. Bill Slim was very hard to beat.

There was one further memorable encounter between Slim and Wingate. On 5 March, as the fly-in of two of Wingate's LRP brigades was about to begin, Slim joined Wingate at Hailakandi, the airfield in eastern Bengal where the loaded Dakotas, each towing two loaded gliders, waited to depart. With the Dakota engines revving, a two hour old aerial reconnaissance photo was brought to Slim: one of the three places chosen for glider landings was now covered with teak logs. Wingate, already keyed up, immediately decided that the Japanese must have foreknowledge of "Thursday," which therefore ought to be scrubbed.[45] Slim took him aside, told him that the fact that the other two landing sites were not obstructed argued against any leaks and that on balance, there was good reason to push on. Wingate told Slim the decision was his. "I knew it was," Slim later wrote; he then launched "Thursday."[46]

44 Slim, *Defeat Into Victory*, p. 220.
45 In fact, the obstruction was fortuitous: some Burmese loggers had dragged the tree trunks into the clearing to dry out.
46 What happened at Hailakandi that evening has become one of the disputed points in the controversy-strewn saga of "Thursday." Slim's version, given above was directly contradicted

As the Dakotas and their gliders lifted off from Hailakandi, Special Force leaves the story of XIV Army's battle around Imphal. Special Force had come into existence to help Stilwell's advance – for that reason only had the Americans supported it so lavishly. Therefore its focus was on the rail and road link that supplied the Japanese 18th Division confronting Stilwell.

Wingate was a distraction for Slim (as for SEAC, Auchinleck and India Command!) before Thursday was launched, but after Special Force took the field it was mainly because of its air resupply needs that it impinged on Slim and XIV Army. One last major issue arose however. On 24 March Wingate died in an air crash and it fell to Slim to name his successor. Slim chose Brigadier W. D. A. Lentaigne, a Gurkha officer who, he felt, was the "most balanced" of Wingate's commanders. Under Lentaigne, Special Force, in an epic of courage and endurance moved north along the "railway corridor" to assist in Stilwell's capture of Myitkyina.

The question of how much Special Force contributed to XIV Army's victory is controversial. The answer delivered by the official historians was, in essence, "not much," an answer bitterly resented by Wingate's partisans, but hard to refute. Faulty Japanese planning had more to do with Fifteenth Army's logistical woes than did Special Force.[47]

As that force wrote its epic in Burma, XIV Army, having absorbed the initial Japanese blows (two of which were considerable tactical surprises) and stabilized its situation, was ready to take the offensive. IV Corps was ordered to go over to the offensive by Slim on 10 April. By that time the Dakotas had brought Scoones another division, Harold Briggs' 5th Indian, shifted from the Arakan. Frank Messery's 7th Indian, victors in the Admin Box fight, had been airlifted to join Stopford's XXXIII Corps pushing south toward Imphal along the Dimapur-Kohima- Imphal road.[48] The ability to rapidly reposi-

by a memo Wingate subsequently wrote, in which his role and Slim's are reversed. The most dispassionate analysis of Thursday, Shelford Bidwell's *The Chindit War* (New York, 1979) pp 105-106 supports Slim – as does any comparative view of Slim's personality and Wingate's.

47 When Japanese offensive began, Giffard had put two of Wingate's three reserve brigades at Slim's disposal. One of them, Brigadier Lance Perowne's 23rd LRP Brigade played a significant, if unsung, role in the battle.

Slim would later muse in his memoir (*Defeat Into Victory*, p. 268) that since Imphal was the decisive battle, he ought to have focused Special Force on aiding IV Corps. This reads oddly. Slim knew that Special Force had been created with American aid to assist Stilwell. Changing its mission would have sent sharp tremors right to the top of the Anglo-American alliance. And the Americans still owned most of Slim's invaluable Dakotas.

48 XXXIII Corps' other division, Major General J. M. L. Grover's 2nd British Division was trundled across India by rail. The strain that active operations in Assam placed on India's internal transportation system in which the railroads were key was enormous and one of the unwritten stories of the war is the way the Indian railroads coped. Another is how little London did to help. In March 1944, the Quartermaster General of the British Army was dumbfounded to be told by Auchinleck's Principal Administrative Officer that in all of India there were fewer locomotives than were owned by the London, Midland, and Scottish Railway, itself one of several rail operating companies in Britain. India's stock of locomotives had been raided in 1941 to beef up the Iraqi railroads. Replacements promised from Britain did not arrive. Yet the Indian system somehow coped.

tion reserves, crucial in any battle, was utterly dependent on the Dakotas whose crews and ground staff, working in monsoon conditions, performed prodigies.

At the same time, the divisions at Imphal were being sustained by an airlift – Operation Stamina. It was the largest sustained aerial resupply operation of the war: 7,500 sorties between April and June brought in 12,250 reinforcements and 18,800 tons of supplies while flying out 13,000 sick and wounded plus 43,000 noncombatants. All the while, in the background SEAC, London, and Washington argued about who would provide how many Dakotas and for how long. At one point when the return date of borrowed Dakotas became contentious, Slim, backed by Giffard, told Mountbatten that if the Dakotas were not retained he would not be responsible for the consequences. The Dakotas remained. Securing Slim's flying supply line was one of Mountbatten's best performances at SEAC.

The Imphal battle was a Stalingrad in reverse for the Japanese. IV Corps was effectively supplied. There were precautionary ration cuts in both early April and May but rations for Scoones' 155,000 men and 11,000 animals remained adequate. There were sporadic ammunition shortages. But operational efficiency was not impaired. Morale was sustained by effective medical care and the knowledge that sick and wounded could be flown out to India. At the end of the siege IV Corps, thanks to Stamina, had more supplies than at the beginning. The Japanese on the other hand were poorly supplied and "poor" turned into "very badly" quickly. Their logisticians concentrated on getting ammunition forward; food was not a priority. Medical care, scanty to begin with, was as bad as food supply. And yet they fought relentlessly, attacking when they could and fighting to the last man on the defensive. Japanese military culture became Slim's ally in the destruction of Fifteenth Army – as he had always assumed it would.

In three months of confusing small scale engagements – a contest of platoons, companies, and battalions – Slim's divisions simply chewed up their opponents. Cowan's 17th Indian held the southern gate to the plain while the Japanese 33rd Division battered at it frontally and tried to outflank it. Neither move succeeded. Gracey's 20th Indian held the east gate, at the Shenam Pass, against the Japanese 15th Division (which had most of Fifteenth Army's armor and artillery).

Again the Japanese attacked repeatedly, penetrating into the 20th's positions but never breaking through. On the north side of the plain, Briggs' 5th Indian and Ouvry Roberts' 23rd pushed steadily north towards the oncoming XXXIII Corps, grinding down more of 15th Division.

Stopford's Corps made slow progress. The tangled country south of Kohima lent itself to Japanese defensive tactics and one of Stopford's divisions, 2nd British, was inexperienced in the type of fighting it was asked to do.[49] But with the arrival of Messervy's 7th

49 The division was a regular division that had fought in France in 1940 returning home via Dunkirk. Shipped east in 1942, bits of it had been involved in both "Ironclad" – the taking of Madagascar – and the Arakan fiasco. But for nearly two years the division had been training in South India for amphibious operations (which SEAC planned constantly and cancelled as routinely). Railed across India to Dimapur, it had to immediately reorganize,

Indian, the pace of Stopford's advance picked up. Imphal was about attrition – and XIV Army had become very good at inflicting it on their enemy – or as Slim put it: "We had learned how to kill Japanese."[50]

In the end, the Japanese 31st Division, with Stopford bearing down remorselessly, that cracked first. Mutaguchi and his superior, Burma Area Army commander Lieutenant General Kawabe Shozo still could not bring themselves to order a retreat. When they met at Mutaguchi's headquarters at Kaleymo on the Chindwin on 5 June, Mutaguchi could not make himself admit failure – he hoped Kawabe would understand the situation from the tears in his eyes. Kawabe had no intention of carrying the can for Muaguchi. Ignoring his dewy eyes, he ordered renewed attacks. It was the last straw for Major General Sato Kotoko of the 31st Division. Facing remorseless pounding by XXXIII Corps, his logistics in a state of collapse and without reinforcements, Sato rebelled. Telling Mutaguchi his failure to supply 31st Division absolved it of loyalty to him, he organized a die in place rear guard and ordered the division to retreat – a withdrawal that turned into a rout. Mutaguchi sent his chief of staff to bring the situation under control – that worthy was aghast to find a Japanese division in "unprecedented…headlong retreat." Mutaguchi's other divisions soon followed suit. Finally on 25 June, Mutaguchi made it official, asking Kawabe for permission to retire. The Japanese chain of command was merely rationalizing what was already happening – Fifteenth Army was finished.

Around mid-morning on 20 June, a patrol of the 1/7 Dogra Regiment, part of Briggs' 5th Indian, accompanied by tanks of the 254th Indian Tank Brigade, met the 2nd Durham Light Infantry of Stopford's 2 British Division. The siege of Imphal was over – exactly when Slim had predicted. XIV Army had won overwhelmingly. Of Mutaguchi's 84,000 men, 55,000 were lost. The survivors, staggering back to Burma in monsoon downpours, abandoning their wounded and sick to die, riddled with a medical text-book's worth of diseases, had ceased to be a coherent fighting force. But Slim was not done with them yet.

The monsoon season (May-September) had always been considered a closed season for major military activity. This was particularly true in an area like India's northeast frontier. The primitive roads were washed out or swept away by landslides – as were railway lines and bridges. Tracks became muddy quagmires; "hills," usually mountains thousands of feet high, became unclimbable because the sodden vegetation was slippery and the earth underfoot a soggy morass. Disease proliferated. Slim was convinced that it would be

giving up its motor vehicles for mules and Naga porters. It then had to tackle Assam's jungle-covered, mountainous terrain, amid monsoon downpours that made scaling heights dauntingly difficult. It also had to tackle formidable Japanese bunker complexes, without the full measure of artillery and armor support it was trained to expect. All things considered, its slow start is not surprising. It also seems to have made matters more difficult for itself by ignoring the lessons painfully learned by the veteran Indian units it fought alongside. Of its dour determination there can be no doubt – its three brigades lost four brigadiers, the highest senior officer casualty rate of any British division in the war.

50 Slim, *Defeat Into Victory*, p. 369.

possible to move ahead during the monsoon, and he intended to do so.[51] He wanted to give the Japanese no breathing space; he intended to be poised on the edge of the north Burma plain at the beginning of the dry season of 1944-45, ready to make full use of XIV Army's mobility and firepower which could be used there to fullest effect. He would retake Burma overland from the north in the next campaigning season. Although he never said so, there may have been something else in the back of Slim's mind. SEAC, reflecting London, wanted to pursue an amphibious strategy – Rangoon, and then Malaya. If the resources to do this were forthcoming from Europe (which depended on the German war ending in 1944), XIV Army's campaign might well be limited to making sure Stilwell's road went through. If XIV Army continued to move forward during the monsoon and was poised to launch a decisive thrust into Burma when the dry season came, it would be harder for any of Slim's layers of superiors to put the brakes on. And so was launched perhaps the most remarkable chapter of the Imphal story: the monsoon pursuit.

To push after the retreating Japanese 15th and 33rd Divisions – there was almost nothing worth pursuing left of the 31st – would involve driving south along the Tiddim road, and, to the east, through the Kabaw Valley, in the teeth not only of sacrificial Japanese rearguards but of the full fury of the monsoon. Moreover, the Kabaw Valley was one of the most unhealthy spots a region rich in health hazards. To conduct the monsoon pursuit, Slim restructured his forces. IV Corps' Indian divisions and the 2nd British Division were pulled back to healthier locales around Imphal and Kohima for rest and refitting. Stopford's XXXIII Corps was responsible for the pursuit, with Briggs' 5th Indian on the Tiddim Road and Major General C. C. ("Fluffy") Fawkes' 11th East African in the Kabaw Valley.

Briggs' Division had a daunting task. The Tiddim Road, built by 17th Indian and then demolished by them, patched up by the Japanese and then wrecked again as their 33rd Division fell back, was now assailed by the most effective road destruction agent in the theater, the monsoon. There was no point trying to maintain the road behind the division – it was allowed to wash away and the 5th Indian depended on air supply by the Dakotas which, somehow, always got through. It was impossible to hack out landing grounds, so casualties could not be flown out – XIV Army's nurses volunteered in large enough numbers so they could be carried along and treated as 5th Indian squelched forward, often at no more than two miles a day. Briggs, exhausted after months in command, went back to India on leave. Geoffrey Evans, the defender of the Admin Box, took over and, when he went sick, D. F. W. ("Daddy") Warren, whose brigade had played a key role at Kohima, replaced him. Whoever was in command, 5th Indian kept relentlessly on – not the monsoon, not the "last man, last round" Japanese rearguards, nor terrain features like the "Chocolate Staircase" (where, in 7 miles, the road climbed through 38 hairpin turns, and 3,000 feet in a 1:12 gradient) could now stop Slim's divisions.

51 With his incurable itch to annex credit, Mountbatten later claimed that fighting through the monsoon was his idea. It wasn't – something Slim's official biographer clearly established. Lyman, *Slim: Master of War*, pp. 134-136.

The story of the 11th East African Division in the Kabaw Valley is equally remarkable. It was chosen for this role because of the "believed higher resistance," in the careful phrasing of the official historians, to the malaria endemic there.[52] The monsoon simply closed down the Kabaw Valley. Even the Dakotas had difficulties; weather sometimes shut down radio communications. Wheeled and tracked vehicles could not move. 11th East African depended on its porters, who even carried disassembled artillery pieces. Sappers built "corduroy" roads, surfaced with logs, but even on them four-wheel drive vehicles, like the invincible jeep, could only make about five miles in 24 hours. Nonetheless, and despite a steadily mounting sick list, 11th East African pressed doggedly on. By November, as the rains ended, 11th East African and 5th Indian were closing in on the Chindwin River port of Kaleymo, which they entered on 13 November. The monsoon pursuit was over; XIV Army was poised, as the landscape dried out, to reenter Burma – just as Slim planned.[53]

But the cost had been high – XXXIII Corps recorded 50,000 casualties (55 percent of its average daily strength). Ninety percent of those casualties were illness caused by ghastly climatic conditions, and Kabaw Valley's collection of diseases. A successful general has to have a touch of ruthlessness and the monsoon pursuit demonstrates Slim's – as had his order in Persia that one of his units preempt Russian occupation of points in the zone assigned to Britain no matter now many vehicles and their Gurkha passengers were written off doing so. In both cases, he got the result he wanted. Once Kaleymo was in XIV Army hands, a 1,500 foot Bailey bridge was quickly thrown across the Chindwin. The 11th East African fanned out on the east bank securing the bridgehead and creating the springboard for the dry weather offensive that would take XIV Army to the Irrawaddy and Mandalay – destroying the Burma Area Army en route.

52 Slim says (*Defeat Into Victory*, pp. 354-55) that he was "interested to be told" that Africans had higher resistance to malaria than British or Indian troops. It would be interesting to know by whom and on what evidence he was so briefed.

53 Slim, in *Defeat Into Victory* (p. 354) wrote, slightly defensively, that given a choice he would have fought in the healthiest, not the most disease-ridden, environment he could find but that the Kabaw Valley was tactically and operationally the best route. He acknowledged what 11th East African had accomplished: "a great achievement which… a year before would have almost universally have been proclaimed impossible" (p. 356). However, he felt 11th East African should have gotten to Kaleymo while the Japanese 33rd Division was still trying to delay 5th Indian, thus trapping the Japanese rear guard. He also had reservations about the organization of all three of his African divisions (81st and 82nd West African Divisions also served in Burma) feeling that there were too many European officers, who sapped the ability and initiative of the African NCOs. Slim also disliked the train of unarmed porters who were part of the African divisions – although they came in quite handy in the Kabaw Valley. On the whole, the complaint of one British officer who served in the 81st West African division – John A.L. Hamilton, *War Bush: 81 (West African) Division in Burma, 1943-45* (London, 2001), passim – that Slim and his fellow Indian Army officers had a poor opinion of African units and underplayed their achievements seems to have more than a grain of truth to it. Certainly, the trek of 11th East African down the pestilential Kabaw Valley deserves a book to itself.

In mid December, Shwegyin on the east bank – where Burcorps withdrew across the Chindwin – was cleared. Slim – now Sir William, knighted, appropriately on the Imphal plain, together with his three corps commanders by the Viceroy, Lord Wavell, on behalf of the King Emperor – revisited it immediately: "There were the burnt-out and rusted tanks that I had so reluctantly destroyed… Much had happened since then. Some of what we owed we had paid back. Now we were going to pay back the rest – with interest."[54]

## Burma: Payback

The campaign in Burma had always been carried on against a background of Anglo-American discord over its purpose, discord intensified by Stilwell's acerbic presence and the constant drizzle of denigration in his reports to Washington about British competence and courage. Moreover, neither the prime minister nor the British Chiefs of Staff had proved themselves consistently supportive. The Americans wanted a restored road to China, period. Churchill wanted SEAC to develop a maritime/amphibious strategy whose goal was the reconquest of Singapore which, he asserted in a note to his Chiefs of Staff in September 1944, "is the only prize that will restore British prestige in this region,…"[55] The British Chiefs of Staff were not enthusiastic about the Burma campaign either. Like Churchill they looked to a future in which Anglo-American relations would be a paramount factor. While Churchill sought to prepare for this by reestablishing British prestige in Asia, the Chiefs of Staff wanted a significant British role in the main theater, the Pacific (where the Americans did not want them). A bitter argument about which option (neither of which could be resourced) to choose had consumed much time and emotional energy in London over most of 1944. The point to note here is that neither strategy envisioned a significant role for XIV Army beyond clearing North Burma to ensure completion of the Ledo (or Stilwell) Road to the point where it would tie into the old Burma Road and thus reach an American, not a British, goal.

As the monsoon pursuit inched its way forward, this was the background against which Slim and his staff had to plan. The Americans, who owned most of the Dakota squadrons supporting XIV Army were on the eve of reaching their objective. Myitkyina, the goal of Stilwell's campaign, fell in August. Its airfield, in American hands, provided complete security for the China airlift. Thanks to XIV Army victory, Stilwell's road would be completed in short order. Would the Americans then continue to support XIV Army's campaign? SEAC had developed, and London had approved, as the centerpiece of the 1944-45 campaign, another of Mountbatten's amphibious projects, "Dracula," a seaborne assault on Rangoon, a way station on the way back to Singapore. The clearance

54 Slim, *Defeat Into Victory*, p. 369. Interestingly, Slim never mentions his knighthood in his memoirs.
55 Winston S. Churchill, *Triumph and Tragedy* (Boston, 1953), p. 167.

of North Burma and the acquisition of defensive depth in front of the new road to China was XIV Army's (subordinate) role in this plan. No one in Washington, London or Kandy envisioned what Slim and his staff were already revolving in their minds – the total reconquest of Burma, culminating in the recapture of Rangoon by an overland drive from the north.

As had been so often the case, whatever the intentions of planners at the strategic level, events on the ground resolved the issue in Slim's favor. That ground however was not in Burma, or anywhere else in SEAC, but in Dwight Eisenhower's far away theater in Northwest Europe.

Since January 1944, the planning assumption in London had been that the German war would end in 1944. British industrial and manpower mobilization had both passed their peak. It would be increasingly difficult to keep the British war effort going at the same level of intensity in Europe and there was nothing to spare for the Far East – until the German war ended. Then, to mount Dracula, the three Indian divisions in the Mediterranean theater would have to return home, and three British divisions, two independent brigades, substantial numbers of naval vessels and amphibious craft plus 190 transport aircraft would have to be transferred to SEAC as well – and even then nearly 400 more transports would have to be borrowed from the Americans (Dracula's planners were clearly rather optimistic about the "special relationship.") But by the late autumn of 1944 it was quite plain that the German war would linger into 1945.

Eisenhower's advance was stalled on the borders of the Reich by logistic exhaustion and the Wehrmacht's last rally. In Italy Field Marshal Sir Harold Alexander's armies had stalled before the Gothic Line. Nothing could now be spared for SEAC. "Dracula," like previous SEAC amphibious designs, was interred in the filing cabinets at Kandy. All this was made official when the British and American Chiefs of Staff met at Malta in January, 1945. SEAC was told simply to clear all of Burma and prepare to then liberate Malaya. Slim's campaign thus became, finally, SEAC's priority. By the time this directive was issued, Slim – the only senior commander in Burma whose plans invariably worked out – was well on his way to the battlefield triumph that would ultimately see him mentioned in the same breath as Wellington.

As XIV Army turned to planning its dry season campaign, the framework within which it operated changed – a few things improved while in one major respect things grew much worse. Mountbatten finally rid himself of Giffard who left in October. In his place commanding the new Allied Land Forces South East Asia (ALFSEA) Lieutenant General Sir Oliver Leese, Bart., Monty's successor as Eighth Army commander, arrived. Leese was a soldier of modest attainments – Monty, one of whose favorites he was, liked his subordinates to stay that way. He had not shone on his own as an army commander in Italy. But his greatest weakness was that he arrived with his own bubble. His superior in Italy, Alexander, had cautioned him about taking his Eighth Army staff with him – and Alex knew Slim from the 1942 retreat. Slim later noted of Giffard's departure: "We saw him go with grief." Of Leese he wrote "I found him easy to serve under" but he was more pointed about Leese's Eighth Army imports, noting "his staff… which replaced most of our old friends at General Giffard's headquarters, had a great deal of desert sand in its shoes and was rather inclined to thrust Eighth Army down our throats. No doubt we provoked them, for not only were my people a bit sore at losing General Giffard, *but… we also thought Fourteenth Army was now quite something*."[56] Faced with the overpromoted Guardsman and his patronizing staff, Slim's provocation took the form of a tactic he had successfully employed since outflanking the RAMC in 1915. He worked around the obstacle. He later said that, as an army commander, he felt that plans made and actions taken within the terms of his directive were matters for him alone. Leese and ALFSEA were informed rather than consulted. Thus was lit the long fuse that produced a spectacular explosion in May, 1945.

The other major – and entirely positive – change was Stilwell's recall. At daggers drawn with Chiang, he had virtually ceased to function as SEAC Deputy Supreme Commander, immuring himself in his NCAC headquarters and focusing obsessively on driving through his road. His relations with the British were close to poisonous. But, as the 1944-45 dry season approached, he was no longer needed for the attainment of American objectives – the road would go through. Marshal recalled him – and named him to command an army in the closing stages of the Pacific War. The emollient American Lieutenant General Raymond Wheeler became SEAC's Deputy Supreme Commander and Lieutenant General Dan Sultan (who Slim "knew and liked") took over NCAC.

But, whatever may have been happening in the command stratosphere there was one unchanging factor: the hair-raising logistics of XIV Army – which were about to get even more complex. The capacity of the Assam line of communications had grown exponentially since the dark days of 1942. But that enhanced capacity had been focused on supporting IV Corps on the Imphal plain. Now IV and XXXIII Corps were moving forward to the Chindwin and, as the dry season set in, would be conducting intensive operations further and further away from Imphal. When Eisenhower's armies broke out of the Normandy beachhead and surged to the frontiers of Germany they had behind them the dense road and rail network of Northwest Europe, damaged to be sure, but repairable, especially since his armies had at their disposal engineering and transportation resources lavish by XIV Army standards. It was far otherwise for Slim. From the railhead at Dimapur, it was nearly 200 miles to Imphal and as far again to the Chindwin crossing at Kaleymo (Rangoon was 1,000 miles away). Most of the roads were fair weather only and even the imaginative idea of surfacing them with tar coated jute sacking – "bithess" – would not really completely monsoon-proof those roads. When the Chindwin was reached, timber could be felled, rafts built, outboard motors air-dropped and an improvised fleet assembled to use the river as an alternate to road haulage for part of the distance to a front that would be moving steadily eastward toward the Irrawaddy. The XIV Army's assortment of trucks, jeeps, mules, elephants, improvised rivercraft and (in the East African units) "carriers" – porters with head loads – would however not be quite enough. The Dakotas would remain, as they had been since the Admin Box battle,

56 Slim, *Defeat Into Victory*, p. 385. Italics mine.

vital. And the Americans still controlled most of them. The background music to Slim's 1944-45 campaign would be the constant effort required see that XIV Army had access to enough of them, for long enough, to get to Rangoon.

The plan that would take XIV Army there was taking shape at Slim's headquarters as the monsoon pursuit ground its soggy way forward. Operation "Capital" whose aim was to carry XIV Army to Mandalay, envisioned a major battle with Burma Area Army (now commanded by Lieutenant General Kimura Hyotaro) in the open plains around Shwebo, west of the Irrawaddy, where Slim's now veteran divisions could utilize their hard won skills in combined arms tactics to the fullest. Slim's plan called for IV Corps, now commanded by Frank Messervy, and consisting of the new 19th Indian Infantry Division commanded by the dynamic Major General Pete Rees and the veteran 7th Indian, to drive east toward Shwebo from a Chindwin bridgehead near Tamu. Further south, at Kalewa, the 11th East African was still enlarging its bridgehead through which Stopford's XXXIII Corps would break out heading for a rendezvous with Messervy in the Shwebo plain. Each corps had an armored brigade to take advantage of the more open terrain into which they were now moving.

Slim expected that the Japanese would defend the line of the Zebyu Taungdan range, hills running north-south and 1,000-2,000 feet high located about thirty miles east of the Chindwin, a natural stop line which, defended with the Imperial Japanese Army's trademark tenacity, would buy the time necessary to reorganize Burma Area Army for the impending battle with XIV Army in the Shwebo plain. Slim would remark in his memoirs that battles in which he was engaged "rarely went according to plan."[57] Kimura was a much smarter soldier that Mutaguchi and understood that facing XIV Army on ground that played to its strength with the mile-wide, unbridged Irrawaddy behind him might well be fatal. So he elected to simply delay XIV Army with rearguards while he pulled his forces back to the east bank of the Irrawaddy thus posing for Slim the operational and tactical problem of an assault crossing of a far more formidable obstacle than the Rhine. Within a week of the opening of XIV Army's offensive on 3 December, Slim began to suspect from the speed at which Rees' division was advancing that Kimura was not going to offer battle west of the Irrawaddy, and that his plans would have to be recast.

As Slim and his staff began to revise their design, creating what would be the most imaginative – and risky – maneuver any British general would undertake during the war, the army he led was assuming its final form, one light years away from the Burcorps he had take command of in March, 1942. The changes that had begun in the aftermath of the retreat from Burma had culminated in 1944 in exactly the army Slim had always wanted – well trained, well led, able to go anywhere, do anything and keep on doing it on a logistic shoestring as long as necessary. The training and doctrine revolution of 1943; the work of Savory and Auchinleck at army headquarters and the now smoothly functioning machine that harvested "lessons learned" from the battlefield, digested them and produced the necessary training and doctrinal adjustments were producing a

57 Ibid., p. 295.

very capable, adaptable and flexible force. Even as Slim planned and launched "Capital," two of his best divisions, Cowan's 17th Indian and Warren's 5th Indian had been rotated back to India to re-equip and retrain as mechanized divisions in anticipation of a forthcoming campaign on north Burma's plains.[58]

This well-oiled military machine was also, increasingly, an Indian military machine. The rule that every Indian brigade contain a British battalion had been quietly shelved during the war – there were simply not enough British battalions any longer, as Britain's war effort far exceeded what its demographic base could support, and first priority for the increasingly scarce infantry replacements had gone to Montgomery's 21st Army Group (which, nevertheless, would inexorably shrink). Moreover those British units present in XIV Army were now chronically understrength for lack of replacements. Finally, in September 1944, the War Office, concerned about the morale of British troops serving in the east (many having been there for years) shortened the length of service necessary to quality for repatriation from five years to three years and eight months, thus stripping thousands more from already attenuated ranks. British troops consumed far more supplies than Indian *jawans* and this in a situation where logistics would grow steadily tighter. The weakness of British battalions meant more tactical pressure on Indian battalions – which noticed the increased burden they were carrying. As XIV Army's final campaign unfolded British units were swapped out of Indian divisions for full strength, easier to maintain Indian units. By the time the British XIV Army reached Rangoon it would be only 13% ethnically British.

The Indian Army on the other hand had come into its own as a modern force. Despite the huge role it played in the 1914-18 imperial war effort, the pressure for modernization created by that war largely evaporated after 1918. The army shrank back to its bedrock – long service, martial race professionals – and its traditional duties: policing the Northwest Frontier and "aid to the civil," backing up the police in dealing with political or communal unrest (increasingly, overlapping categories). Modernization meant expense that the Government of India did not wish to incur. Indianization of the officer corps was accepted, grudgingly in many cases, but proceeded slowly. On the eve of the war, the Indian Army still looked very much like the army Kipling knew. What happened next is best described by the leading historian of the Indian Army's final years:

> It would be difficult to overstate how far-reaching and fundamental were the changes the Indian Army went through in the Second World War. In 1945, it was a highly professional and modern force that included in its ranks representatives of ethnic groups that had traditionally been ignored as 'non-martial' as well as Indian commissioned officers (ICOs) in positions of command on the battlefield, and was

58 Both divisions had of course been mechanized originally: 5th Indian served in the desert campaigns and 17th Indian had been originally destined for the Middle East as well. Their remechanization in 1944-45 was therefore the third configuration they had adapted to in three years.

> bonded by a hard won *espirit de corps*. It had played the leading role in the destruction of the Imperial Japanese Army in Burma, as well as significant supporting roles in… North and East Africa and Italy… In almost every way, the Indian Army of 1945 – battle-seasoned, imbued with regimental *espirit de corps*, and above all victorious – was a different force from the one that suffered crippling defeats in the difficult early days of the Second World War.[59]

The army Slim led in the 1945 campaign was already the army of a new nation (or, as it turned out, two nations) not yet quite born. Auchinleck, who in December 1944, had indicated that no more British officers should be appointed to the Indian Army, would say, at the end of Slim's campaign, that every Indian officer "worth his salt" was a nationalist.

It was this army that Slim would launch on the great gamble that was the revised "Capital" plan. Originally both corps were to launch from bridgeheads across the Chindwin. Rees' 19th Indian, already through the Zebyu Taungdau passes and driving hard for the Irrawaddy was to have led IV Corps. Now Slim converted that drive to a mask for the core of his design. 19th Indian was transferred to Stopford's XXXIII Corps. Together with 2nd British and 20th Indian, it would push to the great river, and seize crossings. Messervy' IV Corps, was now made up of 7th and 17th Indian (the latter rejoining after converting from a jungle configured light division to a mobile, mechanized force with one brigade organized to be air portable). IV Corps' two divisions, plus the accompanying 255th Indian Tank Brigade would drive not east but south down the Myittha Valley, which ran parallel to the Irrawaddy about fifty miles further west. At a point about 150 miles south of where they would have crossed the Chindwin, IV Corps would wheel east, close up to the Irrawaddy and 7th Indian would cross at a point well below Kimura's prepared defenses (which were oriented to face a crossing of the Irrawaddy by XIV Army, aimed directly at Mandalay). Once across, Messervy would pass 17th Indian and his tank brigade through 7th Indian's bridgehead to drive on the nodal point of Kimura's communications, Meiktila, south of Mandalay. With that in his hands, Burma Area Army's position would be as hopelessly compromised as the allied armies in Belgium had been when the German panzers reached the channel in May 1940.

Preserving the illusion that XXXIII Corps was the entire XIV Army was vital to Capital's success. Operation "Cloak," Slim's deception scheme, pivoted on creating a dummy corps headquarters at Tamu, where IV Corps had been located. All radio traffic between XXXIII Corps and Rees' division was routed through this bogus headquarters, maintaining the fiction that both XIV Army corps were advancing side by side towards the Irrawaddy. Radio deception games, although complicated to operate successfully, were a standard feature of the war by this point. Much more challenging would be concealing the long trek of Messervy's corps down the Myittha Valley. Two divisions

59 Daniel Marston, *The Indian Army and the End of the Raj* (Cambridge, UK, 2014), p. 45.

and a tank brigade (the latter moving whenever possible on tank transporters to save the track wear on the already hard used Shermans) would travel the 328 miles that separated Tamu from Pakokku (where IV Corps would cross the Irrawaddy) on a rough dirt track with hill sections that offered daunting curves, especially for the tank transporters. They would have to carry both their own supplies, material for an opposed river crossing (including numerous small craft) and reserve supplies to support 17th Indian's dash to Meiktila that would begin the minute 7th Indian's bridgehead was secure. All this amid choking clouds of dry season dust on a track that could never be shut down for repair – and without the Japanese discovering what was going on.

Keeping the Japanese in the dark was aided by the near total air supremacy the RAF and USAAF had by this time achieved but it was unlikely that the Japanese would totally fail to notice something was moving in the Myittha valley. Slim therefore preceded IV Corps down the valley with two formations the Japanese might well expect to see there. The Lushai Brigade had been part of the monsoon pursuit of the Japanese 33rd Division down the road that led to Tamu on the Chindwin. The 11th East African Division had led the pursuit down the Kabaw valley to the Chindwin. Now the Lushai Brigade pushed down the Myittha valley and, when pulled out for a well earned rest, was replaced by the 28th East African Brigade, while IV Corps, observing radio silence – except when it came on the air as 11th East African Division – ground its way south behind it. The hope was that the Japanese would write off anything they noticed as a subsidiary operation that Kimura would evaluate as no immediate threat. It would work but that should not obscure the fact that it was an enormous gamble – the greatest taken by any British or American general during the entire war. One stray Japanese plane spotting the dust clouds that marked IV Corps line of march; one lucky Japanese patrol; one agent in the right place at the right moment, and Slim's plan would unravel. He had decided after Gallabat that the boldest choice was best; the revised "Capital" plan was a choice so bold that, but for Slim's well grounded, absolute confidence in his army, would have been rash.

Once the ease and speed of 19th Indian's advance convinced Slim that Kimura would not, like Mutaguchi, cooperate in his own destruction, Slim had switched gears very quickly, something made easier because since July discussion at XIV Army had revolved around all the variants of the next step on the road back to Mandalay – and Rangoon. An advance, via the Myittha valley to the Irrawaddy and thence to Meiktila had been one of those possibilities. On 18 Dec. 1944, Slim met Messervy and Stopford at IV Corps headquarters and laid out the new design. The following day he issued his formal Operation Instruction. At the conference with his corps commanders, Slim "made clear… that the forthcoming battle would be followed by a dash south to take Rangoon before the monsoon."[60] XIV Army was going to end the war its way during the 1944-45 dry season, driven by the fact that Slim knew it was the last chance for his army to do so.

60 Slim, *Defeat Into Victory*, p. 394. Queried later by one of the official historians, Slim would say of the birth of the idea for the seizure of Meiktila that "he didn't think he did think of it

The check on Eisenhower's advance in September 1944 and the subsequent Fall-Winter pause in the allied advance into Germany had opened the door for Slim's '44-45 campaign, but the European war was unlikely to last beyond the Spring of 1945. Eisenhower would cross the Rhine, the Red Army, already on the frontier of East Prussia, would crumble the eastern defenses of the Reich – and when the German war ended, SEAC would at last have the resources it needed to pursue the strategy it had always yearned to implement. Already, in the heady days following the Normandy breakout, Montgomery had agreed to the withdrawal of an infantry division, an airborne division, a tank brigade and a corps headquarters for transfer to Burma.

The idea died as SHAEF's front congealed but clearly the War Office planned to make SEAC's war a British war in every sense.[61] An advance guard had already arrived. In addition to Leese and his Eighth Army crew, Mountbatten's Chief of Staff, the talented but acerbic (at least in the privacy of his diaries) Lieutenant General Sir Henry Pownall, who had fallen ill, was replaced by Lieutenant General F. A. M. ("Boy") Browning. Browning, a Guardsman like Leese, had not attended staff college and never held a staff job but after his none too effective command of 1st Allied Airborne Corps in Market-Garden "effectively ended his operational career" another post had to be found for him.[62] If XIV Army was not to be sidelined as more British troops – and senior officers – became available for service east of Suez, and a maritime/amphibious strategy finally became possible for SEAC, it had to win before the 1945 monsoon. Slim never alluded to any of this but it is unlikely that someone so determined and shrewd about institutional politics – as well as so sure of both his own and his army's abilities – would have missed the signs.

But these concerns were future possibilities, only to come into play if Rangoon was not taken before the 1945 monsoon broke. Slim's biggest concern, as he replanned Capital was the logistics of his operation (which consume more and more space in *Defeat Into Victory* as Slim recounts the 1945 campaign). How precariously these were balanced became painfully clear to Slim early on the morning of 10 Dec. 1944 when he was woken up at his new headquarters at Imphal by the roar of Dakotas passing overhead. Three USAAF Dakota squadrons (75 aircraft) assigned to support XIV Army (whose advancing XXXIII Corps spearheads were already on air supply) had suddenly been ordered to China. Dumping supplies already loaded for XXXIII Corps on the airstrip,

first: the whole Fourteenth Army staff was continually thinking about it and he didn't know who first said Meiktila…" The idea came from "joint thinking and discussing…" Brigadier Michael Roberts to Ronald Lewin, May 5, 1974, Roberts Papers MRBS 1/4, Churchill Archive Center, Churchill College Cambridge. Slim never felt the need to claim the spotlight for himself.

61 The armored brigade was the 6th Guards Armored Brigade. If it had deployed to India or Burma, it would have been a first. Unlike the regiments of the line, the Guards never rotated to India, nor did any Guards units serve east of Suez in either World War.

62 John Buckley, *Monty's Men: The British Army and the Liberation of Europe*, paper ed., (New Haven, CT, 2014), p. 230.

they unceremoniously left, their departure the first indication Slim had that he was facing a major logistic crisis.

Once again the shadow of the United States' China policy had fallen across Slim's campaign. American B-29 bombers, based mostly in India but staging through bases in China had become a problem to the Japanese who launched a major offensive to overrun the USAAF's Chinese airfields. Stilwell – who hated the USAAF commander in China, Major General Claire Chennault, as badly as he hated the British – had pointed out that this would be the consequence of USAAF strategy. He warned as well that Chiang's army would not be able to stop a major Japanese offensive. He was right on both counts. Chiang asked for two of his divisions fighting in NCAC to be returned. American trained and equipped, their greater fighting power was now (the Burma Road being again open) needed at home. The three Dakota squadrons were required to shift them.

Mountbatten and Leese had known for several weeks this was likely to happen. It is hard to credit that Slim got no forewarning but his assertion in *Defeat Into Victory* is categorical. (It certainly must have been in his mind when he chose to cut Leese out of the loop subsequently). Slim and his staff, juggling transportation assets furiously began to cope with the new situation while Mountbatten tried to claw back the squadrons. Eventually, after a classic exercise in "Dakota politics" involving SEAC, the British Chiefs of Staff, Washington and Stilwell's replacement as Chiang's American military advisor, Major General Albert Wedemeyer, two squadrons were returned. The British Chiefs of Staff, who had been oddly passive throughout the argument, then found two more RAF Dakota squadrons and added five more planes to each of the eight RAF Dakota squadrons in SEAC. But by then it was the third week in January; 1,300 supply sorties had been lost and the pace of XIV Army's advance had been perceptibly slowed. The 2-3 weeks (by Slim's estimate) this lost him would ultimately cost XIV Army the chance to actually march into Rangoon before the onset of the monsoon.

While all this was going on, XIV Army drove forward. Only a commander with iron nerves and adamantine determination would have pressed on while his American allies removed a key factor in his logistic plan. But Slim may well have calculated that Mountbatten could not afford to let SEAC's only offensive stall and would exert every effort to get him what he needed. He had operated since Gallabat on the principle that the boldest course was best – and so it again proved to be. Even though the loss of the three Dakota squadrons slowed XIV Army's advance, Pete Rees' 19th Indian continued to lead the XXXIII Corps advance toward the Irrawaddy building its own road as it went.[63] 20th Indian and 2nd British, south of Rees, were clearing the Shwebo plain.

63 Road building had, perforce, become a XIV Army specialty – and largely in the absence of the engineering resources so readily available in Europe. For the '44-45 campaign XIV Army planned to concentrate on only one road forward of Imphal: the one that ran down the Kabaw Valley – the site of 11th East African's monsoon trek – to the Chindwin River port at Kalewa. That road would be surfaced with "bithess," the brainchild of Slim's Chief Engineer, Major General W. F. "Bill" Hasted. Strips of asphalt-covered jute sacking, it could stand up, continually patched, to dry season traffic. Forward of the Chindwin, divisions built

As they closed on the Irrawaddy, Kimura saw (and his radio monitors heard) what he expected: XIV Army, two corps abreast, taking the shortest straightline distance back to Mandalay. Meanwhile the deadly threat to his Burma Area Army was crawling steadily southward.

The movement of IV Corps was not the least of the XIV Army's remarkable feats. It was over 300 miles from Tamu on the Chindwin to Pakokku on the Irrawaddy. The dirt track had to be widened and maintained, while in continuous use. The sections that traversed hilly terrain required special work to create curves and gradients negotiable for the tank transporters carrying the armored brigade's Shermans and the assault craft for the river crossing. Even so, the tanks had occasionally to tow their own transporters. All this amid dry season heat and massive, choking clouds of dust. Slim rightly in his memoir singled out for special praise the Indian drivers (many of whom had never even seen what they were now driving before joining the army). To further complicate matters, halfway down the Myittha valley was the village of Gangaw, still held by the Japanese. The lightly equipped Lushai Brigade and 28th East African Brigade, screening the IV Corps advance, would need help clearing Gangaw but to involve IV Corps leading division, Geoffrey Evans' 7th Indian, would compromise the secrecy of the operation. Instead, the heavy bombers of SEAC's Strategic Air Force were called in. "Earthquake" put roughly ten tons of bombs for every Japanese defender onto Gangaw; the Lushai Brigade and the East Africans occupied the rubble and IV Corps rolled on. Overhead the Hurricanes and Spitfires of 221 Group RAF, XIV Army's tactical air support, sealed the skies over it.

By 9 January 1945, 19th Indian was on the west bank of the Irrawaddy. Within a week, Rees had two bridgeheads on the east bank, Kimura was redisposing his troops to meet what he took to be the spearhead of the British drive, and 20th Indian and 2nd British, who had to tackle stubborn Japanese rear guards, slowly closed up to the west bank south of Rees' bridgeheads. Meanwhile, Messervy's corps continued to move remorsely down the Myittha valley, preceded by the East Africans and flanked by a protective screen of British officered tribal levies – the Lushai and Falam Scouts and the Chin Hills Battalion. As it moved south from Gangaw, the lead division, Evans' 7th Indian was stretched out over 350 miles of road and track stretching back to Kohima (approximately the distance from London to Cologne). Small Japanese rearguards confined themselves to mining the track and felling trees across it – in one three mile stretch hundreds, cleared in a day by Messervy's sappers, whose mechanical equipment was supplement by ten elephants. On 28 January 1945, one of Evans' brigades, marching parallel to the track, supported by pack transport swung back onto the track, seizing Pauk, where IV Corps would turn east to the Irrawaddy. Evans' men began hacking out airstrips for the Dakotas, while another of his brigades closed up to the Irrawaddy by 10 February.

roads behind them – one of 19th Indian's cantilevered out from a hillside on timber supports. The three-week shortfall in airlift forced more traffic onto roads thus requiring more men committed to maintenance with minimal equipment. But the advance never faltered.

The East Africans were sent down the west bank to feint at crossing forty miles further south. Slim had told Messervy and Evans they had to be across the Irrawaddy by 15 February – the timetable for getting to Rangoon before the monsoon was inexorably tightening. And still Kimura had not noticed.

Slim was very concerned about his army's shortage of appropriate equipment: "I do not think any modern army has ever attempted the opposed crossing of a great river with so little," adding "the only equipment my army had in full supply was, as ever, brains, hardihood and courage."[64] XIV Army and its commander would need all three. Slim admits in *Defeat Into Victory* to being heavily stressed as his design began to unfold – the chances for failure were multiple. On the night of 12/13 February, 1945, Gracey's 20th Indian began to cross the Irrawaddy. By the evening of 13 February two of his brigades were firmly established on the east bank. Far to the south, IV Corps began to cross that night. Because they had to cross diagonally it would be the longest opposed river crossing of the war, and at first, it seemed that all of Slim's dark forebodings would come true. The main crossing was led by a battalion of the South Lancashire Regiment. One company got across. Then chaos set in. The rest of the battalion – despite previous amphibious experience – fumbled their embarkation; some of the boats (carried hundreds jolting miles on tank transporters) were found to be damaged and leaking; then some of the tired outboard motors refused to start. Japanese machine gun positions on the east bank woke up and raked the boats with fire. The attempt had to be abandoned.

Further downriver a secondary crossing was attempted by a Sikh unit, using commandeered Burmese rivercraft (and impressed Burmese boatmen). When Japanese posts on the east bank opened fire, the Burmese crews panicked, lost control of their craft and although the crews "urged by the sepoys" as Slim delicately put it, brought the boats under control, the attempt had to be abandoned. By breakfast time on 14 February, Slim was looking at failure. Only one South Lancs company had gotten a precarious toehold on the east bank.

Then professionalism and good luck (which Napoleon had said always attended good generals) came to Slim's aid. The sappers patched the boats and resuscitated the cranky outboards; the commander of the assault brigade decided the South Lancs could not sort themselves out quickly enough and substituted the 4/15th Punjab Regiment, who Slim noted, embarked with "great calmness and in excellent order."[65] Then, anticlimactically,

64 Slim, *Defeat Into Victory*, pp. 409-410. For operation "Plunder," the British Second Army's crossing of the Rhine in late March, 1945, the build up involved 32,000 vehicles (including 4,000 tank transporters) stockpiling 118,000 tons of stores. Royal Navy amphibious craft, "Buffalo" amphibious vehicles and "duplex drive" swimming tanks were available. Ten thousand aircraft stood ready to support the operation. One corps alone had 8,000 Royal Engineers in support. A supporting airborne drop on the east bank of the Rhine was launched by two airborne divisions. Over 2,000 guns and mortars supported the operation. XIV Army, by contrast, crossed the Irrawaddy with an assortment of badly worn equipment and could not even get enough reliable outboard motors for the craft they had.

65 Slim, *op. cit.*, p. 429.

it turned out most of the Japanese defenders had moved off. By evening IV Corps had not one but two bridgeheads. The Sikhs, forced back to the west bank, saw a boat, under a white flag, crossing to them. The occupants were members of the woebegone Indian National Army, who brought the news that the Japanese unit that had beaten back the Sikhs had moved out, leaving only INA troops to guard the shoreline. They in turn wanted to surrender. By nightfall the Sikhs also had a bridgehead on the east bank.[66]

IV Corps had successfully sprung Slim's surprise. Like the penetration of the Ardennes and crossing of the Meuse by the Germans in 1940, XIV Army's success now put it in position to completely unhinge its opponent. Kimura was convinced he faced the whole of XIV Army, a conviction reinforced when, on the night of 24/25 February, the third of Stopford's division, Major General Cameron Nicholson's 2nd British, began crossing south of Gracey's bridgehead. Expecting the British to drive on Mandalay from their bridgeheads, Kimura began reinforcing his front facing them. The disappearance of the Japanese defenders who had stymied the initial IV Corps attempts to cross was due to Kimura's assessment that XIV Army would attempt no serious crossings south of the confluence of the Chindwin with the Irrawaddy. Japanese units were pulled north therefore to thicken Burma Area Army's defense against Stopford. Kimura assumed that whatever the British were doing on the west bank south of the confluence was not very important – indeed Japanese intelligence bought the idea that the 28th East African Brigade was an entire East African Division which might try to cross well to the south, near the Burmese oil fields. The few Japanese units that were not ordered north went south to meet his non- existent threat, leaving only the INA. Its speedy collapse opened the door though which Slim delivered the death blow to Kimura's army.

The month after IV Corps' successful crossing was the hinge of the campaign. XIV Army seized Meiktila; Mountbatten finally abandoned "Dracula" which had maintained a shadowy existence as an option for taking Rangoon if XIV Army bogged down in central Burma. On 23 February, as 17th Indian crossed into 7th Indian's bridgehead, SEAC formally cancelled Dracula – taking Rangoon before the monsoon now rested on XIV Army alone. At the same time Slim's always precarious logistics were again worsened by his nominal Chinese and American allies.

The first order of business for Slim was Meiktila. He and Messervy had originally planned to assemble 17th Indian inside Evans' bridgehead before beginning the drive into Meiktila. However to do so would lead to a pause in operations and rather than give the Japanese a chance to reassess and realize what Slim really intended, the crossing and forward deployment of Cowan's division proceeded simultaneously. On 21 February, the drive on Meiktila began. Of all Slim's divisions the Black Cats best embodied the

66 The Japanese military never took the INA seriously as a military force and its role in the 1944 Imphal campaign had never been anything but marginal and inglorious. It is a testimony to the success of XIV Army's deception efforts that Kimura left the task of watching the east bank of the Irrawaddy at the point where IV Corps proposed to cross in the hands of INA units, whose rapid surrender, as Slim caustically observed, was its major contribution to the 1945 campaign.

trajectory of XIV Army. Raised in 1941 for the Middle East; committed instead to Burma under a sick commander, it had been nearly annihilated at the Sittang River – in the aftermath of that debacle, it mustered 3,484 officers and men (41% of normal establishment) with 1,420 rifles and 10 light machine guns. Cowan took command, nursed it through the 1,000 mile retreat and brought it to Imphal where it was rebuilt and retrained. It conducted a 160 mile fighting retreat at the beginning of the Imphal battle, badly damaging the pursuing Japanese 33rd Division. Then it fought for three months to seal the southern approaches to Imphal. Now, reshaped as a mechanized infantry division, it was poised to go for Kimura's jugular. Cowan's two brigades and his accompanying armor went across country to Meiktila in blitz fashion, rolling over or sweeping around Japanese defenders who, Slim noted, "had no experience of these massed armored attacks and seemed quite incapable of dealing with them."[67] By 28 February, Cowan had reached, encircled and was assaulting Meiktila. In a week, he had covered eighty miles, over wretched terrain, fighting every step of the way, and in the process overrunning an airfield into which, while still under repair and occasional Japanese fire, 17th Division's third brigade was flown. Slim would later say, "if you wanted an 'up Guards and at 'em' show you couldn't do better than leave it to Punch."[68] Cowan and his division delivered on the drive to Meiktila.[69] It gave Slim the advantages he had had in the Admin Box fight and at Imphal: the unwavering Japanese commitment to the offensive would erode Kimura's strength as he sought in the face of XIV Army's firepower both to contain Stopford's bridgeheads and retake Meiktila. Then, as XXXIII Corps pushed out of its bridgeheads and IV Corps grip on Meiktila tightened, the hammer and anvil effect seen at the Admin Box fight and at Imphal came into play: "have you ever seen a walnut crushed by a piledriver?"

As the jaws of XIV Army closed on Kimura, Slim confronted a major logistic crisis whose roots lay in the troubled Anglo-American relationship in SEAC. There had been a foreshadowing, as we have seen, in December when three USAAF Dakota squadrons were suddenly removed from XIV Army's air transport pool. The crisis that broke on Slim as Stopford closed on Mandalay and Cowan fought first, to take, and then to hold, Meiktila was far more serious. As the Japanese pressed on in their offensive against the American airfields in China, Chiang's government asked for the return of the remaining Chinese forces serving in Burma; pending that the forward movement of the Chinese and American units in NCAC would stop. The Burma Road had reopened in January (in its brief life it would carry less than the airlift moved it its last full month of operation). Defensive depth in front of it had been achieved – and the Japanese were clearly now in no position to take the offensive in north Burma. But the cessation of NCAC operations freed those Japanese units that had been containing it to redeploy against XIV Army while Slim became responsible

67 Slim, *op. cit.*, pp. 441-442.

68 Brigadier Michael Roberts, a close friend of Slim's, recounted this to Slim's official biographer, Ronald Lewin in a letter of 5 May 1974. Roberts Papers, MRBS 1/4, Churchill Archive Center, Churchill College, Cambridge.

69 Cowan's son, like his father (and Slim), a 1/6 Gurkha officer, serving with Rees' 19th Indian, was killed as his father took Meiktila.

for the Road's security; the redirection of American air transport squadrons to shifting Chinese units homeward would present an even bigger problem. Air supply to XIV Army would be sharply constrained while Slim's remaining Dakota squadrons would have to handle supply to NCAC units pending their shipment back to China. It is hard to see how Chiang – and American decision makers – could have been less helpful. Slim's memoir account of this period with its constant recurrence of his logistic concerns and reference to the intense stress he was under (which does not appear in his account of the long, complex Imphal battle) is a reflection of how, on the eve of a victory that would vindicate him and his army the whole precariously balanced logistics of the campaign threatened to collapse because the Americans were not fighting the same war as XIV Army.

It took iron nerves to deal with the situation he faced. Slim however had one important card in his hand: XIV Army's campaign was now SEAC's sole offensive endeavor (and Britain's) in the war against Japan. Could Mountbatten (and Churchill) afford to allow it to stall in Central Burma, leaving it stranded with the monsoon eight weeks away and the certainty that its impact would force a withdrawal for logistic reasons? So he did what he had consistently done since Gallabat – took the bolder course. He compensated for the increase that Chinese action had made possible in Kimura's strength by bringing forward his remaining division, Warren's 5th Indian, which like 17th Indian, had recently converted into a mechanized and air transportable division. Doing so would compensate for any increase in Kimura's strength made possible by the closing down of NCAC as well as positioning his other highly mobile division to pair with Cowan's 17th in a dash for Rangoon as soon as the current Mandalay-Meiktila battles were concluded. It would also, of course, although "cruelly overworking the men who drove, flew, sailed and maintained our transport of all kinds" keep intense pressure on SEAC to win the battle to retain for XIV Army enough Dakotas.

In the end that issue had to go right to the top of the Anglo-American alliance. When the US Joint Chiefs of Staff responded to British requests to leave with Slim with the Dakotas on which he had counted with the assertion that the removal of the transports would not affect XIV Army's campaign, Churchill was stung into action. The European war was in its final stages and the prime minister faced a host of pressing issues but, although he did not know Slim, distrusted the Indian Army and had largely ignored Burma since his sponsorship of Wingate, he did understand the importance of the prestige that would result from what he thought of as Mountbatten's campaign. On 30 March, he sent a message to Marshall, now largely managing the American war effort as Roosevelt faded away. It was one of the bluntest of his wartime messages. We did not want to fight in Burma, he told the US Army Chief of Staff, but we did so because you wanted a road to China. We are about to win the campaign on which you insisted. It is therefore only "fair and right… to let Mountbatten have the comparatively small additional support which his air force requires to enable to decisive battle now raging in Burma to be won."[70] Churchill's shrewd appeal to Marshall's sense of honor got

70 Winston S. Churchill, *Triumph and Tragedy* (Boston, 1953), p. 618.

home. On 3 April, the US Joint Chiefs told their British counterparts that the Dakotas could stay with XIV Army until Rangoon fell or 1 June – whichever came first. A small, grudging concession but a crucial one – and possibly Churchill's greatest contribution to Slim's victory.

As the messages flew back and forth between Kandy, London, and Washington trying to keep the air over Burma full of Dakotas, Slim and his army had a sprawling complex battle to win. With Cowan's seizure of Meiktila, and the breakout of Stopford's divisions from their beachheads, Slim again had his Japanese opponents between a descending hammer and an anvil – or to use his metaphor, about to be hit with a piledriver. He and his army continued moreover to find in Japanese military culture an unwitting ally. Kimura had, despite allied air supremacy, concentrated very quickly against XXXIII Corps' bridgeheads but the advantages of this concentration were then negated in part by the tendency, noted by Slim, for Japanese generals to hurl their units into battle as they came to hand rather than waiting for complete formations to assemble. This, and their relentless commitment to the attack, piled up both casualties and disorganization. When suddenly 17th Indian and a tank brigade materialized in his rear and seized a vital communications hub, Kimura had to turn his heavily engaged units around and try to clear his communications.

XXXIII Corps, emerging from its three bridgeheads, drove east and southeast towards Meiktila. Rees' 19th Indian retook Mandalay while 20th Indian and 2nd British pressed Kimura's forces, beginning to lose cohesion if not determination steadily backwards. Cowan having secured Meiktila in four days of ferocious combat – as intense as anything in the war in Slim's opinion – then prepared to face Kimura's counterattack, delivered from all directions by a corps sized force that however lacked the coherence of a corps, consisting as it did of a miscellany of units hastily ordered to Meiktila and hurled into action the moment they arrived. Furthermore the marriage of allied air mastery with a very efficient wireless intercept service meant that Japanese headquarters could be pinpointed and then harried, further degrading the cohesion of Kimura's forces. Nonetheless, 17th Indian and its tank brigade had several weeks of intense fighting. To keep the Japanese off balance Cowan launched tank-infantry sweeps around Meiktila to disrupt planned attacks. Even so, Japanese infantry reached the edge of the crucial airstrip. 17th Indian's overland communications had been cut by the Japanese and everything had to reach Cowan by Dakota. The air-portable brigade of Evans' 5th Indian deplaned under fire.

But the Dakotas kept coming and by 28 March, the Japanese, hammered relentlessly from the air, shredded by Slim's gunners and armor and outfought by XIV Army's now highly professional infantry, began to retreat amid unit disintegration.

Now it was time to launch the drive on Rangoon that would seal XIV Army's victory by denying Kimura any opportunity to rally and reform his army – and solve XIV Army's otherwise impossible logistic quandary when the monsoon broke, in about six weeks. XIV Army's "SOB" (Sea or Bust) plan, which first took shape as the Imphal battle wound down, depended entirely on the Dakotas. XIV Army would drop overland communications and rely on air supply alone to get it to Rangoon. As Burma Area Army retired in confusion, Slim did not yet know whether Mountbatten (and Churchill) had won the latest round of the Dakota war, but he pushed ahead as if they would – the boldest course had always been for him the best course. And, at this crucial moment, the grinding Arakan campaign, where his career had almost ended, finally paid dividends.

After the Japanese assault on the Admin Box had been repulsed in February 1944, Slim's old XV Corps, now commanded by Lieutenant General Sir Philip Christison, had resumed the offensive, paused for the monsoon and then pressed on as the '44-45 dry season began. His two West African and two Indian Divisions made steady progress against weakening Japanese resistance, as units were pulled out to face XIV Army's drive on Mandalay. By Boxing Day 1945, 26th Indian had reached the tip of the Mayu Peninsula and then taken an island within striking distance of Akyab. That long sought island fell, ironically, not to XV Corps but to the RAF. A reconnaissance flight over Akyab on 2 January, carrying an artillery spotter, noticed local inhabitants waving. Assuming they would only do so if the Japanese were not present, he landed and single-handedly "captured" the island. The last Japanese had left two days previously.

However anti-climactic the retaking of Akyab was, it was also supremely important to Slim. Since XIV Army had begun, in July 1944, to envision the retaking of Rangoon by an overland drive from the north, air supply had been central to the design. Slim's Dakotas, from their bases in East Bengal and Assam would not have the range to supply XIV Army's spearheads all the way to Rangoon. XV Corps' occupation of Akyab, and the adjacent islands of Ramree and Cheduba in January 1945, meant that, even before XIV Army crossed the Irrawaddy, he was certain that airfields would be available to allow the Dakotas to sustain SOB – if the Americans could be persuaded to let him keep them.

The clearing of the Mandalay-Meiktila area – SOB's jumping off point – and the rearranging of units took several weeks. The 2nd British division left XIV Army, being flown back to India, its units understrength and its supply demands now an undue burden on Slim's logistics. SOB would be a two pronged drive: Messervy's corps (5th and 17th Indian and 255 Indian Tank Brigade) would drive straight down the road-rail corridor from Meiktila to Rangoon. Meanwhile Stopford's XXXIII Corps (7th and 20th Indian) would drive down both banks of the Irrawaddy also aiming for Rangoon. In addition to concerns about his Dakota support, Slim had mounting concerns about his armor, crucial to Messervy's drive. All XIV Army's tanks were American-built. The "Stuart" light tanks and the "Lee Grant" mediums were obsolescent and had long disappeared on European battlefields. The workhorse Sherman was more modern but all of XIV Army's tanks were nearly worn out, and only kept going by the same prodigies of maintenance that characterized the rest of Slim's logistics. And, of course, beyond all logistic concerns there remained the Japanese – beaten and disorganized but still formidable and still willing to die where they stood. "Our best hope," Slim reflected," was to rush him off his feet before he could regain balance – and to pray for a late monsoon."[71] And, just in case

71 Slim, *op. cit.*, p. 475.

those prayers went unanswered, Slim conjured up the ghost of "Dracula" in the form of a modified amphibious assault on the city if the monsoon came early.

At the beginning of April all the pieces of his design finally clicked into place. The Akyab airfields had opened on 20 March. On 2 April, Mountbatten ordered an insurance policy for XIV Army, a single division "Dracula," not later than 5 May (the latest date the navy felt prudent in view of the impending monsoon). The next day Slim learned that he had the Dakotas until Rangoon fell. Only one obstacle remained: Lieutenant General Honda Masaki's 33rd Army (three divisions weakened by weeks of fighting) dug in at Pyawbwe south of Meiktila, barring entrance to the road-railway corridor that led to Rangoon. Cowan's 17th Indian, in a three day battle (7-10 April) crushed Honda's defenses. Two brigades looped around Pyawbwe, while the armored brigade cut Honda's withdrawal route. With a brigade pressing against Pyawbwe from the north, while two more closed on his rear, accompanied by the armor, 33rd Army was pulverized: "have you ever seen a walnut crushed by a piledriver?" The road south was open.

On the morning of 11 April, Major General E. C. R. Mansergh's 5th Indian (Warren had recently been killed in an air crash) passed through 17th Indian. The most quoted account of that moment is in the memoir written by John Masters of the 4th Gurkha Rifles who witnessed it.[72] It is however Slim's memory that is most fitting to recall.

> They were off! I stood beside the road outside Pyawbwe and saw them go. Three hundred miles and, with luck, thirty days to do it in… They certainly meant to and they looked like it;… there was an air of purpose in every truck that rolled dustily by… loaded with Indian soldiers grasping their weapons and on their faces was the same look as on their commander's, alert and eager. I had begun the war as a brigadier in this division in 1939, and I was proud of them. We should get there all right![73]

It is sometimes overlooked how remarkable XIV Army's final spurt was. When Guderian drove from the Meuse to the Channel in May 1940 he had something over 200 miles to cover; when Montgomery's 2nd British Army drove from the Seine to Brussels in late August- early September 1944, the distance was comparable. Both confronted disorganized resistance and had manageable logistics. XIV Army had 300 miles, over poor roads with worn equipment and barebones logistics, utterly dependent on Dakotas and therefore on the weather, more capricious the closer the monsoon drew. The opposition, although increasingly disorganized, retained the adamantine determination to die where they stood rather than yield an inch that had always characterized the Imperial Japanese Army. That furious resistance, however unavailing, cost precious time to overcome. But XIV Army now had the bit in its teeth and went over or around any opposition simply refusing to be stopped. At Pyinmana, finding the town strongly held, the armored brigade bulldozed a bypass road around the town, rolled ten miles further,

72 John Masters, *The Road Past Mandalay*, paper ed., (New York, 1961), pp. 306-307.
73 Slim, *op. cit.*, p. 475.

overran an airfield, and quickly repaired it. Then the Dakotas appeared and SOB rolled on. The armored brigade nearly caught Honda who barely escaped, an experience that could have done little for 33rd Army's disintegrating command and control structure.

Traveling with the spearhead units were airfield engineers who carved out emergency landing fields, 2,000 yards by 50 yards, for the Dakotas, now working well above what had been considered their maximum effort level, but who nevertheless continued to fuel Messervy's drive. Slim was now racing not only the monsoon but a new date for Dracula – 2 May, the navy having gotten increasingly worried about the monsoon. Kimura's last chance of dislocating SOB was to hold Toungoo, some 50 miles south of Pyinmana. Driven off the main road the Japanese were moving south parallel to IV Corps but on hill tracks to the east. Those hills were the home of the Karens, a hill people who had remained loyal to the British and had suffered badly for it.

Britain's Special Operations Executive (known in SEAC as Force 136) had been dropping organizers and arms into the Karen Hills for some time. Building on Karen veterans of the pre- war Burma Rifles, SOE had created a "secret army" of Karens which Slim now ordered into action. All around Kimura's units as they struggled south the Karen Hills exploded. The hillmen took their revenge while the British officers advising them called in punishing air strikes. Fifty miles from Toungoo the Japanese faltered to a halt. On 22 April, having covered 50 miles in three days, 5th Indian rolled into Toungoo, the lead tank running over a Japanese military policeman directing traffic. The next day the division covered another 30 miles, then Cowan's 17th took over the lead. There were 114 miles to go and a week to do it in. Despite heroic efforts by the Dakotas many forward units were on half rations, fuel and ammunition being prioritized over food. By 1 May, Cowan was 40 miles from Rangoon, but that afternoon the pre-monsoon showers turned into a torrential downpour and 17th Division was bogged down, its forward movement reduced from gallop to crawl. Dracula launched the following day. But, once again, a long desired goal was reached first by the RAF. A Mosquito on reconnaissance over Rangoon encountered no anti-aircraft fire, saw no sign of Japanese activity and saw a choice piece of RAF slang spelled out with laundry by POWs on the roof of Rangoon Gaol. The pilot landed on Rangoon's badly battered main airfield, wrecking his plane, walked into the city, confirmed with the POWs that the Japanese were gone, commandeered a small sampan and sailed down the river to meet the advancing 26th Indian. Four days later, at 4:30 pm on 6 May, a 26th Division patrol met Cowan's leading unit north of Rangoon. The 1/7 Gurkha Rifles had fired in January 1942 the first shots of the longest land campaign of the British Empire's war. It was a fitting final act for them and the army that had borne the brunt of the campaign.

The triumphant conclusion of SOB was, of course, overshadowed by VE Day – the end of the war that to which Britons, and their dauntless leader, were emotionally committed to. But while it did not command headlines in Britain, no one could have predicted that Slim's dazzling feat of arms would be immediately followed by an attempt to sack him. This was, and remains, one of the stranger episodes in Britain's war: Churchill, when at the Admiralty, had forced out both Admirals and staff officers he found uncongenial. More famously, he had fired Wavell as Middle East commander-in-chief in 1941 and Auchinleck from the same position a year later.

But Churchill had nothing to do with the drama that unfolded beginning the day after the linkup north of Rangoon that marked the conclusion of SOB. Nor could Slim in any way be considered to have failed. What XIV Army had done was little short of astounding and Slim was that army's beating heart. On 7 May, Leese arrived at Slim's headquarters at Meiktila, congratulated him – and told him he was to be replaced as XIV Army commander. "This came as a complete surprise to me," Slim rather mildly commented in an account he later wrote of the episode but did not use in *Defeat Into Victory* which says nothing about the crisis which hung over him for the next fortnight. Turning down the sop of commanding an occupation force in Burma, he told Leese he would retire, and assured him "as far as I was concerned, there would be no fuss either in or outside the Army." Leese seemed taken aback – although it is a measure of his failure to understand Slim that he was – by Slim's refusal to accept relegation to a lesser command. He asked Slim to think matters over. Slim simply asked for his designated successor, Christison, to be made available quickly – there was still a war going on. Slim told his staff on the 9th, then made a flying visit to his wife at Shillong in India. Returning to Meiktila he found no Christison but briefed Stopford and Messervy on the impending change. Then he wrote Leese, reiterating his decision to retire and again asking for Christison's speedy arrival. After several days of silence, Leese's Chief of Staff, Brigadier G. P. Walsh, known for his tactlessness arrived at Meiktila on the 17th to talk Slim around. Slim simply reiterated his intention to retire "quietly."[74]

By this time news of his removal had spread throughout XIV Army and, if Slim eschewed fuss that was not his army's reaction. His chief of staff, Brigadier "Tubby" Lethbridge threatened to lead XIV headquarters staff on a "sit down strike" to force the issue into the open; a corps commander and two division commanders threatened resignation. One XIV Army staffer denounced Leese as an "affected, silk-handkerchief-waving guardsman." The ripples by this time had reached London where Auchinleck, the professional head of the Indian Army, was meeting with Brooke, the professional head of the British Army. After hearing Auchinleck, Brooke went to Churchill and told him the Indian Army would not fight without Slim. The prime minister asked what had caused the crisis. Leese, he was told. "Sack Leese," said Churchill.

Meanwhile, Slim's repeated requests for Christison's arrival had gone unanswered by ALFSEA (where doubtless consternation reigned). Slim, whose tactics throughout were as masterly as his battlefield performance, ratcheted up the pressure by announcing that in five days he would hand over XIV Army to Stopford and leave for India. This brought, on 23 May, a complete capitulation. "It was all a misunderstanding," Slim wrote in his unpublished account, doubtless with tongue firmly wedged in cheek, "I was to retain command of Fourteenth Army in future operations." The next day he flew to Calcutta, saw Leese, who told him he was "anxious" that Slim remain with XIV Army, and then

74 The account of Leese's attempt to shelve Slim in this and succeeding paragraphs is based on my *Churchill and His Generals* (Lawrence, KS, 2007), pp. 226, 231-33 and the sources cited there, as well as Robert Lyman's *Slim: Master of War* (London, 2004), pp. 255-58.

on to Mountbatten's headquarters in Ceylon, where "Dickie" asked him if he was willing to continue to serve under Leese, to which Slim agreed (doubtless with the feeling that Leese was now effectively and permanently neutered).

What was it all about? Clearly, it went back to Leese's arrival with his accompanying posse of 8th Army staffers displacing Giffard and his staff who Slim trusted. Leese was clearly affronted by Slim's openly expressed opinion that XIV Army was as good as 8th Army, with the implication that his generalship stood comparison with Monty's (a position surely anathema to Leese). Furthermore, Leese, like Monty and many British Army officers, thought the Indian Army inferior. Finally, there was Slim's action in very successfully reducing ALFSEA to a fifth wheel. He dealt whenever possible directly with Mountbatten, shaped "Capital" and SOB without much reference to Leese. "Bill was quite frankly insubordinate in his dealings with Leese," Brigadier Michael Roberts, a fellow Gurkha officer and Slim's researcher for *Defeat Into Victory* told Slim's official biographer years later, adding, "but he was an expert in knowing when he could be insubordinate – and for 'could' you could substitute 'should.'" The attempted sacking can therefore be seen as the revenge, when it seemed safe to exact it, of an affronted mediocrity.

But was there something more? What about Mountbatten? Leese saw the Supreme Commander before visiting Slim on 7 May and expressed the view that Slim must be tired and in need of a rest. Mountbatten – according to Lieutenant General Sir Frederick Browning, his Chief of Staff – apparently told him he could sound Slim out but "extremely carefully." Either Leese ignored this entirely – or there was something else, perhaps only a nod and wink. We know that Mountbatten was avid for laurels, and a spotlight shared is less impressive than one occupied alone. We also know that Leese was a Guardsman for whom the chain of command was sacred – and that he told Christison before leaving for Meiktila that Mountbatten had sanctioned sending Slim on indefinite leave. We also know that when Christison in retirement wrote up an account of this conversation he showed it to Leese, who agreed it was accurate.

Finally we know that Slim, in his later years, came to believe that Mountbatten was behind Leese's *coup*. Definitive proof is unlikely at this point to come to hand, but a very strong suspicion lingers that "Dickie" was at least willing to let Leese try to move Slim aside. If so, he should have known better – no one ever beat Bill Slim.

The commander of XIV Army returned to Meiktila to hand over to Stopford who, with the newly created Twelfth Army would wind up the war in Burma. He then flew to Delhi where XIV Army headquarters would plan for "Zipper," the invasion of Malaya. First however he went back to the UK. On the long flight home, he shared a plane with General Sir Richard Gale, the commander of the British Airborne Corps. Slim had with him a draft of his official Dispatches on the Burma campaign, which he shared with Gale, who was fascinated by the story and told Slim so. "Yes," was the reply, "you wouldn't think they'd sack a chap for doing that."[75]

75 Ronald Lewin, *Slim: The Standard Bearer* (London, 1976), p. 254. Lewin had this story from Gale.

## Afterwards

The country to which Slim returned in mid-Summer 1945 was very different from the one he had left seven years before. Exhausted, battered and bankrupt by six years of total war, it was in the midst of a general election – act one of the social revolution that would transform Britain over the next five years. The victor in a campaign that had always been marginal to the attention of an embattled nation, Slim nonetheless received recognition from civic authorities in London, Edinburgh and Birmingham, where he had begun his military career. Most important for his future career prospects however was a visit to Chequers. The armed forces vote had not yet been tallied and the prime minister, in common with nearly everyone else, believed he would be returned to office. During a burst of rhetorical optimism by Churchill, his shrewd wife reminded him that the service vote remained a great unknown. Perhaps remembering that the boldest course had always served him well, Slim added, "well, Prime Minister… *My* Army won't be voting for you."[76] Whether it was Slim's record, his personality or his candor that won Churchill's approval, shortly afterwards, having meanwhile been promoted full general, he was informed he would replace Leese at ALFSEA (Mountbatten fired Leese, who was on leave in Kashmir, by telegram).

While in London, Slim had been briefed on the atom bomb, which was dropped as he prepared to return. By the time he reached his new headquarters in Kandy (where he retained nearly all Leese's staff) Japan had surrendered – and his old Fourteenth Army had mopped up the remnants of Burma Area Army as it tried to cross the Sittang River, hoping to reach Thailand. Slim thus presided over no more active operations – although SEAC's long sought and oft frustrated plans for an amphibious operation finally bore fruit – after the Japanese surrender. Operation Zipper was thought the quickest way to get units into Malaya where no one was yet quite sure whether the untouched Japanese Seventh Area Army would accept surrender. Launched by XXXIII Indian Corps commanded by Ouvry Roberts it was far from flawless – but it was 9 September and there was no opposition. The faults in the Zipper plan were down, of course to Leese. Slim's tasks at ALFSEA were however almost as stressful as active operations had been. Three quarters of a million Japanese soldiers, scattered across South-East Asia had to be disarmed and repatriated. More urgently, 125,000 allied POWs, many *in extremis* and also scattered across the theater had to be located, cared for and evacuated. Moreover huge and very delicate problems loomed in French Indochina and the Netherlands East Indies (NEI). In both territories there were militant anti-European nationalist movements armed, in the case of Indochina in part by the American Office of Strategic Services (OSS) as a wartime measure, and in the case of the NEI, by the Japanese to frustrate a European return. Thus Japanese forces had to be disarmed, allied

76 Ronald Lewin, *Slim: The Standard Bearer* (London, 1976), p. 246. Dr. W. J. Reader, then a Royal Signals officer attached to the Indian Army, told me he knew how the service vote would break when he discovered that all the British sergeants in his unit were voting Labour.

POWs urgently succored while anti colonial insurgencies erupted in both places. And, of course, France and the Netherlands, British allies in Europe expected British support as they strove to assuage war-battered national pride by reclaiming their Asian empires. This complex and dangerous task fell largely on the Indian Army, as the new Labour government sought to repatriate and demobilize as rapidly as possible British forces in the East. This, the Indian Army's last twilight fight under the British flag, would last into 1946, involving many of Slim's old XIV Army units – Gracey's 20th Indian in Saigon and 5th and 23rd Indian in Java.[77] Slim had to manage all this while also fighting health problems. He had had a stressful war in an unhealthy theater and suffered several bouts of illness – he was being treated for dysentery when the Admin Box battle began and was hospitalized for a bout of malaria during the monsoon pursuit. The flying trip to the UK after his victory over Leese was certainly not a rest cure and shortly after he took over ALFSEA he had to be hospitalized for surgery. It was a draining operation from which he only slowly recovered, while still carrying on the trying business of ALFSEA with its frequent lengthy flights. At the end of 1945 however his career suddenly moved in a new direction.

During the crisis precipitated by Leese, Auchinleck had told both Churchill and Brooke that Slim ought to succeed him as the Commander-in-Chief of the Indian Army. Barely six months later it was becoming increasingly clear that the Raj was in a terminal state and that Auchinleck would be unlikely to have a British successor. However the Imperial Defence College, where Slim had spent a happy year before the war, was being reopened after six years of dormancy and Slim was invited to become its refounding Commandant. Mountbatten later told Slim's official biographer, Ronald Lewin, that he persuaded Slim to accept the offer, foreseeing that becoming familiar with the British Army would inevitably lead Slim to the post of CIGS.[78] This, like Mountbatten's many other claims to prescience and accomplishment, may be taken with a large pinch of salt. Slim was tired and still recovering from serious surgery. He was in his 55th year and, never in possession of the cushion of "private means" available to many British (but few Indian Army) officers, must have been wondering how he would finish out his career. He was more clear-eyed than Auchinleck about the limited future of the Indian Army he had served in for a quarter century. The IDC would be a much lower stress job and a good one in which to move towards retirement. In December 1945 he bade farewell to India, landing at Liverpool on Christmas Day. The restart of the IDC went smoothly and Slim had two years to recover from the strains of high command. As the Raj wound to an end, there were back to back offers from both of the successor states. Nehru wanted him as the first commander-in-chief of independent India's army (and, in a sense, the Auk's successor) while Jinnah, rather oddly, offered him the governorship of East Bengal (now Bangladesh). There is no indication Slim found the latter in the least bit tempting.

77 The best account of the Indian Army's "post war wars" in Indochina and the NEI is Daniel Marston's *The Indian Army and the End of the Raj* (Cambridge, UK, 2014), chap. 4.

78 Lewin, *Slim*, p. 256, quoting a 1975 letter from Mountbatten.

The former, he explained in a letter to Mountbatten, would inevitably involve him in a conflict of interest if British and Indian policies differed. He turned Nehru down. On 15 August 1947, the Raj vanished at the stroke of midnight and Slim's army was cut in twain.[79] At the end of 1947 his term at the IDC ended, and, on 1 April 1948 General Sir William Slim, the greatest of Britain's "sepoy generals" retired from the Indian Army.[80]

79 The first two commanders-in-chief of Pakistan's army were Fourteenth Army stalwarts: Frank Messervy and Douglas Gracey. Pete Rees commanded the last functioning formation of the old army, the Punjab Boundary Force, which had the thankless – and hopeless – task of trying to control to murderous violence in the province that was the epicenter of the partition massacres. The first commander-in-chief of India's army was General Sir Rob Lockhart.

80 Of course Slim had still a long career ahead of him. After a brief stint as deputy chairman of the Railway Executive – the agency set up to manage Britain's newly nationalized rail system – Slim was tapped by Attlee to succeed Monty as CIGS, the professional head of the British Army. Monty tried and failed to prevent this, showing the same capacity for intrigue as his protégé, Leese. Slim, now a field marshal, remained CIGS, shaping Britain's Cold War army, until his term ended in 1952 – when he was named to the still important ceremonial post of Governor General of Australia. While there he wrote *Defeat Into Victory*. The lower middle class boy who had dreamed of a seemingly unattainable military career, then ended it as Field Marshal Viscount Slim, K. G., Constable of Windsor Castle.

3

# The Trainer: Lieutenant General Sir Reginald Savory

## Introduction

> I regarded the Indian Army as one of the most remarkable military achievements of the whole of history… In the Second World War they took on the Japanese, Italians and Germans fighting battles for us and we would have never won the war without them. Two million volunteers, no national service.[1]

This interview excerpt from 1972 underpins the importance of the Indian Army to the outcome of the Second World War. Lieutenant General Sir Reginald Savory both acknowledges and was instrumental in this process but he is practically unknown amongst Second World War generals. Very few historians have heard of him or consulted his voluminous papers held at the National Army Museum, London. I first came across him when researching training in the Indian Army.[2] Since then, I have been determined to make him better known to a wider audience and especially his important training role in the Indian Army that was vital to the Burma campaign.[3] My co-author Raymond Callahan is one the few who had noted his significance in the development of the Indian Army,

1 Transcript of interview with Peter Liddle, Leeds University Library, tape 47.

2 Alan Jeffreys, *Approach to Battle: Training the Indian Army during the Second World War* (Solihull: Helion, 2017).

3 Savory was interviewed by Peter Liddle about his First World War service. See Special Collections, Leeds University Library, Sir R. Savory (GS 1429) interview transcript. He was also interviewed by Charles Allen for a Radio 4 series *Plain Tales from the Raj* on life in India between the wars and again on his First World War service, see Imperial War Museum (IWM) SA 4957. However, he was never interviewed on the most important part of his career during the Second World War and up until the independence of India. His extensive papers are held in the National Army Museum (NAM), see the Private Papers of Lieutenant General Sir Reginald Savory, NAM, 1976-03-93. Savory's nephew and literary executor was in correspondence with Major General James Lunt with regards to a possible biography of his uncle, letter from Tony Savory to James Lunt, 1 February 1990, NAM, 2009-08-51-60. Andrew Willett is currently undertaking a PhD on Savory's army career.

corresponding with Savory in the 1970s.[4] Indeed, he has written that, along with Slim and Auchinleck, Savory was responsible for adapting the Indian Army to make it capable of defeating the Imperial Japanese Army in the Burma campaign of 1944-1945.[5] In addition, Daniel Marston has highlighted Savory's important role as one of the first instructors at the Indian Military Academy when the first Indian officers were commissioned in India as well as his role in the run up to independence in 1947 as Adjutant General.[6]

It would generally seem that Savory is largely remembered, if at all, for his First World War experience with the 14th Sikhs when the regiment was almost wiped out at Gully Ravine and more recently during the Second World War East African campaign.[7] During the latter war he also served in North Africa, before commanding a division in Assam in 1943. From whence he was made Inspector (later Director) of Infantry until 1945 and retired in 1947 as the Adjutant General of the Indian Army. Thus, like Slim, he served in East Africa and, like Auchinleck, in North Africa. Although he did not reach the same heights as Auchinleck and Slim in his career, he was instrumental in the development of Indian Army from the 1920s until the independence of India. This extended essay also draws a picture of life as an officer in the Indian Army during the first half of the twentieth century, serving in both world wars as well as on the North West Frontier during the interwar period.

Savory was educated at Uppingham School, an English public school, which did not have a traditional army connection until the establishment of the Officer Training Corps in 1908 when a small number of pupils went on to either Sandhurst or Woolwich. As a result the school produced seven senior officers during the First World War.[8] Brian

4 See the correspondence between Sir Reginald Savory and Professor Raymond Callahan, 1976-1979, NAM, 1976-03-93-71A.

5 See Raymond Callahan, *Churchill and His Generals* (Lawrence: University Press of Kansas, 2007), pp. 201-206. See also Raymond Callahan, *Burma 1942-1945* (London: Davis-Poynter, 1978), p. 98. See also Daniel Marston, *Phoenix from the Ashes: The Indian Army in the Burma Campaign* (Westport: Praeger, 2003), p. 4; Tim Moreman, *The Jungle, the Japanese and the British Commonwealth Armies at War, 1941-45* (London: Frank Cass, 2005), pp. 86, 159, and Jeffreys, *Approach to Battle*, pp. 159, 188-189. Kaushik Roy in his *Sepoys against the Rising Sun* (Leiden: Brill, 2016), pp. 228-248 refers to the infantry liaison letters produced by Savory and his team but never actually mentions his name.

6 See Marston, *Phoenix from the Ashes*, pp. 20-21 and Daniel Marston, *The Indian Army and the End of the Raj* (Cambridge: CUP, 2014), pp. 29-30, 146-147, 221, 254, 263, 268, 271-273, 280. See also John Kiszely, *General Hastings 'Pug' Ismay: Soldier, Statesman, Diplomat: A New Biography* (London: Hurst, 2024), pp. 214, 235-236.

7 For Gallipoli, see for example Peter Hart, *Gallipoli* (London: Profile, 2011), pp. 242, 321-327 and Peter Stanley, *Die in Battle, Do Not Despair: The Indians on Gallipoli, 1915* (Solihull: Helion, 2015). For East Africa, see Andrew Stewart, *The First Victory: The Second World War and the East African Campaign* (Yale University Press, 2016), pp. 158-170.

8 Timothy Halstead, *A School in Arms: Uppingham and the Great War* (Solihull: Helion, 2017), pp. 50-54 and Simon Robbins, *British Generalship on the Western Front* (London: Routledge, 2005), p. 206. Five old boys from Uppingham went on to be awarded the Victoria Cross serving with the British Army. See Mike Garrs, *Valiant Hearts: The Story of Upppingham School V.C.s* (Stamford: Spiegl Press, 2010).

Horrocks and Eric Dorman-Smith were contemporaries who served in the First World War and became senior officers in the British Army during the Second World War.[9] However neither his school nor family had any particular connections with the Indian Army.[10] He left Uppingham early and spent 18 months at a crammer in Hannover, Germany. He wrote in his autobiography 'A Subaltern of the Sikhs':

> The eighteen months I spent in Germany broadened my outlook in a way that a similar period at Uppigham could never have done. They gave me an inclination to learn foreign languages, a sense of history, and a capacity for seeing other people's points of view. I made many German friends at an age when I had no prejudices.[11]

Afterwards he became a cadet at Sandhurst. His father told him that he could not afford to put him through a British cavalry regiment as a private income was required. He suggested that if he wanted to join a cavalry regiment Savory would have to go to the Indian Army and join the Bengal Lancers.[12] It was quite clear that the status of the Indian Army was high amongst Savory's fellow cadets at the Royal Military College at Sandhurst. From seventeen prizes awarded on passing out in December 1913, fourteen were won by those destined to join the Indian Army. Savory won two prizes for German and the combined scheme and his fellow cadet and Indian Army officer, Francis Tuker, won the prize for Hindustani. Tuker, like Savory, went on to play an equally important role in the development of the Indian Army during the Second World War.[13] The Commandant at Sandhurst, Brigadier General Lionel Stopford, remarked on Savory's abilities in his report, stating he 'will make a fine leader of men' and 'should go far in his profession and will make a really first class officer'.[14]

Even though Savory had no family connections with the Indian Army his Uncle Bertie, of whom Savory writes 'The Admiral, you know' (in a footnote to his diary transcription for 1914), wrote a letter of introduction for him to General Sir James Willcocks. The importance of patronage in the armed forces was paramount in this period, as Peter Robinson states of the British Army, was equally true of the Indian Army, 'the officer

9 Horrocks was also at Sandhurst with Savory. See photograph of F Company, Royal Military College, Sandhurst, May 1913, NAM, 2003-04-261.

10 Only 55 Old Uppinghamiams served in the Indian Army during the First World War, out of 2,343 old boys who served in the armed forces from the school, Halstead, *A School in Arms*, Appendix I, pp. 166-241.

11 Reginald Savory, 'A Subaltern of the Sikhs' (Unpublished autobiography), chapter 1, NAM.

12 See Charles Allen (ed.), *Plain Tales from the Raj* (London: Futura Publications, 1977), p. 40. Even smart infantry regiments required a private income. Major General Oliver Nugent joined the King's Royal Rifle Corps in 1883 and got into serious debt, even though his father gave him an annual allowance of £120 on top of his pay of £95 per annum. See Nicholas Perry, *Major-General Oliver Nugent: The Irishman who led the Ulster Division in the Great War* (Ulster Historical Foundation, 2020), p. 7.

13 See Jeffreys, *Approach to Battle*, pp. 48-49, 58-67, 95-98.

14 Confidential report, 1913, NAM, 1976-03-93-02.

corps of 1914 was made up of people who were very familiar with each other'.[15] Rear Admiral Herbert Savory even saw Savory off for India as he remembered in Charles Allen's *Plain Tales of the Raj*:

> I had an uncle who was an admiral who happened at that time to be director of transport, and he, no less, came along to see me off. The result was that Second Lieutenant Savory, when he boarded Her Majesty's Transport *Dongola*, was seen off by this gold-braided gentleman who put the fear of God into the Captain and the Officer Commanding Troops and everybody else![16]

On arrival in India Savory found it 'a very ordinary, rather unpleasant, dusty country'. Although it was also 'the first time in my life I saw an officer dressed up in khaki drill, which thrilled me to the marrow. I had visions of Piper Finlayson and Kipling and all those chaps'.[17] He was gazetted as a Second Lieutenant on 13 January 1914 and was attached to a battalion of the Duke of Wellington's Regiment (West Riding). Initially Savory put down to join the Guides because they had cavalry and infantry, with the Gurkhas as his second choice. He later commented:

> As my second string I put down the Gurkhas; they were also very smart, very *pukka* indeed, and I spent a week with them in their mess. However I was not selected – and I only found out the reason why after I retired. I sent them a cheque in payment of my mess bill and I forgot to sign it. It was sheer forgetfulness but I think the Gurkhas thought, "Here's a pretty crooked sort of chap, we don't want him!"[18]

After a year with the Duke of Wellington's, Savory joined the 14th King George's Own Ferozepore Sikhs on 12 October 1914. He recollected his first night in the mess:

> I remember the night we joined after a long and dusty train journey from Calcutta. We were allowed to dine in the mess in our plain clothes because we hadn't time to unpack our mess kit, but we dined in what was in those days called the "dirty dining room". The mess was pretty stuffy. I was terrified of the commanding officer, we all were. I was equally terrified of the majors. The captains we treated with some respect and the senior subaltern put the fear of God into us. Altogether we were a little bit – to use a civilian word – regimental, but then all this was pre-1914, when the army was a little more blimpish that it was later on. The war taught us a thing or two.[19]

15 Peter Robinson (ed.), *The Letters of Major General Price-Davies VC, CB, CMG, DSO: From Captain to Major General, 1914-18* (Stroud: Spellmount, 2013), p. 7.
16 Quoted in Charles Allen (ed.), *Plain Tales from the Raj* (London: Andre Deutsch, 1975), p. 45.
17 Quoted in ibid., p. 54.
18 Quoted in ibid., p. 176.
19 Quoted in Allen, *Plain Tales*, pp. 176-177.

Then he was given the military handbook on the Sikhs by the Adjutant and handed over to a Sikh officer to learn the language, customs and culture of the Sikhs.[20]

Pay for a subaltern was Rs 220 a month and Savory's father gave him a yearly allowance of £100. As a result he was able to enjoy the sporting activities available to a young officer such as rugby, football, cricket, polo, as well as hunting, shooting and fishing. Savory's diary for 1914 is full of these activities as India was deemed 'a sporting paradise' for impecunious officers with time on their hands.[21] He also enjoyed the social life, although the atmosphere was still very formal, even in the Himalayas he recollected:

> If you dined out pre-1914 anywhere in India privately, it was a tail coat, a boiled shirt and a white waistcoat, with a stiff collar and a white tie. Long after they gave this up in England we continued to do it in India. I even remember up in the Himalayas where we had to ride about five miles to get from our camp to the station club where we danced, we would ride in on ponies in our tail coats. We'd put our tails into our trouser pockets and trot in and dance there. Then we'd stick our tails back into our trouser pockets and gallop home in tails, white waistcoats and boiled shirts, the lot![22]

However, this all changed by the end of 1914 with the onset of the First World War.

## First World War

In early 1915, Savory left India with a draft of 75 Sikhs, thinking he was destined for the 15th Ludhiana Sikhs on the Western Front, but was diverted to the Middle East.[23] He was initially involved in the tail end of the Turkish attack on the Suez Canal.[24]

The Expeditionary Force G was created for the Gallipoli campaign, after the Indian troops had been sent. It comprised one Indian Army brigade and a mountain artillery brigade.[25] Savory was a junior officer with the 14th Sikhs, in 29th Indian Infantry Brigade. His mother asked him how warfare first struck a man. In his reply, Savory commented:

20 IWM, SA 4957, reel 1. See also 'A Subaltern of the Sikhs', chapter 2, NAM.
21 Tony Mason and Eliza Riedi, *Sport and the Military: The British Armed Forces 1880-1960* (Cambridge: CUP, 2010), pp. 32, 59. See also Major General J. G. Elliott, *Field Sports in India 1800-1947* (London: Gentry Books, 1973). Elliott was a contemporary of Savory who joined the Indian Army in 1916.
22 Quoted in Allen, *Plain Tales*, p. 112
23 Stanley, *Die in Battle*, p. 49.
24 For more on the defence of the Suez Canal, see Adam Prime, 'Keeping the "Highway to India" Open: The Indian Army and the Defence of the Suez Canal 1914-15' in Jeffreys (ed.), *Indian Army in the First World War*, pp. 110-130.
25 See Stanley, *Die in Battle*, p. 303.

> I rather imagine that depends on the man: but it has not struck me yet as being anything particularly awful: except that a dead man, after a week or so unburied with his face turned black and his body swollen as far as his trousers will permit it to swell, is a distinctly unpleasant spectacle, and the stench is damnable. But one thing I know, and that is that all the twaddle one sees in the papers about men becoming full of sentimental "high souled" (to use their own word) patriotism is bosh. One hasn't the time or inclination to indulge such rot.[26]

He quickly adapted to conditions of the midday heat followed by the cold of the night by wearing his thin khaki drill during the day, and managed to avoid dysentery with Gelantine Lamel sent out from Britain. He also grew a beard so that he did not stand out from the Sikh soldiers under his command.

The main action for the 14th Sikhs was the attack on Gully Ravine on 4 June 1915 during the Third battle of Krithia. Savory was in No. 4 Double Company, commanded by Lieutenant Fowle. The unit advanced and found the ground in front of them more open and were able to make good progress. Covered by the adjacent 88th Infantry Brigade, Lieutenant Fowle pushed forward with his men for 250 yards and approached the Turkish front line trench when serious enfilade fire from Gully Spur began to cause casualties. Fowle was shot dead, and Savory was hit in the head. When he was interviewed by Peter Liddle in 1972, Savory recalled the attack:

> When we got over the top I have never known anything like the roar of fire that came over. Well, I was young, fit and I had all the bravery of the novice you know. It is always the novice who is the brave chap and I ran ahead of my men. I had a rifle and bayonet and I suddenly found myself standing on the edge of a Turkish trench with a Turkish soldier down below looking at me rather surprised. So I stuck my bayonet into him. I got it through his shoulder and I skewered him to the back of the trench. I can see that chaps face today. I don't know what happened after that. I got my bayonet out and popped into the trench and I went along a bit somewhere.
>
> The next thing I remember was lying on my back on the Turkish parapet with some Turks using my body as an aiming rest and firing at the rest of my chaps coming up. Not very pleasant. I suppose I must have fainted a bit and then I came to on and off. Then the fire stopped and I looked round and got up.[27]

Savory was picked up by Sepoy Udey Singh, one of the regimental wrestlers, and taken to the field ambulance.[28] At the end of the battle, only the commanding officer, Lieutenant

26 Letter to his mother 31 May 1915, NAM, 1976-03-93-09.

27 Transcript of interview with Liddle, tape 47.

28 Even when Savory was Adjutant General in 1946-47 his private secretary, Miss Felice Pereira, was given instructions that no matter who might be waiting for an audience a retired Sikh gentlemen should be ushered in immediately as it was him who saved his life at Gully Ravine. See foreword by Rana Chhina in Stanley, *Die in Battle*, pp. xiii, 137. See also

Colonel Palin, with the battalion's medical officer, Lieutenant Heerajee Curtsejee, and 47 Sikhs remained. The situation was clearly untenable. During the morning, Palin started to withdraw his men and by midday the remnants of his battalion were back where they had begun twenty four hours earlier. Savory wrote to his mother a week after the battle:

> Our methods here seem to be based on a theory that all tactics are rot, that the only way to do anything at all is to rush forwards 'bald-headed' minus supports, minus reserves, and in the end probably minus a limb or two. Hence, the almost total wiping out of the 14th Sikhs on 4th June. We had our own special task, to advance up a nullah (a thing which one has always learned should never be done until all the ground commanding it is first seized) against the Turks who were in a wired trench at the end, and also on both sides, and at the top, and their machine guns took us in front and rear, and from practically from every side. Needless to say, we had no supports whatever! Not a damn thing! Well at 12 noon, we got up out of our trenches, got through their barbed wire (the only regiment that did) and bagged their first trench: total time taken, roughly twenty minutes: we hung on there all night, unable to go forward because of having only two British officers left (the C.O. And a Capt. Engledue of 89th P.I, [Punjabis] who is attached to us) and also because of their machine-guns: their infantry being rotten: no one gives a damn for them. Not a single reinforcement did we get, after repeated messages had been sent, and so about 9am next day we had to come back: having had 9 officers killed, and three wounded out of fourteen: and the regiment being 135 strong. The general who ordered the advance up the nullah is in everyone's opinion responsible for the whole thing. So, bang goes one of the finest regiments of the Indian Army, and certainly the best on this old Peninsula. We knew we were in for a hot time before we started, and it turned out to be right. I had a bayonet in my forehead, which luckily just went in under the skin and did little harm except for stunning me for a few hours, and giving me occasional headaches, but I am perfectly alright now. [29]

He told his mother that 'every single officer who came out with the Regiment has either been wounded or killed'.[30] Indeed the shortage of Indian Army officers continued to be a problem in the early years of the war.[31] Savory himself was reported dead, with a tele-

diary entry 29 May 1944 'Ude Singh came yesterday. Gave him a good feed', the previous day Savory who had been busy visiting the frontline and had just attended a conference at Comilla, leaving for Delhi at 1330, NAM, 1976-03-93-64. For more on Udey Singh see Colonel Tejinder Hundal, *We Too Were There: Indians at Gallipoli* (New Delhi: Manohar, 2025), pp. 405-411.

29 Letter to his mother, 11 June 1915, NAM, 1976-03-93-9.

30 Ibid.

31 See Alan Jeffreys, 'The Expansion of the Indian Army Officer Corps during the First World War' in Alan Jeffreys (ed.) *The Indian Army in the First World War* (Solihull: Helion, 2018), pp. 174-186.

gram sent to his parents officially reporting his death. Although seven days later another telegram reported him wounded and 'very much regretted' the error.[32] His parents received another telegram two years later reporting the death of Savory's older brother on the Western Front. Ernest Harley, missing and subsequently reported dead on 10 August 1917. He served as a second lieutenant with the 7th Battalion of the Queen's (Royal West Surrey Regiment).

After Gully Ravine, due to the aforementioned severe shortage of officers, Savory was made adjutant, aged twenty years old. One of his responsibilities was writing up the regimental war diary, which Savory remarked to his interviewer that he wrote up about once a fortnight. He continued:

> I don't think an awful lot comes out of war diaries you know. It may possibly from brigade and divisions but in a battalion the real value [is] in diaries and letters and all that kind of thing…A soldier isn't bothered about paper and writing and all that sort of thing. Our war diaries were very cursory things. Probably just nothing except 2 men killed and 13 wounded, something like that. They weren't worth much.[33]

A comment that might dishearten military historians and especially coming from someone who after his retirement wrote military history with a very well-received volume on the Seven Years War.[34]

The 14th Sikhs were in reserve during the breakout from ANZAC, which in turn was to support the landings at Suvla Bay. As Peter Hart writes:

> The breakout from Anzac was the centrepiece: the very heart of the August Offensive that was the last chance for the Gallipoli campaign of 1915. There were three main elements of the operational plans as prepared by Lieutenant General Sir William Birdwood and Brigadier General Andrew Skeen. The first was a major diversion centred on the assault by the 1st Division on Lone Pine in the late afternoon of 6 August; then the main event was the dramatic breakout from Anzac, intended to seize the key heights of Chunuk Bair and Hill 971 by dawn on 7 August; and finally concerted attacks to be launched on The Nek and Chessboard. Depending on your viewpoint, this was either a brilliantly imaginative programme that left little to chance, or a farrago that substituted optimism for realism.[35]

The 29th Indian Brigade fought alongside the 4th Australian Brigade, commanded by Brigadier General John Monash, under the overall command of Brigadier General

32 Telegrams to Savory's parents dated 10 June and 17 June 1915, NAM, 1976-03-93-11.
33 Transcript of interview with Liddle, tapes 47 & 108.
34 See Reginald Savory, *His Britannic Majesty's Army in Germany during the Seven Years War* (Oxford: Clarendon Press, 1966).
35 Hart, *Gallipoli*, p. 292.

Vaughan Cox. The 29th Indian Brigade's objective was Hill Q but they initially got lost in Aghyl Dere. Eventually Major Cecil Allanson and the 1/6th Gurkha Rifles did manage to get to the crest of the hill on 9 August but the Australians got equally lost and were not able to reach their objective of Hill 971. Thus the Indian troops were isolated as the New Zealanders did not take Chunuk Bair to the right of Hill Q and the Australians failed in their attempt to take the overlooking heights of Hill 971. There were too few troops to defend the hill, even though they had been reinforced by the 6th South Lancashires. The following day, a Turkish counterattack under the command of Colonel Mustafa Kemal on the remaining positions on Chunuk Blair meant that the Anzac breakout attack 'had been for nothing'.[36] Savory witnessed the retreating soldiers on 10 August:

> The sheer terror of some men, the bewilderment of others; none of whom had slept for four days; all of whom were at the end of their physical tether; all mixed up together; with strange officers trying to control men whom they had never seen before; with men looking for officers they could not find; with shouted orders merely adding to the uproar; with some unashamedly running away; with others trying to slip past, as if on some duty or errand, but intent only on putting as much distance as possible between themselves and the enemy; it was like the bursting of a dam. Yet, as the waters of a flooded river eventually spread out, slow down, and come to a trickle, so, in due course, the rush was stopped and the men led back. All this was only on a very narrow front, and for a very short time, but it was nasty while it lasted. Those like us who were in the trenches on the sides of the ravine, watching their front and facing the enemy, were the lucky ones; not only did the torrent miss them, but they were dealing with the tangible and could see the Turks were not following up. It is the fear of the 'unknown' that matters. Most of those who had run, when the panic started, were not engaged directly with the enemy, but were in reserve in the clefts and gullies behind.[37]

The ANZAC Corps lost 12,500 men over the four-day battle. Savory commented on the lessons learnt at Gallipoli and Suvla bay in particular, stating: 'By God, if we had one World War Two brigadier in Suvla Bay we would have got Gallipoli without the slightest trouble at all', the implication being that senior officers were more tactically aware and better trained during the later war.[38] Savory went on to become one of this generation of senior Indian Army commanders who was very influential in establishing an 'institutionalised training framework' and a professional officer corps during the Second World War.[39]

36 Ibid., p. 327.
37 Quoted in Hart, *Gallipoli*, pp. 326-7.
38 Transcript of interview with Liddle, tapes 47 & 108.
39 Jeffreys, *Approach to Battle*, pp. 209-210.

Savory was later awarded a Military Cross when the Sikhs were supporting the 5th Gurkha Rifles holding off an attack on 22 August. When no volunteers came forward Savory carried up ammunition under fire, an example that led other soldiers to follow suit.[40] His twin brother, Kenneth, also served during the First World War. He joined the Royal Naval Air Service and as a Squadron Commander was awarded the Distinguished Service Order, as well as a later bar in 1917, for bombing the German ships Goeben and Breslau.[41]

Savory served briefly in Mesopotamia but his battalion was kept out of any severe fighting as the sister battalions of the 36th and 45th Sikhs had suffered heavy casualties in the fighting on the River Hai, and thus there were not enough Sikh reinforcements available to make his unit up to strength.[42] Savory continued to serve as battalion adjutant but he was not impressed by his commanding officer.[43] At the end of 1917, he was attached to 17th (Indian) Division as GSO III. Savory describes 1918 as a 'dull year', spending the first two months in hospital due to an injured knee. He volunteered for Dunsterforce, led by Major General Lionel Dunsterville, with the purpose of infiltrating the Caucasus, which was in disarray after the Russian Revolution.[44] They never quite made it to their original objective of Georgia and Savory was left behind because of his knee. He returned to his regiment until April, when he spent three months on leave in Kashmir, as he noted in his diary, 'My first real leave in three years'.[45] In July and August 1918, he was briefly attached to the HQ of 51st Indian Infantry Brigade under Brigadier General Andrews, where he first came across Claude Auchinleck, who was brigade major. The following month, he became an instructor at the Platoon Commanders School. Indeed, his annual confidential report for 1919 marked him out as 'a good trainer of men'.[46] However, he was not really enjoying his service in India, writing in his diary for March: 'I had been getting very "stale". In order to get away from 'The East" I contemplated transferring to the British Service'.[47] His uncle, Captain Alec Fraser, had

40 Stanley, pp. 253-4.
41 Diary entry for 30 April 1916, NAM, 1976-03-93-12.
42 For an overview of the campaign in Mesopotamia which was largely an Indian Army campaign, see Kristian Coates Ulrichsen, 'India and the Mesopotamia Campaign' in Jeffreys (ed.), *The Indian Army in the First World War*, pp. 249-269. See also Charles Townshend, *When God Made Hell: The British Invasion of Mesopotamia and the Creation of Iraq 1914-1921* (London: Faber & Faber, 2010).
43 1917 diary, NAM, 1976-03-93-17. The regimental CO was Lieutenant Colonel E. S. Earle.
44 For more on Dunsterforce, see Robert Johnson, *Spying for Empire: The Great Game in Central and South Asia, 1757-1947* (London: Greenhill Books, 2006), pp. 230-232 and Major General M.H. Dunsterville, *The Adventures of Dunsterforce* (London, 1920).
45 1918 diary transcript, NAM, 1976-03-93-19.
46 Annual confidential report of 1919, Service record of R. A. Savory, British Library (BL), IOR/L/MIL/14/2623.
47 1918 diary transcript, NAM, 1976-03-93-19. Frank Messervy had similar doubts and considered resigning from the Indian Army, see Henry Maule, *Spearhead General: The Epic Story of General Sir Frank Messervy and his Men in Eritrea, North Africa* (London: Odhams, 1961), p. 15.

died as adjutant of the 2nd Battalion, Argyll and Sutherland Highlanders. He applied for a transfer to the Argylls, but it seems he was unsuccessful, perhaps due to the age-old prejudice and snobbery of British Army officers towards Indian Army officers.[48] Instead, he applied for the British Military Mission in Siberia.[49] Savory became a staff officer based at Vladivostock – much to his disappointment.[50] He was responsible for dealing with supplies, ammunition and transport. Whilst there, he socialised with many of the White Russians including General Zourabov (Director of the Trans-Siberian Railway) and his family. Very much later, in 1969, he married his daughter Maria.[51] He married his first wife Myrtle Richardson in 1922.[52]

## Interwar years

In 1923 Savory was back with the regiment in Iraq. He philosophically wrote from South Kurdistan to his mother: 'A regimental officer is frequently doomed to periods of lengthy and enforced activity: very often without books, or anything to help him pass the time. What a pawn in the game he is: how much does the success (or otherwise) of an action depend upon him almost entirely'.[53] He had just returned from a '"punitive expedition", burning, pillaging and killing. It's too cold-blooded…for me to take to it'.[54] At the same time, Savory was trying to study for the Staff College entrance examination and managed to read military manuals, strategy, political economy, European history and even ancient history.[55] However, he was also having second thoughts about his Indian Army career:

> You see all my service I have not liked India, nor been particularly keen on the Indian Army and I have tried all sorts of ways of getting out of the life, either by applying for jobs in other countries, or by varying the monotony by a change

48 See Callahan, *Chuchill and his Generals*, p. 192 when Brigadier Michael Roberts, for example, 'reflected years afterward that there was a "prevalent" belief in the British Army "that the Indian Army was a second class army fit only for what they looked on as guerrilla warfare on the N.W.F. [North-West Frontier]."

49 1918 diary transcript, NAM, 1976-03-93-19. See also Damien Wright, *Churchill's Secret War with Lenin: British and Commonwealth Military Intervention in the Russian Civil War, 1918–20* (Solihull: Helion, 2017).

50 Transcript of Liddle interview, tapes 47 & 108. For a detailed description of Savory's time in Vladivostock see A.C.S. Savory, 'Vladivostock: 1919-20' *Journal of Army Historical Research*, Vol. 1, No. 285, Spring 1993, pp. 8-23.

51 Transcript of Liddle interview, tapes 47 & 108.

52 Myrtle died in 1965. Some of Savory's wartime correspondence with Myrtle was published in Alastair Massie and Francis Parton, *Wives and Sweethearts: Love letters sent during Wartime* (London: Simon & Schuster, 2014), pp. 156-167.

53 Letter dated 23 May 1923, NAM, 1976-03-93-28.

54 Ibid.

55 Letters dated 13 and 20 June 1923, NAM, 1976-03-93-28.

> of employment. I've felt almost suffocated in the narrowness of my surroundings; and my lack of steadfastness has been more lie the fluttering of a captive bird than anything else…It has been the loneliness of it all. Everyone I met seemed to be a robot without any sense of beauty or culture: their interests centred round polo and games and dancing: and I all the time was longing for beauty and love and the wilds. That is why I have travelled about so much, always searching for something and being restless and unhappy, not knowing what it was that I was seeking. In other words, I became a Robot myself; purely external; with all my longings and secrets locked away in my heart and never shown…[56]

His attitude to the army and even another war was quite understandable considering what he had been through: 'I never want to see another war; it's too damned inhuman and ruthless nowadays; and the next one will be ten times worse with all the new mechanical contrivances which are being invented and tested now.'[57] He had been an avid enthusiast of hunting, shooting and fishing, but he noted in 1923 after shooting sand-grouse: 'I'm not as keen on shooting as I used to be and much prefer to watch the habits of birds and animals than kill them'.[58] He obviously had much time for introspection in Iraq. He also considered transferring to one of the Guards regiments but then realised: 'I am too well placed out here to give up everything and start again; also in the Indian Army one is much more one's own master off parade that one would ever be in the Guards, where one would have to live a life strictly according to the conventions'.[59] His sense of humour comes across with the recounting of a visiting general to his wife:

> …The General arrived on Wednesday to inspect us: of course he brought a staff-officer with him; and there was the usual rush and preparations prior to the arrival of a senior officer! It really is most amusing to see the way in which colonels and majors get flustered when they hear a general is coming to inspect them. The regiment at his instigation lashes itself into a regular fury; officers and men go frantic over the cleaning of the barracks and equipment; the preparation of accounts; the washing of uniforms; anything which may strike the eye of the inspecting officer! Then, when the general does arrive and has been received with a guard of honour and a blare of trumpets, he usually turns out to be a very mild old gentleman, much keener on getting his inspection over and eating his breakfast than anything else.
>
> I always feel a little sorry for men in that position. Nobody is ever natural with them and they too must find it difficult to be their natural selves. At dinner that evening military subjects formed the topic of conversation, when all the old man really wanted to talk about was carpets and china, and his family. I found this out,

56 Letter dated 4 July 1923, NAM, 1976-03-93-28.
57 Letter dated 4 August 1923, NAM, 1976-03-93-28.
58 Letter dated 6 August 1923, NAM, 1976-03-93-28.
59 Letter dated 10 August 1923, NAM 1976-03-93-28.

> and the old boy yarned away after dinner to his heart's content, so pleased to have got on to common ground with someone. He talked about where he would live when he retired and what he should buy and all the china he was going to collect. I told him about your lovely china and cut-glass and he was so pleased. It was almost pathetic to hear him. Eventually he tried to get me to go on his staff, but I refused as it would have done me no good, and would have meant staying on in this country, which would never do![60]

Savory was obviously glad to leave Iraq and did not particularly enjoy the experience. Although his time had provided plenty of opportunity for reading, as well as preparation for the staff college examinations, which impressed his superior officers as his confidential report for the following year remarked 'A wide reader & thinker who should, with training, do well on the staff'.[61]

By the end of 1923, Savory was back in India at the Training Battalion of the new 11th Sikh Regiment. These new 'super' regiments were formed as a result of the recommendations of the Esher Report, following the example of the British Army. Savory's 14th Sikhs became the 1st Battalion (King George's Own) (Ferozepore Sikhs) 11th Sikh Regiment in 1922. The 10th Battalion was the training battalion which meant that battalion commanding officers no longer had responsibility for recruitment and basic training: a lesson that had been learnt during the First World War. These reforms of the regimental system made a big impact not only at the time but were adapted to important effect during the Second World War.[62] Savory, however, found the work 'rather narrow and very dull'.[63]

The Army School of Education was established in 1924 with British and Indian wings. Savory was asked to be an instructor at the school whilst acting commander of the training battalion. His commanding officer (CO) was on leave so Savory accepted the post and left immediately, much to the annoyance of his returning CO.[64] He became an instructor in the Indian Wing where he noticed a change in those joining the Indian Army. Prior to the First World War recruitment had largely been from agricultural workers from the Punjab region who were less likely to be politically aware, but with the demands for more mechanisation of the army a higher standard of education was required from recruits after the war. Savory taught young Viceroy's Commissioned Officers (VCOs) and senior Non-Commissioned Officers (NCOs). He wrote: 'The students worked like beavers. Their thirst for knowledge was unquenchable. They surprised their instructors by their intelligence and potential capacity'.[65] His commanding officer at the

60 Letter dated 25 August 1923, NAM, 1976-03-93-28.
61 Confidential report 1925, NAM, 1976-03-93-2.
62 Jeffreys, *Approach to Battle*, pp. 37-39.
63 The Indian Wing of the Army School of Education, NAM, 1976-03-93-29.
64 Ibid. The CO of 10th Battalion, 11th Sikh Regiment was Lieutenant Colonel B. W. Shuttleworth from *Indian Army Lists* for April and October 1924.
65 Ibid

Indian Wing was his firm friend and fellow Sikh Regiment officer, Major Lewis 'Piggy' Heath, who remarked that Savory was 'unusually popular with all ranks'.[66] On return, the students passed on their knowledge to their units. Later, Savory noted that students from the school were essential for the modernisation and mechanisation of the army at the beginning of the Second World War. He thought: 'The Indian Wing of the Army School of Education was as important a milestone in the development of the Indian Army as the Indian Military Academy was later to become; possibly even more so'.[67] These developments along with a new generation of Indian Army officers, such as Savory and Francis Tuker, who developed a battalion training infrastructure in the 1930s, were instrumental in the development of the army, where battalions continually learned the lessons from frontier operations and maximised the educational opportunities for Indian soldiers.[68] The concurrent Indianisation of the officer corps scheme received much criticism and was later abandoned at the beginning of the Second World War.[69]

Savory attended the Staff College at Camberley in 1927-28. Attendance was becoming almost obligatory for anyone wanting to reach senior command in either the British or Indian armies.[70] The directing staff, whilst Savory was at Camberley, included Bernard Montgomery, Richard O'Connor, Bernard Paget, Henry Pownall and George Giffard, who all became generals during the Second World War. These connections and networks not only helped careers but could prove essential when fighting together.[71] Those attending had 'a common language of staff and command methods' across the British, Indian and dominion armies.[72] Savory returned to India and the North West Frontier spending most of the next decade there. Initially Savory was in command of his company at Dargai Fort, along with two Indian officers.[73] His wife, Myrtle, accompanied him where:

> She instituted "ladies evenings" to which she invited the Indian officers' wives. They were brought by their husbands, who would join me in a separate room and

66 Annual confidential Report, 1926, BL, IOR/L/MIL/14/2623.
67 The Indian Wing of the Army School of Education, NAM, 1976-03-93-29.
68 Jeffreys, *Approach to Battle*, pp. 39-52.
69 Marston *Indian Army and the End of the Raj*, pp. 22-33.
70 Mark Frost, 'The British and Indian Army Staff College in the Interwar Years' in Douglas E. Delaney, Robert C. Engen and Meghan Fitzpatrick (eds.), *Military Education and the British Empire, 1815-1949* (Vancouver: University of British Columbia Press, 2018), pp. 154-174.
71 Ibid., pp. 165-167. Also on Savory's course were Eric Dorman-Smith, William Penney, Oliver Leese, Richard McCreery and John Hawkesworth. Although he does not seem to have particularly stood out on the course, see Staff College, Camberley, Final Report, BL, IOR/L/MIL/14/2623.
72 Ibid., p. 169. See also Douglas E. Delaney, *The Imperial Army Project: Britain and the Land Forces of the Dominions and India, 1902-1945* (London: OUP, 2017).
73 These Indian officers would have been Viceroy's Commissioned Officers rather than Indian commissioned officers who are grudgingly commissioned from 1920 onwards with only just over 400 Indians commissioned as officers by the beginning of the Second World War.

> drink whiskey, while the women swapped yarns. My wife was no linguist. Not one word of Punjabi could she speak! But sounds of revelry would percolate through the intervening doors and it seemed that signs and smiles and a considerable amount of play-acting were more effective than grammar and vocabulary. On one occasion my wife came out of the room blushing furiously, having been asked by mime and gesture a question of a most intimate nature.[74]

One time she dressed up as a Sikh Woman and Savory did not recognise her. What is interesting about these encounters is that this was not the usual practice for a 'memsahib' in India.[75] Savory spent most of his time on the Frontier in non-family stations. He commented that officers on the Frontier got three months leave with full pay 'but we earned it. The remaining nine months were spent surrounded by a barbed wire fence, away from your wife, longing for the post to arrive. I lived that kind of life for ten out of the twenty years which separated World War One from World War Two'.[76] It was in this period that his enduring friendship continued with his battalion commanding officer, Lieutenant Colonel Lewis 'Piggy' Heath. He thought very highly of Savory, writing in his annual confidential report for 1930:

> An excellent commander who inspires his subordinates with keenness and who commands the high respect of all with whom he has dealings. Extremely reliable: possesses marked initiative. A most energetic and conscientious officer with great powers of application and drive.
>
> Captain Savory is, in my opinion, much above the average in all round efficiency. A forceful efficiency. A forceful personality who should go far in his profession.'[77]

He also encountered Bill Slim when he 'dined with the 6th Gurkhas in their mess on the Malakand... a year or so my junior'.[78]

Cantonment life could be stifling and restrictive, particularly as it was 'not the done thing' to take a career as a soldier seriously.[79] It generally started with a 6.30am parade, followed by breakfast and then office administration and the commanding officer's conference. At midday lunch was served followed by a rest afterwards before tea and then various sports such as hockey, which was very popular in the Sikh regiment.[80] For some officers, this was enough stimulation, with many becoming obsessed with sports. Promotion in the army was very slow, it took nine years to become a captain, eighteen

74 Dargai Fort 24 Feb – 13 Mar 1930, NAM, 1976-03-93-30.
75 See Margaret MacMillan's chapter on Unconventional Women in *Women of the Raj* (London: Random House, 2007), pp. 237-268.
76 Quoted in Allen, *Plain Tales*, p. 202.
77 Annual Confidential Report, 1930, BL, IOR/L/MIL/14/2623.
78 Dargai Fort 24 Feb – 13 Mar 1930, NAM, 1976-03-93-30.
79 IWM, SA 4957, reels 3 & 5.
80 Ibid., reel 3.

for major and twenty six to become a lieutenant colonel. Opportunities for promotion in the British Army were quicker.[81] However, for Savory and some of his fellow Indian Army officers, this was not enough. From the 1930s onwards, they trained their battalions to a very high level in order to be effective on the North West Frontier in particular. This helped make the esprit de corps of units extremely high, enhanced by the 'highly competitive' nature of the units and soldiers fighting there.[82] They also advanced their own careers by applying for staff college and extending their horizons further than their regiment. Savory went on to become one of a number of these professional middle-ranking officers during the 1930s who had shown themselves to be highly capable.[83]

The Peshawar Riots of 1930 has almost gone unnoticed by historians. It was one of the most serious incidents of the interwar period in India.[84] Abdul Ghaffar Khan and his Khuda Khidmatgars (called Red Shirts by the British) organised a non-violent demonstration against British rule in Peshawar when he was arrested on 23 April. Riots ensued and military assistance was required. Savory's battalion was called in as two platoons of the 2/18th Garwhal Rifles refused to board the buses, although 'there had been no direct subversive influence at work' according to the subsequent report.[85] The situation flared up across the region. Savory wrote to his wife: 'No one likes these civil disturbances, nor having to quell them. They create racial hatred and the worst possible atmosphere in which to commence a new constitutional regime'.[86] Thus he was well aware of the increasing tension in India with the arrest of Mohandas K. Gandhi, along with the impending publication of the Simon Report. He concluded once the report was published, 'At times I feel like chucking it and taking my first pension. Living in a country which, through no fault of one's own, one is hated, has few attractions and the future will probably deny what little status we have at present'.[87] However, he was offered a new job as GSO II in the Intelligence Branch at AHQ that perhaps solved his dilemma as he wrote to his parents: 'My new appointment I find of enthralling interest and the difficulty is to tear oneself away from it. I am solely responsible for intelligence regarding the Middle East including Russia, and, as you know, there is nothing which suits me better. In fact, my work and one of my hobbies coincide'.[88]An opinion that was backed up by his annual confidential report.[89]

81 IWM, SA 4957, reel 3.
82 Ibid., reel 11.
83 Jeffreys, *Approach to Battle*, pp. 48-52.
84 Daniel Marston, 'The Culture of the Indian Army, 1900-1947' in Peter Mansoor and Williamson Murray (eds.), *The Culture of Military Organizations* (Cambridge: CUP, 2019), p. 138.
85 Philip Mason, *A Matter of Honour* (London: Jonathan Cape, 1974), p. 452. See also letter from Savory to his parents, 24 May 1930, NAM,1976-03-93-30. He considered the aid to civil power role in Peshawar to be unpleasant and nasty in his oral history interview, IWM, SA 4957, reel 6.
86 Letter to his wife, 7 May 1930, NAM, 1976-03-93-30.
87 Letter to his wife, 24 June 1930, NAM, 1976-03-93-30. See also Allen, *Plain Tales*, p. 249.
88 Letter to his parents, 4 July 1930, NAM, 1976-03-93-30.
89 Annual confidential report, 1932, BL, IOR/L/MIL/14/2623.

## Indian Military Academy

In 1932, Savory wrote in his diary: 'Looked up Punch Cowan who told me that he & I had been applied for by Peter Collins as GSO II's at the new Indian Sandhurst : a great honour & a great opportunity. I jumped at it. It should be intensely interesting and I know we will be able to turn out a good show and confound the pessimists'.[90] This appointment as an instructor at the newly established Indian Military Academy (IMA) was a post which Savory thought was one of the most important of his career.[91] He continued in his diary in early January: 'I must now think out my attitude towards Indianization. It has always been "liberal" rather than otherwise: and my time as an instructor at Belgaum taught me that there is little that the Indian cannot be taught to do well'.[92] Indeed, when interviewed in 1974, Savory considered the Indianisation process of the 1920s had been 'not really or sincerely applied' and was 'approaching Indianisation in a dishonest way' with command of the Indianised units given to British officers who were not really up to the job.[93] The IMA was the first permanent officer training academy in India that continues to function in commissioning officers into the Indian Army. It was established for Indian cadet officers in 1932 on the recommendation of the Indian Military College Committee, chaired by Field Marshal Sir Philip Chetwode, C-in-C India.[94] Savory, alongside Major David 'Punch' Cowan, were crucial in making the academy successful under the leadership of the commandant Brigadier Lionel Collins, who Savory thought was an 'outstanding man'.[95] After his two year stint, Collins retired and on his way back to the UK he wrote to Savory: 'I count the Academy very fortunate in having yourself & Cowan as its first GSOs II & noone realises better than I do the contribution you have made towards its success &, what is far more important, towards establishing it on sound lines'.[96] Savory and Cowan wanted to prevent the IMA from being set up along the lines of an English public school. He wrote in his diary: 'What we want to produce is a tough sporting and hard soldier … We want to produce a Military Caste which shall stand above politics and communal hatred; and be the backbone which India wants'.[97] Ten days later he remarked in his diary: 'Punch and I at last won our Case for the "military" as opposed to the "academic" character of this Academy'.[98] They had six months to prepare for the first intake of cadets. Although there was internal politics within the staff, Savory thought it had proved useful helped by 'my training at the

90 Diary entry for 4 January 1932, NAM, 1976-03-93-36.
91 IWM, SA 4957, reel 6.
92 Diary entry for 7 January 1932, NAM, 1976-03-93-36.
93 IWM, SA 4957, reel 6.
94 See Vipul Dutta, *Making Officers out of Gentlemen: Military Institution-Building in India, c. 1900-1960* (New Delhi: OUP, 2021), pp. 89-91. For the wider political background of the IMA see chap 2.
95 IWM, SA 4957, reel 6.
96 Letter to Savory from Brigadier L. P. Collins, 30 December 1934, NAM, 1976-03-93-35. See also Jeffreys, *Approach to Battle*, pp. 46-47.
97 Diary entry for 31 May 1932, NAM, 1976-03-93-35.
98 Diary entry for 10 June 1932, NAM, 1976-03-93-35.

Staff College for having taught me my level among my fellow men and my capacity for self-expression. The period has not been pleasant, but it has been instructive and I shall not forget its lessons'.[99] He taught at the academy for two years. Some cadets, such as the future Lieutenant General Harbakhsh Singh, were inspired, who wrote in his memoir:

> I remember an incident in our military history class, being taken by Captain Savory, an officer of high calibre whom I greatly admired. He was always upright and perfectly dressed, both in uniform and civil dress, and I must admit that it was due to him that I put in for the 5th Battalion of the Sikh Regiment, as he belonged to the 1st Sikh. The incident I am about to relate illustrates his many qualities. When Captain Savory noticed that a few heads in the last two rows in the class were nodding away he quietly sent for the Gurkha bugler on duty and asked him to stand at the rear of the class and play the 'Reveille'! The poor cadets who were nodding off woke up to a start while the rest of us had a good laugh. What a way to teach a lesson! But then Captain Savory was an exceptional man.
>
> I remember yet another occasion when he was taking a class outdoors on military history and wished to teach the cadets the meaning and effect of 'covering fire'. He divided the class into two halves, with one representing the enemy and the other were 'our' troops. He asked them to occupy two opposite trenches at a stone's throw from each other and armed 'our' troops with brick-bats. He ask the 'enemy troops' to pop up from the trench and pretend to shoot at their opponents, while 'our' troops were instructed to pelt any head they saw with stones. The demonstration was very pragmatic and effective, though it was at the expense of a few battered heads'.[100]

In addition to the academic lectures, Savory also provided talks on such subjects as shikar, safe shooting, big game shooting in India, life in cantonments, dress, mess customs, regimental distinctions and the academy.[101] Collins was extremely impressed by Savory in the three annual confidential reports he signed between 1933 and 1935, commenting in 1934:

> Major Savory is an officer of marked professional ability, wide outlook, high ideals & great energy, both mental and physical. He has imagination & enthusiasm – qualities of particular value in his dealings with young Indians on whom his influence is of the best.
>
> A very loyal subordinate who has worked unceasingly to promote the best interests of the Academy.[102]

99 Diary entry for 30 September 1932, NAM, 1976-03-93-35.
100 Lieutenant General Harbakhsh Singh, *In the Line of Duty: A Soldier Remembers* (New Delhi: Lancer, 2000), p. 40.
101 Bound collection of lectures given at the IMA, November-December 1934, NAM, 1976-03-93-38.
102 Annual confidential report, 1934, BL, IOR/L/MIL/14/2623.

In an article on the IMA, Savory remarked that "Cooperation and no politics' was the motto of the academy, stating 'that if the Cadets of to-morrow maintain those of to-day, the Indian Army should have no cause for the future'.[103] Savory encouraged and kept up with the cadets he taught throughout his career.[104] One joined his regiment, and when Savory put him up for his club but 'they turned him down. I put the club out of bounds to all my officers from that minute. Eventually the penny dropped and this man was allowed to become a member of the club'.[105] Savory considered his time at the IMA 'as one of the few achievements of my Indian Army career that I am proud'. He saw it as a 'watershed in my military career and my political thinking so far as India was concerned'. As he noted in later life, British Indian Army officers only really knew the soldiers and servants in India; this was the first time Savory came across the middle class of India, who he found to be very outspoken and highly intelligent.[106]

After attending the Senior Officers School, Savory achieved command of his battalion, the 1st Battalion (King George's Own) (Ferozepore Sikhs) 11th Sikh Regiment, in Waziristan. He coped well with the 'loneliness of command'.[107] He even gave up the chance of seven months leave in England in order to command his battalion in action.[108] He quickly became competent as a commander in frontier warfare:

> I am getting my hand in this frontier warfare game. It is an experience which (professionally) I would not have missed for anything; and I now feel I could command a battalion or even a brigade up here with confidence. I find the responsibility is great and that I am not so ready with my laugh as I used to be, but that will return as soon as I feel the lives of my men are no longer in my hands: I mean when we return to our peace stations.[109]

At this stage of his career he had achieved the aim of most Indian Army officers, which was to command their battalion. He trained his battalion to a high standard.[110] According to his brigade commander:

> Lieut-Colonel Savory took over a very good battalion and has already improved it. He is thoroughly up-to-date in his professional knowledge and he exercises imagination

103 See Reginald Savory, 'The Indian Military Academy', *Fighting Forces* December 1933, p. 475.
104 See *Indian Military Academy Journal* Vol. 1, No. 2, June 1933, NAM, 1976-03-93-39, where Savory wrote up what happened to some of the cadets – Smith C-in-C Burma, M Musa C-in-C Pakistan, S Manekshaw COAS India, M.F. de Mellow All India Radio, R Rai killed Kashmir 47. He also hosted a dinner for his ex-cadets, see for example diary entry 27 January 1938, NAM, 1976-03-93-42A.
105 Quoted in Allen, *Plain Tales*, p. 123.
106 IWM, SA 4957, reel 6. See also Allen, *Plain Tales*, p. 236.
107 Letter to his wife from Waziristan, 4 September 1937, NAM, 1976-03-93-41.
108 Letter to his mother 6 December 1937, NAM, 1976-03-93-41.
109 Letter to his wife 11 September 1937, NAM, 1976-03-93-41.
110 Jeffreys, *Approach to Battle*, p. 50.

> in training his unit and in framing exercises...By staging demonstrations etc. he has given very valuable assistance in the training of other units of the Brigade.[111]

Savory could perhaps be accused of becoming too close to his regiment and his Sikh soldiers. He considered them the equivalent of Cromwell's Ironsides during the English Civil War – 'a military caste' with 'some of the finest military material in the world'.[112] This was not unusual in the Indian Army, with British officers often becoming very attached to the troops they commanded. In the Gurkha regiments, for example, it was sometimes called 'Gurkhaitis'.[113] At the same time, however, Savory does not seem to be such an advocate for the British in India, commenting after a dinner party he attended in 1938 that it was 'noisy and uninteresting' with 'too much alcohol' and 'typical Anglo-India'.[114]

## Second World War – North and East Africa

It was with the onset of the Second World War that this forward-thinking generation of Indian Army officers came to the fore and were responsible for making the Indian Army a professional fighting force that by 1945 was capable of adapting to all forms of warfare. Savory was at the forefront of this network of officers. He took over as brigade commander of 11th Indian Infantry Brigade on 16 March 1940. The brigade was in 4th Indian Division based in North Africa. The division, albeit comprising only two brigades, had been in Egypt six months. It went on to fight throughout the campaign in North Africa, with the exception of a stint in East Africa.[115] The division trained hard, alongside 7th Armoured Division, in the desert. Both formations were designated Western Desert Force, comprising veteran regular soldiers.[116] In the brigade, for example, the 2nd Queen's Own Cameron Highlanders formed a special 'assault company' to clear a way through minefields and anti-tank obstacles, together with the 18th Field Company Royal Bombay Sappers and Miners, which would prove essential in the ensuing action.[117] The plan was for 11th Indian Infantry Brigade to lead the attack

111 Annual Confidential Report, 1939, BL, IOR/L/MIL/14/2623.
112 Letter to his mother, 6 December 1937, NAM, 1976-03-93-41. See also Allen, *Plain Tales*, pp. 241-242.
113 Patrick Rose 'British Army Command Culture 1939-1945: A Comparative Study of British Eighth and Fourteenth Armies' (King's College London: PhD thesis, 2008), p. 80.
114 Diary entry for 8 February 1938, NAM, 1976-03-93-42A.
115 The other brigade was 5th Indian Infantry Brigade (commanded by Brigadier Wilfred Lloyd from July 1940) and they were joined by 7th Indian Infantry Brigade (commanded by Brigadier Harold Briggs) in October 1940. Both brigadiers later became divisional commanders.
116 Jeffreys, *Approach to Battle*, pp. 89-92.
117 Brigadier R. A. Savory, 'An Account of the 11th Indian Infantry Brigade of the 4th Indian Division in the Western Desert Force of Egypt from 6th to 12th Dec. 1940', p. 2, NAM, 1976-03-93-44.

and capture the Italian camp at Nibeiwa with artillery support, alongside the 7th Royal Tank Regiment. It was planned by Savory, and this first phase of the attack during the Battle of Sidi Barani was achieved in a hour and a quarter, with 2,000 prisoners taken for eight officers and 48 men as casualties.[118] In the ensuing report, Savory's effective command of the operation is very apparent. Two days before the operation he separately saw each individual unit commanding officer, going through all the orders and instructions and making alterations to the plans where necessary. On the morning of the operation he saw all his commanders to go through the orders again. When the 7th Royal Tank Regiment and 31st Field Artillery started off on a wrong compass bearing, Savory ordered the units to adjust their position but the wireless of 7th Royal Tanks liaison officer was not working. Savory, along with his brigade major and unit liaison officers, were just behind the Cameron Highlanders and the 7th Royal Tanks. They kept in contact as the R/T of his other liaison officers were all working when he ordered the attack, which meant that control of the action was through these liaison officers and R/T, which was standard operational procedure. Similarly the unit commanders kept in contact with Savory throughout the action.[119] Savory's first action at brigade level demonstrated his adaptability, encouragement of his commanding officers and keeping in touch with his units as far as the W/T and liaison officers allowed. He was later awarded the Distinguished Service Order for this action: 'Brigadier Savory commanded the Brigade which, after an amazing night-march round the rear of the enemy position, attacked NIBEIWA camp. Although the odds were more than 5-1, the Brigade gained complete success in the space of less than an hour. Later, it participated in the attack on Sidi Barrani, again with complete success.'[120]

The subsequent report on lessons from the operation covered 27 points ranging from the high standard of training and night marching to the inadequate greatcoats used by Indian troops. The most important lessons were that all officers and men knew of the plan and what was expected of them, which increased morale. This was backed up by realistic rehearsals where secrecy was maintained. Reconnaissance, good intelligence, air control, armour, artillery and mobility were also of vital importance. Command of the operation by Savory was increased by his consultation with commanding officers twice before operations and then his close contact both up and down the chain of command throughout the action with liaison officers and W/T. This was very important for the future as one of the lessons learnt in the report was:

118 Major P. C. Bharucha, *The North African Campaign* (India & Pakistan: Combined Inter-Services Historical Section, 1956), pp. 91-92. Major General I. S. O. Playfair, *The Mediterranean and Middle East: Volume I: The Early Successes against Italy (to May 1941)* (London: HMSO, 1954), pp. 267-268. Of the casualties 3 officers and 12 other ranks died – see '11th Indian Infantry Brigade: Report on Operations 6-12 December 1940', p. 7, NAM, 1976-03-93-44.

119 'Report on Operations', pp. 2, 5-6, NAM, 1976-03-93-44.

120 Quoted in a letter to his wife, 30 August 1941, NAM, 1976-03-93-43.

> The fact that Brigade Groups will in future be the normal fighting formation, the Commander and Brigade Major will normally have to deal with eleven subordinate commanders. During actual operations this is too much for one 'G' Staff officers and a second is necessary. For the operations 6-12 December the senior liaison officer was made a assistant to the Brigade Major.[121]

Savory's brigade major was Major Geoffrey Evans, who went on to command 7th Indian Division in the Burma campaign. They made a very capable team as Evans wrote of Savory:

> He was short in build, big chested and extraordinarily dapper. He had the knack, whatever the situation, of always appearing well turned out; he was never without his stick and pipe. His manner of speech was staccato and he was excellent at giving out orders. He planned every operation meticulously and after he had given his clear, careful explanation there was never any doubt in anyone's mind as to what he was expected to do. As a commander he was energetic and thrusting; personally, he was quite fearless…He enjoyed life thoroughly and he was excellent company. In every way he was an ideal commander to serve under.[122]

This is borne out further by the thoroughness of Savory's notes from the action, together with his command of the brigade at the front. The subsequent report on lessons learned noted, 'The commander must be well forward. At Nibeiwa the Brigade Commander was in such a position that he could see the objectives and assaulting troops and so was able to make decisions quickly and control the battle personally'.[123] As his first command of a brigade in action, it was highly successful due to his own action, as well as those under his command and in divisional command. It proved to be the basis for future successful brigade command, when 4th Indian Division, not long after Sidi Barrani, was ordered to East Africa.

The brigade's first action in Eritrea was to help capture Agordat along with 5th Indian Infantry Brigade and Gazelle Force, a mobile force from 5th Indian Division under the command of Colonel Frank Messervy. The 11th Indian Infantry Brigade's objective on the right flank of the attack was Mount Cochen, which was achieved against no opposition but then came under increasing pressure from the Italian forces. As a result, it was decided to hold only the top of Mount Cochen. After which, the Italian forces began to retreat along the Keren road, which meant that concerted action by 5th Indian Infantry

121 'Lessons from Operations 6-12 December 1940', p. 5, NAM, 1976-03-93-44.
122 Lieutenant General Sir Geoffrey Evans, *The Desert and the Jungle* (London: Kimber, 1962), p. 11.
123 Ibid. The divisional commander, Major General Noel Beresford-Peirce, was in a similar forward position. See 'Lecture – Operations Western Desert', NAM, 1976-03-93-46B.

Brigade and Gazelle Force led to the occupation of Agordat without opposition on 1 February.[124] Savory's report summed up the fighting:

> The action on Mount Cochen was the first battle to be fought in the mountains of Eritrea by troops organised on a mechanised basis, and the difficulties, particularly those of maintenance became at once apparent. It was a hard battle and only partially successful, but with 2 rather weak Battalions we had taken on 2 Colonial Brigades and one Blackshirt Battalion.[125]

Thus, very soon after Sidi Barrani, the brigade was back in action, but not to the same level of success as previously. Once again, Savory took command at the forefront of the action on top of Mount Cochen.[126] According to Geoff Evans: 'Reg Savory and Skrino, commanding the Rajputana Rifles, had both got hold of rifles and personally joined in the fight. Under cover of darkness Reg ordered the two Indian battalions off the summit of Cochen. He and Skrino, keeping up a steady covering fire with their rifles, were amongst the last to come down'.[127]

The Battles for Keren in February and March 1941 were crucial in the development of the Indian Army.[128] It was the first time during the war that two Indian divisions fought alongside each other. Although initially unsuccessful, they regrouped, retrained and proved ultimately victorious, despite being outnumbered by well-supplied Italian troops equipped for mountain warfare. In addition, they came up against the difficult climatic conditions, and mountain warfare whilst equipped for mechanised warfare. More significantly, for Savory and his fellow brigade commanders, nearly all of whom held divisional or higher command in the later Italian and Burma theatres, it was the only occasion when Indian formations fought and trained together and then applied the lessons learnt.[129]

The 11th Indian Infantry Brigade led the advance from Agordat towards Keren. The formation captured Brigs Peak, named after Savory, but not Mount Sanchil.[130] Savory himself was suffering from a poisoned arm.[131] However, they were pushed back to Cameron's Ridge, named after the brigade's 2nd Battalion Queen's Own Cameron

124 Bisheshwar Prasad, *East African Campaign 1940-41* (India & Pakistan: Combined Inter-Services Historical Section, 1963), pp. 443-46, Stewart, *First Victory*, pp. 158-160.
125 Brigadier R. A. Savory, 'Account of the Operations carried out by the 11th Indian Infantry Brigade of 4th Indian Division. Mount Cochen in Eritrea from 28 to 31 January 1941', p. 4, NAM, 7603-93-44.
126 Evans, *Desert and the Jungle*, p. 34 and Stevens, *Fourth Indian Division*, p. 33.
127 Ibid., p. 35. Skrino was Lieutenant Colonel P.R.H. Skrine who commanded the 5th Battalion, 6th Rajputana Rifles in 11th Indian Infantry Brigade.
128 For more on the East African campaign generally see Stewart, *First Victory*.
129 Jeffreys, *Approach to Battle*, pp. 115-116.
130 Letter to his wife, 29 October 1941, NAM, 1976- 03-93-47.
131 Evans, *Desert and the Jungle*, p. 39.

Highlanders.[132] This was tenuously held by the brigade for the next six weeks.[133] Another unsuccessful attack on Brig's Peak and Mount Sanchil was attempted on 15 March but was also unsuccessful.[134] Casualties were extremely high throughout the battle, with the Camerons losing 8 officers and 250 other ranks.[135] On 17 March, the 10th Indian Infantry Brigade made an equally unsuccessful attack on Brig's Peak and Mount Sanchil when the defending Italian troops surrendered on 27 March.[136] Afterwards, Savory and Evans climbed Mount Sanchil, and Evans wrote in his memoir:

> Now, all was quiet, but the sun was beating down fiercely. Clad in shirts and shorts and along stick to help, we found the going hard and sweat poured off us profusely. More and more was it brought home to us that the assaulting troops, in their battle equipment and in the face of the enemy fire, had almost achieved the impossible. It had to be seen to be believed. Dead lay everywhere and parties were working flat out to bring away the bodies for proper burial. In the enemy position, efforts had been made to bury our dead, but with little success, as it was impossible to dig in the rocky ground. A head protruded from under a pile of stones while feet emerged from the other end. The stench and flies were nauseating.
>
> Sanchil itself was a natural fortress, a cluster of enormous boulders, some the size of a house, and it was easy to see that behind these the defenders had been safe from any artillery fire.
>
> How anyone even got up to the position, let alone into it, is difficult to understand. Yet the bodies of three Camerons were evidence that they had penetrated the heart of the defence before they lost their lives.[137]

The fighting at Keren was ultimately a successful action for both Indian Divisions, but not for 11th Indian Infantry Brigade. Savory wrote to Major General Jim Elliott:

> I was beginning to have my doubts because I had a fairly stiff fight to take Mount Cochon at Agordat, and realised that (as we had no animal transport) it would take nearly half a battalion to keep the remaining half in action.

132 Brigadier R. A. Savory, 'Summary of events outside Keren (Eritrea) during the period 10th to 12th February 1941 with units of the 11th Indian Infantry Brigade', NAM, 1976-03-93-44 and Prasad, *East African Campaign*, pp. 52-56.
133 Peter Cochrane, *Charlie Company: In Service with C Company 2nd Queen's Own Cameron Highlanders 1940-1944* (London: Chatto & Windus, 1977), p. 76.
134 'Summary of events which took place outside Keren (Eritrea) during operations carried out by units of the 11th Indian Infantry Brigade of 4th Indian Division during the period 15th to 17th March 1941', NAM, 7603-93-44 and Prasad, *East African Campaign*, pp. 92-95, 101-103. Brig's Peak was actually named after Savory see letter from Savory to his wife, 15 August 1942, NAM, 1976-03-93-50.
135 Stewart, *First Victory*, p. 176.
136 Prasad, *East African Campaign*, pp. 104, 107-108, 117 and Evans, *Desert and the Jungle*, p. 55.
137 Evans, *Desert and the Jungle*, p. 56.

> I think the Italians did put up a much stiffer fight at Keren than we had anticipated.[138]

He went on to say that there was high morale in the brigade after Sidi Barrani, but Frank Messervy had warned him that 'You cannot apply your desert tactics in these mountains'.[139] The brigade was not at its strongest either. Savory replaced 3rd Battalion, 14th Punjab Regiment as they had been bombed on the train to Kassala on their way to join the brigade, and the commanding officer was evacuated. He described it as a 'shaky' battalion and took them out of the line at Keren, being replaced by the 2nd Mahrattas. He told the divisional commander, Beresford-Peirse, and had 'to be rather firm about this'.[140] As brigade commander, Savory did not shy away from making difficult decisions and was very aware that his brigade would not be as effective as previously due to porterage duties.

Shortly afterwards, 11th Indian Infantry Brigade returned to North Africa, where it underwent re-training for the desert, training at night and studied German methods and organisation.[141] The brigade, as part of Operation Battleaxe, attacked the Halfaya Pass on 15 June. But early tank losses meant that the 'attack now completely changed its character. From being primarily a tank attack supported by infantry and some artillery against what had been previously reported as a weak position, it became an infantry attack supported by inadequate artillery against a position held obviously in some strength'.[142] The Camerons achieved their objective but had to withdraw due to the lack of tank support and anti-tank guns. In addition, their communications with the artillery support had broken down. A second attack followed the next day but was also unsuccessful.[143] A third attempt was not made as the brigade was ordered to withdraw on 17 June by Major General Frank Messervy, the new commander of 4th Indian Division, due to a threatened major German counterattack. During the battle, Savory had to delegate command to his unit commanders due to the lack of radio communications, but soon resumed leadership in person with his unit commanders, through radio communication, the use of liaison officers and conferences.[144] Thus, despite the difficulties of little tank and artillery support as well as the breakdown in communications, the brigade was initially successful and then withdrew orderly. Moreover, the regular troops of the brigade had lost men and equipment in East Africa and needed to be brought up to

138 Letter from Savory to Major General J.G. Elliott, 27 March 1974, NAM, 1976-03-93-46E.
139 Ibid.
140 Ibid.
141 11th Indian Infantry Brigade, 'Notes of Brigade Commander's Conference, 15 May 1941', The National Archives (TNA), WO 169/5351.
142 'Outline of the Operations of the 11 Indian Infantry Brigade Group from 15 to 18 June 1941', p.1. NAM, 1976-03-93-44.
143 Prasad, *North African Campaign*, pp. 178-180, 182-183.
144 'Diary of Events during Operations 15-17 June 1941', pp. 4-5,7, NAM, 7603-93-44. See also Stevens, *Fourth Indian Division*, p. 63.

strength and then given the time to acclimatise and assimilate the reinforcements, some of which arrived at a very late stage, such as the Camerons, who received two hundred reinforcements on 12 June.[145]

After Messervy had taken over command of 4th Indian Division, Savory wrote to his wife 'my time may not be so very far away'. Indeed, he thought his command of the brigade had been successful, writing in the same letter, 'I can honestly say to you (what I would say to no one else) that I feel I have filled the bill so far and earned some small reputation for myself'.[146] To his mother, he remarked about the troops under his command, writing: 'The Indian troops have a very high reputation out here and we are all very proud of them'.[147] However, in his next letter to his wife he wrote: 'I am not really a keen soldier. Everyone thinks I am. If I were, I should have gone further than I have and been cast for almost any height in the military world'.[148] He obviously fluctuated according to his mood, as he was particularly pleased with the announcement of his award of the Distinguished Service Order (DSO), writing again to his wife:

> I have got my DSO at last. You know I have hankered after that decoration. I had begun to think that as a brigadier my chances of getting an award which must be for service under fire, were becoming slim; and now I have it, and am so pleased; and I know you are too. Isn't it grand. That was for "Operations in the Western Desert, Libya and Cyrenica, December 1940-February 1941", or so it is described.[149]

Nevertheless, in his next letter he questions himself and is obviously feeling the strain from both command and almost continuous action since late 1940:

> The more I approach the higher ranks of my profession, the less does rank appeal to me. I begin to see the hollowness of just rank unless it is accompanied by true worth, and I sometime wonder if I am the calibre for a major-general. I sometimes feel very tired. The last battle in June took it out of me more than I knew and I felt lazy in mind and body; and sometimes wonder if I ought in all fairness even to continue to hold my present appointment. But it is all probably just a passing phase of war-weariness. My brigade has been through much [during] the past eight months and the strain has been great for us all.[150]

145 'The Ultra Secret: Battleaxe 15-17 June, 1941', NAM, 1976-03-93-45. See also Report by Commander 4th Indian Division on Operations in the Western Desert 15-18 June 1941, TNA, WO 169/3289.
146 Letter to his wife, 15 May 1941, NAM, 1976-03-93-43.
147 Letter to his mother, 16 September 1941, NAM, 1976-03-93-43
148 Letter to his wife, 26 June 1941, NAM, 1976-03-93-43.
149 Letter to his wife, 10 July 1941, NAM, 1976-03-93-43.
150 Letter to his wife, 24 August, 1941, NAM, 1976-03-93-43.

Both Messervy, 4th Indian Division CO, and Beresford-Pierse, CO Western Desert Force, recommended Savory for promotion, with Messervy writing that he was fit to command a division. He commented in Savory's special confidential report: 'A first class B[riga]de C[om]m[an]d[e]r – Energetic, thorough & determined. Puts his heart and soul into his work – an excellent trainer of troops – a fine leader in action.'[151] In September 1941, he got his promotion to major general as GOC Eritrea, which 'means that I shall be in military command of all troops in Eritrea, a large country, and shall be concerned with many problems of administration and internal security; a new line for me'.[152] Brigade command 'had been one of the highlights of my career', 'I think I am correct in saying that we have been in action longer and fought more continuously than any brigade out here'.[153] At the same time, Savory was again feeling the strain of front line command. He remarked to Myrtle, his wife:

> It does mean that I give up command of my brigade and leave action operations for a bit. That is a matter I regard with mixed feeling, as there is nothing like the command of troops in action; and I have been in contact with an enemy, off and on, for 18 months now. All the same, it is a strain, as you may imagine, and I cannot stop admitting to myself that I shall be glad of a rest from the constant watchfulness which the presence of an enemy imposes on a commander.[154]

It is clear that Savory was quite self-aware and his next command would provide the much needed rest from action that was required. This promotion mainly consisted of administration and internal security but would provide good preparation for a higher level of command that would eventually follow in India. His surroundings could not have differed more from his previous eighteen months. He described them to his wife: 'My office would befit the King of England. I sit at my desk at the end of an enormous room, beautifully furnished and lit by reflected lighting.'[155] The tediouseness was reflected in Savory's varied accounts of the experience. The work comprised one long list of visits, lunches, dinners, parties, interviews and inspections.[156] He wrote to his mother, 'I find to my satisfaction that I have some aptitude for administration, both civil and military, and my two months here have not been without results'.[157] But the life could be quite isolating as he wrote to Myrtle: 'Being a general is not all beer and skittles and one has so few friends, though one's acquaintances are legion and visitors are always coming in'.[158]

151 Special confidential report, 1941, BL, IOR/L/MIL/14/2623.
152 Letter to his wife, 29 September 1941, NAM, 7603-93-43.
153 Ibid.
154 Ibid.
155 Letter to his wife, 12 October 1941, NAM, 1976-03-93-47.
156 Diary 20 Oct 1941-12 Jan 1942, NAM, 1976-03-93-48.
157 Letter to his mother, 16 December 1941, NAM, 1976-03-93-47.
158 Letter to his wife, 4 January 1942, NAM, 1976-03-93-47.

He never quite landed on a definitive appreciation of the position, largely fluctuating in his opinions day by day. Indeed, Savory gave his wife an idea of what his days involved:

> To-morrow, Monday, I am off on an inspection of a hospital and prisoner-of-war's camp and get back here about 4pm. Then after tea, I have my office hours until 8pm; and after that have a dinner-party to people who must be "dined". Thank God, my private cinema helps solve the problem of after-dinner conversation. Then on Tuesday (6th) I am off for a very interesting three days tour returning on the evening of the 8th, when I dine officially with a visiting American General, whose dinner I will have to return in due course; and so on. You can picture my life can't you? My greatest satisfaction is when I visit the troops. I have, I think, a knack of getting-on with them; and I would give a lot to be able to get back to a fighting formation and be among fighting men once again.[159]

This wish was granted, as after only three months in the job, Savory was ordered back to India to command a division, at the personal request of Wavell, now Commander-in-Chief, India.[160] There is little evidence of patronage in Savory's career up to this point. This is perhaps the nearest, although from a British Army officer, and most likely due to Savory's service in North Africa under Wavell's command.[161] He was an extremely conscientious brigade commander in North and East Africa, commanding from the front, writing up detailed reports from all the actions he was involved in, as well as continually learning lessons from these encounters. Thus, the early part of his wartime career demonstrated the steep transition from battalion commander to successfully commanding a brigade in the first two years of the Second World War.

## Divisional Command

On his return to India, Savory was given command of 23rd Indian Division. It was established at Jhansi in January 1942 as the only reserve in India, with Savory becoming the first divisional commander.[162] Its original role was to operate alongside an armoured division.[163] On arriving at GHQ in Delhi, Savory was led to believe:

159 Ibid.
160 Letters to his wife, 15 & 16 January 1942, NAM, 1976-03-93-47.
161 For a Second World War example of patronage in the British Army, see Mark Frost, ' "Everyone Thought I was Finished": The Remarkable Comeback of Lieutenant-General Sir Neil Ritchie' *Journal of the Society for Army Historical Research* Vol. 98, No. 395, Winter 2020, pp. 379-397.
162 Diary entry for 24 January 1942, NAM, 1976-03-93-51.
163 Diary entry for 26 January 1942, NAM, 1976-03-93-51.

> I would be given practically anything I wanted and I therefore asked for what I wanted without …including a B[attalio]n of I[nfantry] tanks and a squadron of my own Army co-operation aeroplanes under command as well as a Reg[imen]t of Medium Art[illery]y. To my surprise it looks as if all except the planes will be forthcoming.[164]

However, there was no such smooth and seamless setting up of the division, which comprised 98th Infantry Brigade and the Hyderabad Lancers, Indian State Forces, with one armoured car stationed at Delhi.[165] Savory was unimpressed writing in his diary: 'visited 98 B[riga]de on an exercise and was not by any means impressed, and also saw the Hyderabad Lancers who impressed still less'.[166] The following day he wrote to his wife: 'I have made the acquaintance of my brigade and have talked to all the officers. The next few days I am spending one day with each regiment and getting to know each one of them, so that this division will be second to none. I have it in me I think.'[167] The other brigade was the 46th Indian Infantry Brigade but neither were with the division long and were replaced by 23rd (later renumbered 123rd) and 37th brigades.[168] Both brigades made up the nucleus of the division at Ranchi, although all units were short of equipment and 'few had trained with modern weapons'.[169] Apart from two British Army units – namely the 1st Battalion, the Seaforth Highlanders and the 158th Field Regiment, Royal Arillery – the rest of the division was entirely Indian Army.[170] This was unusual in 1942 as individual infantry brigades usually comprised at least one British Army battalion. This largely remained the case with Indian divisions in the Western theatres of North Africa and Italy but increasingly by 1944 Indian divisions in India and Burma consisted of Indian Army units – not helped by manpower problems in the British Army.[171]

In a continuation of his army career to date, Savory was insistent on intensive training, writing to his wife: 'I am training my division to be as hard as nails and to need no luxuries.'[172] It also seemed that Savory wanted some continuity with familiar faces. He looked into Major Wimberley (GSO1) being replaced by Geoff Evans, who had been his staff officer in Africa.[173] One other factor which was already becoming increasingly apparent and would remain so for the next couple of years was the problem of malaria. Savory noted that there were a hundred cases in the 3/3rd Gurkha Rifles by mid-March 1942.[174]

164 Ibid.
165 Lieut.-Colonel A. J. F. Doulton, *The Fighting Cock: Being the History of the 23rd Indian Division 1942-1947* (Aldershot: Gale & Polden, 1951) p. 1.
166 Diary entry for 4 February 1942, NAM, 1976-03-93-51.
167 Letter to his wife, 5 February 1942, NAM, 1976-03-93-50.
168 Dairy entry for 11 Feb. 1943, NAM, 1976-03-93-51.
169 Doulton, *Fighting Cock*, p. 2.
170 Ibid., p. 15.
171 Jeffreys, *Approach to Battle*, p. 175.
172 Letter to his wife, 23 March 1943, NAM, 1976-03-93-50.
173 Diary entry for 28 January 1942, NAM, 1976-03-93-51.
174 Diary entry for 17 March 1942, NAM, 1976-03-93-51.

Reginald Savory at Sandhurst, 1913. (National Army Museum 1976-03-94-31)

Troops of 29th Indian Infantry Brigade disembarking from a boat at Gallipoli, 1 May 1915. (National Army Museum 1976-05-52-1)

British and Indian instructors, as well as Indian officers, of the Indian Wing of the Army School of Education, November 1925. (National Army Museum 1976-03-94-6)

Savory and his wife Myrtle, on leave relaxing on Dal Lake, Kashmir, 1925. (National Army Museum 1976-03-94-81)

Major General Savory as Director of Infantry, 1944. (National Army Museum 1976-03-94-67)

Savory at the Indian Military Academy where he commanded A Company, 1933. (National Army Museum 1976-03-94-52)

Officers of the 23rd Indian Division at lunch following the visit and parade for General Sir Claude Auchinleck, 13 July 1945. Including, from left to right, Capt Currie, Lt Col William Ridgeway (personal secretary to the Commander in Chief), Col L H D Pugh, Maj Gen Donald Bateman (Director of Military Training), Lt Gen Ouvry Roberts (Corps Command), Gen Sir Claude Auchinleck, Maj Gen Douglas Hawthorn, Air Vice-Marshal the Earl of Bandon, Maj Gen Edmund Beard (Area Commander), Brig R W Andrews, Lt Col R W Atkinson, Col J Sarkis, F/Lt Mullick, Capt H Kay, Lt Col R E Holloway, Col R de Burgh Morris, Lt Col J H Trim, Brig N MacDonald, Capt R C S Garwood, RN, Maj Gen Reginald Savory, Brig Aubertin Mallaby, Brig R C M Kings, Brig Balwant Singh, Lt Col John Mellsop, ADC to C-in-C, Lt Gracia (ADC to Gen Beard) and Lt Forty (ADC to Gen Roberts). (National Army Museum 1981-11-72-66)

Savory preceded his division to Assam and quickly consulted with fellow divisional commanders such as Major General Henry Rich who was commanding 14th Indian Division on the Assam border. His task 'was to get forward to recce positions on or near Burmese border through which Burma Army could withdraw'.[175] He later met up with the retreating commanders Bill Slim (Burcorps), Bruce Scott (CO Burma Division) and his friend 'Punch' Cowan (CO 17th Indian Division), remarking in his diary 'Punch looked well but thin. They have all had a hell of a time'.[176] Slim remarked in *Defeat into Victory:*

> Savory recognized at once that the fighting troops of Burma Corps, who came out in their disciplined ranks, every man with his weapons and little else, were very different from the hotch-potch of improvised units, rear organizationed, non-combatants and military deserters, officerless men, refugees, and riff-raff that had swarmed out of ahead of them.[177]

As with the Fall of Singapore in February 1942, the long retreat from Burma was another signpost in the impending demise of the British Empire in South and Southeast Asia. It included an exodus of civilians, with one report noting 'the condition of the refugees moving along the track is appalling. Nearly every family has lost one or two members through death en route'.[178] Michael Leigh has estimated there were 366,200 evacuees that arrived in India in 1942, with 80,000 deaths en route.[179]

On 20 May, Savory took over command of the front with the objective of preventing 'the Japanese invading India on the line Imphal-Jorhat in force, and to defeat him if he tries to do so'.[180] However, the division were very short of equipment, with the 1st Assam Regiment joining 1st Indian Infantry Brigade with no steel helmets, no respirators and short of about 40 bayonets.[181] Similarly, the brigade had its full complement of tommy-guns, Brens and mortars but had undertaken no training in their use.[182] Savory reviewed the situation four months later and concluded:

> During this period we must ensure that any attempt by the enemy to invade Assam is defeated. In the Imphal area this is the task of 23 Ind[ian] Div[ision]. The situation of the Div[ision] at the moment, however, is not satisfactory. Units are generally

175 Diary entry for 26 April, 1942, NAM, 1976-03-93-51.
176 Diary entry for 19 May 1942, NAM, 1976-03-93-51.
177 Field Marshal Sir William Slim, *Defeat into Victory* (London: Cassell, 1956), p. 112.
178 Report on Refugees from Burma passing through the Kasom Khulem route, 6 June 1942, NAM, 1976-03-95-55.
179 Michael D. Leigh, *The Evacuation of Civilians from Burma: Analysing the 1942 Colonial Disaster* (London: Bloomsbury, 2014), p. 27.
180 Reginald Savory – Appreciation of Situation, 7 May 1942, NAM, 1976-03-95-55.
181 Ibid.
182 Doulton, *Fighting Cock*, p. 12.

> 50% under strength. Animals are so debilitated that out of 7 A[nimal].T[ransport]. Co[mpan]ys only about two composite co[mpan]ys can be made available for operations, second line am[munitio]n is short and there are sup[plie]s for only 5-10 days. Although about 50% under strength the Div[ision] is deployed over a front extending from Mombi to Ukhrul, there are few reserves and in the present circumstances it is doubtful whether it can carry out its task.[183]

Thus, the understrength division had to cover a front of over a hundred miles with inadequate supplies and transport in difficult terrain, a situation that had not really improved in the four months that Savory had commanded 23rd Indian Division in Manipur. Notwithstanding, Savory suggested an aggressive defensive stance to Lieutenant General Geoffrey Scoones, who was commanding 4 Corps. He planned to keep his brigades mobile, operating in small mixed columns of infantry and mountain artillery against known enemy positions. The bases were to be in the hills to minimise the threat of malaria, with attacks in the plains only once the enemy was accurately located. These aggressive raids were also to be co-ordinated with air action. He concluded in a letter to Scoones: 'I should like to be able to do this as I feel it is an aggressive answer to an essentially defensive problem. The alternative (and I can see no other) is to sit in prepared defences and risk all over again what we have recently experienced in Burma and Malaya'.[184] At the end of Savory's time as divisional commander, he received a letter of appreciation which stressed the aggressive divisional attitude, 'inspired by, if I may use your nickname without any disrespect, "Tiger" Savory'.[185] This adoption of a more offensive attitude was commonplace a year later, following the disastrous first Battle of the Arakan, when, for example, 5th and 7th Indian Divisons adopted aggressive fighting patrols in the jungle in order to acclimatise troops to the terrain as well as destroy the myth of the Japanese 'superman' in jungle warfare.[186] Savory continued to keep Scoones in the loop, writing 'I propose writing you an occasional liaison letter such as this from time to time, letting you know what is in my mind, and I hope you will find them useful.'[187] Later, as Director of Infantry, Savory's liaison letters were the method of disseminating doctrine and training across the infantry.

Two months later, the situation had not really improved. The division was 5000 men understrength, with only 30% of its war establishment. This was largely caused by

183 Periodical Review of Situation by Comd 23 Ind Div, 10 September 1942, NAM, 1976-03-93-55.
184 Letter from Savory to Lt Gen G.A.P. Scoones, 29 August 1942, NAM, 1976-05-93-56.
185 Letter from CO 'V' Force to Savory 1 July 1943, NAM, 1976-03-93-60. See also Doulton, *Fighting Cock*, pp. 11-12. Lieutenant E. D. Murray was the CO of 'V; Force. Savory wrote of him to the divisional historian Lieutenant Colonel A. J. F. Doulton: 'Murray was, again, rather like Balwant Singh [CO Patiala Infantry] – a fearless leader and one who was constantly probing out in front. The difficulty I had was in stopping him from going too far.' Letter from Savory to Doulton, 31 March 1947, NAM, 1998-01-153-17-1.
186 Jeffreys, *Approach to Battle*, pp. 169-170.
187 Letter from Savory to Scoones, 22 October 1942, NAM, 1976-03-93-56.

malaria, and exaggerated by the slow rate of reinforcements. For instance, in October 1942, 61st Mule Company received 192 reinforcements, of which 102 went down with malaria on arrival in the Imphal area.[188] The 'milking' of units, where experienced VCOs and NCOs were removed from units to bolster new units, was still occurring in late 1942 due to the continuing expansion of the army. For example, 24th Mountain Regiment was 'milked' of 40% of the unit's VCOs and NCOs, which meant that it was 221 men below strength.[189] The Divisional Commander Royal Artillery (CRA) reported that if it was 'milked' any further he would have to report the unit unfit for operations.[190] The divisional historian remarked: 'Even after two years of improvement and organization, the Assam L[ine]. of C[ommunication]. was unreliable, and in June 1942, it must have been the worst in the world'.[191] However, training continued throughout this period with Savory informing Brigadier Gurdon (who later became Director of Military Training at GHQ India in 1943) that the 7th/14th Punjab Regiment underwent '6 weeks intensive training and the improvement is most marked'. [192]

Towards the end of his tenure as divisional CO, Savory wrote up his thoughts on jungle warfare. He foresaw a need for an increase in infantry, particularly 'if we accept that jungle warfare is an infantry war'. He did not discount the role of artillery in the jungle but noted the slow movement of mountain artillery, such as 3.7-inch howitzers compared to wheeled artillery, as well as being 'terribly expensive in mules and personnel'. Savory suggested that the role of the howitzers could be undertaken by 3-inch mortars, concluding frankly: 'I myself feel that it could'. As a result, he made sure there was a high standard of training in the 3-inch mortar within the division. Similarly, he emphasised the maintenance of the division through light-scale, seven-day supplies carried by brigade groups, in case the lines of communication were cut as well as help prevent infiltration, which Savory described as the 'bogey' of jungle warfare. Furthermore, after the experience of the First Chindit Expedition – Operation Longcloth – led by Brigadier Orde Wingate, fighting behind enemy lines, he wrote: 'we have recently been having considerable experience here of air supply and I think it is one of the answers to our coming campaign against the Japanese'. Fire discipline in the jungle was another important aspect that Savory stressed, accentuated by his experience in East Africa and then the jungles of Assam, stating: 'At the battle of Keren the order was given that there should be no automatic fire but only single shot. I think it was justifield – it saved ammunition and lessoned excitement. Here it is not only justified but essential'.[193] This constant

188 Note on the State of 23 Ind Div (End of Nov 1942), NAM, 1976-03-93-56.

189 'Milking' was the term used for taking experienced officers, VCOs and NCOs from units to help form and bolster newly established units in the expansion of the Indian Army.

190 Some Points discussed between Comd 4 Corps and Comd 23 Ind Div, 15 August 1942, NAM, 1976-03-93-56.

191 Doulton, *Fighting Cock*, pp. 24, 28-36.

192 Letter from Savory to Brigadier E.T.M. Gurdon, HQ Eastern Army, 15 August 1942, NAM, 1976-03-93-56. See also Doulton, *Fighting Cock*, p. 40.

193 Savory, 'Some thoughts on Jungle Warfare', April 1943, NAM, 1976-03-93-57.

assessment of lessons learnt is reccurrent throughout Savory's career, but equally became more widespread across the Indian Army by 1943.[194]

Patrolling continued throughout the period in the Lower Kabaw Valley, Chindwin and Homalin areas, gathering vital intelligence of enemy movements.[195] Savory stressed the need for stronger patrols as well as smaller reconnaissance patrols. Even when soldiers rested, there needed to be constant patrolling, stating 'in fact the rest area itself should be in the form of one large ambush' with the awareness they 'must be prepared for immediate loss of control in a jungle skirmish.' All of these patrols had to be able to react immediately in the jungle, remarking that 'Immediate reaction to surprise is the basis of all tactics in the jungle'. He cited Operation Longcloth as an example where movement, where possible, should be off the tracks, writing 'so far as patrols are concerned it is of course better to avoid the tracks, but there are times when this is not possible though travelling along tracks means a constant danger of ambush'. Uniform was also adapted for jungle warfare. Savory noted that steel helmets were unnecessary and that rubber boots or shoes should be worn on patrol when possible.[196] He had clearly thought about the difficulties of jungle warfare and fighting the Imperial Japanese Army in his time in command of 23rd Indian Division. This introspective assessment was not necessarily standard practice across all British and Commonwealth divisional commanders.

Savory was clearly impressed by the junior officers in 23rd Indian Division, writing to the divisional historian, Lieutenant Colonel Doulton, in 1947:

> In fact, I think I can say in truth that one of the difficulties I had in those days was in controlling the enthusiasm of the junior leaders in their patrol work. They all wanted to penetrate deep into Burma and although I was only too keen to get as much information as I could, and to dominate our particular No Man's Land, I did not want, in my numerical position, to stir up the Japanese to activities with which I might have found it difficult to deal. So I had to hang on to these Subalterns by their coat-tails to some extent, and I take my hat off to them all. There is no question, they were magnificent, and the men under them.[197]

Similarly, Doulton wrote on the departure of Savory:

> On June 13th Major General Savory said good-bye to the formation that he had created out of the rawest of materials that he might, from his new position as Inspector of Infantry at G.H.Q. (I), see that others were properly trained and equipped for warfare in the jungle. We were to see no more that strutting, perky walk which some said had inspired the designer of the "Fighting Cock" [the

194 Jeffreys, *Approach to Battle*, pp. 120-124, 168-170.

195 See for example War diary weekly summary for week ending 23 May 1943, NAM, 1976-03-93-56.

196 Savory, 'Some notes in Recent Patrolling Lessons', 26 April 1943, NAM, 1976-03-93-57.

197 Letter from Savory to A.J. Doulton, Papers of A.J. Doulton, NAM, 1998-01-153-17-1 & 2.

divisional badge] but the owner of the walk left behind a legacy. There are good divisions and there are poor ones. Those that are good have a "soul," a spirit that pulsates through them and causes the individual members to rise above themselves when faced with the perils of war. The 23rd Indian Division had a "soul" and it came, despite appalling difficulties, from the efforts of its first commander'.[198]

## Director of Infantry

After the campaigns in Malaya and Burma, the situation deteriorated further with the First Arakan campaign of 1942-43: the remainder of the cancelled ambitious 'Anakim' offensive to invade Burma and recapture Rangoon. It comprised a limited offensive in the Arakan region, clearing the Mayu peninsula overland with an amphibious operation to take Akyab Island, although this part of the plan was cancelled due to the lack of equipment and manpower. The 14th Indian Division, commanded by Major General Wilfrid Lloyd, attacked on both sides of the Mayu Ridge on 21 September 1942. The advance was very slow due to the supply lines and to avoid exposing the flanks from Japanese counterattacks. However, it meant that Imperial Japanese Army reinforcements were given time to arrive and the British and Indian forces were further slowed down when they encountered well-defended bunkers. On 7 January 1943, a company of the 1st Battalion, Royal Inniskilling Fusiliers reached Donbaik at the end of the peninsula and unsuccessfully attacked the position held by one Japanese company. Another attack launched by the whole battalion two days later supported by field and mountain artillery similarly failed. A series of attacks of increasing strength on the position were made over the next two months. On 1 February, 47th Indian Infantry Brigade attacked Donbaik supported by eight Valentine tanks with artillery support but was equally unsuccessful. The British and Indian forces had encountered Japanese bunkers for the first time to which they had no response. The abortive attacks on Donbaik and other positions gave time for the IJA to mount a counteroffensive. The Japanese forces cleared the Kaladin Valley and both the east and west flanks of the Mayu range combined with encircling attacks on Rathedaung and Donbaik. In stark contrast, it took less than a month, pushing back numerically superior British and Indian troops in demoralising confusion. In addition, the command situation was still in disarray. At one point, Lloyd had five brigades under his command, with Eastern Army commanded by Lieutenant General Noel Irwin. Bill Slim recommended a corps command in the Arakan but Irwin refused. Eventually Lloyd was replaced by Major General Cyril Lomax and Slim formed a corps command but it was too late. Irwin held a press conference on 6 April blaming everyone but himself for the disastrous First Arakan. As a British service officer, he had always been critical of the Indian Army and Slim in particular. Indeed, he tried to make Slim the scapegoat for the

198 Doulton, *Fighting Cock*, pp. 59-60.

campaign and sacked him. But in the meantime, Field Marshal Wavell had replaced Irwin with General Sir George Giffard.[199]

The First Arakan was an utter disaster undertaken by partially trained and demoralised troops, as well as untrained reinforcements, with an inefficient command structure. Morale was further undermined by the huge numbers of soldiers affected by malaria and disease and the problems of evacuation of the sick and wounded back to base hospitals. Generally, the First Arakan caused military and civilian morale in India to plummet. John Prendergast remarked in his memoir, 'Prenders Progress':

> In the minds of the many the Japanese's successes made him into a superman. The number of Japanese prisoners after the Arakan campaign could be counted on one hand for they preferred suicide or death to surrender. Morale in the mass of India was very low as I saw when a closely guarded Japanese prisoner was taken off the train at Chittagong. The platform, crowded with Indians, as only an Indian station platform can be, was bare in a few seconds.[200]

Furthermore, the military situation was hampered by the Quit India movement of 1942 in response to the failure of the Cripps Mission, when the politician Sir Stafford Cripps led an unsuccessful British mission to India to try and persuade the Indian nationalist politicians to support the war in return for promises of full autonomy after the war. This meant that large numbers of troops were required to act as 'Aid to Civil Power'. This, in combination with the Bengal famine of 1943-1944, which killed an estimated three million Indians, meant that much of India was at its lowest ebb during this period.

The turning point in the fortunes of the Indian Army came after the disastrous First Arakan campaign. Sweeping changes were made to senior staff officers and front-line commanders to improve military effectiveness. The C-in-C India, Field Marshal Wavell, was appointed Viceroy of India and was replaced by General Auchinleck to what was his second stint as C-in-C. Operational command for South East Asia now came under the new Supreme Allied Commander, South East Asia Command, Admiral Lord Louis Mountbatten. In the front-line, Bill Slim was appointed commander of 14th Army with a number of experienced corps and divisional commanders also appointed, such as Major Generals Frank Messervy and Thomas 'Pete' Rees who commanded 7th and 19th Indian Divisons respectively.[201] Before his departure, Wavell instigated the Infantry Committee of June 1943, which recommended a large number of changes for the infantry in India, foremost of which was the thorough training of recruits, followed by two months of jungle warfare training with a training division, before going to a reinforcement camp where training continued and then finally joining their infantry battalion.[202]

199 Callahan, *Churchill and his Generals*, p. 201.
200 John Prendergast, *Prender's Progress: A Soldier in India, 1931-47* (London: Cassell, 1979), p. 186.
201 Jeffreys, *Approach to Battle*, p. 159. See also Tim Moreman, *The Jungle, the Japanese and the British Commonwealth Armies at War 1941-45* (London: Frank Cass, 2005), pp. 80-84.
202 Ibid., p. 160

Savory was appointed the new Inspector of Infantry on 11 June 1943. He was instrumental in the transformation of the Indian Army after the disastrous campaigns in Malaya, the retreat from Burma and the First Arakan. He wrote to his wife that the job 'is at GHQ so I shall be at the centre of things, which will be a change after three years as a front-line soldier. It does *not* mean promotion but is in some respects a step forward'.[203] The previous incumbent had been Major General James Scott, who had commanded the Burma Divison in the retreat from Burma. Savory commented that Scott 'had commanded the Burma Division under General Slim and was a wise and experienced officer. But the stresses of the withdrawal had taken their toll. He was so exhausted as not to be capable of the great effort involved in re-training the infantry; and he was the first to admit it'.[204]

Over the next couple of years, Savory travelled widely around India. He wrote: 'I spent most of my time, not only visiting the training establishments, but also infantry units across India. I also made regular trips to the front, so as to acquaint myself with conditions at the time and apply the lessons learnt'.[205] In this new role, he worked closely with the recently appointed Director of Military Training (DMT), Major General Edward Gurdon. Within a few months Savory became the Director of Infantry, with his own small directorate separate from the Military Training Directorate. His remit was extended to include infantry organisation, equipment and arms. Savory remained in this important position for almost two years and, as Raymond Callahan has pointed out, for the first time the senior officers such as Auchinleck, Messervy, Rees, Savory and Slim and Auchinleck were all largely drawn from the Indian Army and 'thus understood the traditions and ways of the Indian Army'.[206]

Savory immediately began to formulate his thoughts on improving the standard of infantry recruits and the infantry generally. He read the latest doctrine, including an Australian pamphlet on jungle warfare which he regarded well, in addition to the training manual *Battle Drill for Thick Jungle*, produced by the Military Training Directorate.[207] Similarly, he watched training films, met Colonel Francis Brink, who had been the US observer in Malaya and written *Japanese Tactical Methods*.[208] The following month he started his tours around India, visiting the Indian Military Academy and the

203 Letter to his wife, 12 June 1943, NAM, 1976-03-93-63.
204 Letter from Savory to Professor Raymond Callahan, 24 October 1974, NAM, 1976-03-93-71A.
205 Ibid.
206 Quoted in Jeffreys, *Approach to Battle*, p. 159. See Callahan, *Churchill and his Generals*, pp. 201-204.
207 Diary entry for 29 June 1943, NAM, 1976-03-93-52 and Savory's 1943 notebook, NAM, 1976-03-93-59B. The training pamphlets were *Military Training Pamphlet (Australia) No. 23 Jungle Warfare Part XX* (Melbourne: Australian Land Forces HQ, 1943) and *Battle Drill for Thick Jungle* (Delhi, GSI, 1943), BL, IOR, L/MIL/17/5/2236.
208 Diary entry for 26, 28 June 1943, NAM 1976-03-93-52. See also Moreman, *Jungle*, pp. 32, 47; Adrian Threlfall, *Jungle Warriors: From Tobruk to Kokoda and beyond, how the Australian Army became the world's most deadly jungle fighting force* (Sydney: Allan & Unwin, 2014), pp. 63-64 and Colonel Francis Brink, *Japanese Tactical Methods Characteristics of Japanese*

three Officer Training Schools (OTS), the Training Divisions, infantry schools, infantry units, Regimental Training Centres and other training establishments. His first visit was to Dehra Dun, where he toured the 2nd King Edward VII's Own Gurkha Rifles (The Sirmoor Rifles) and 9th Gurkha Rifles Regimental Training Centres on 2 July. Savory concluded in his diary that there was a lack of good officers at both. The following day, he visited the 3rd Queen Alexandra's Own Gurkha Rifles Regimental Training Centre, which he praised. The day after, he visited the IMA, now run by Brigadier Jonah Jones, who had commanded 16th Indian Brigade during the retreat from Burma, where they discussed the new *Battle Drill for Thick Jungle* training pamphlet. By the end of the week, he was back in Delhi and had 'smoothed' the way with the Army commanders Lieutenant General Sir Noel Beresford-Pierse and General Sir Edward Quinan, commanding officers of Southern and North-Western Armies respectively. Indeed, Southern Command, which became Southern Army, had initially been a centre for training in India where many training establishments had been created, and continued to be so throughout the war.[209] Savory liaised with Gurdon, DMT, after this first tour to make sure they were both working in collaboration, as well as keeping in touch with his peers, such as Frank Messervy, who relieved Tom Corbett as commander of 7th Indian Division in July 1943.[210]

Savory was quick to set out his initial policy for the new job, which included improving the standard of all infantry battalions and keeping records of all the commanding officers and those who had the potential to do so. His plan was to exert influence on all infantry appointments. Similarly, he wanted to be the one to initiate any changes for the infantry and even suggested a corps of Indian infantry and a corps of Gurkha infantry. Other questions he posed in his notebook included that infantry tactics come under his remit and whether instruction at the various infantry schools was co-ordinated. Furthermore, one of his self-appointed tasks was to see how co-ordinated and how much overlap there was in training at the Regimental Training Centres, the Training Divisions and the Reinforcement Camps. In line with the Infantry Committee proposals, Savory noted the importance of a common doctrine at GHQ, Army, Corps and Divisional level with the 'adaptation of lessons up: down: and sideways'. He also wanted to cut out unnecessary training with the 'abolition of antiquated and useless procedure'.[211]

Savory's last policy note pertained to the overlap with Major General Roland Inskip and whether he should come under his command.[212] Inskip, a retired Indian Army officer, was appointed Inspector of Training Centres in 1943.[213] Savory's wish list for the state of the recruits coming from the Training Centres included that they be generally

*Operations* (Delhi: GSI, 1942) which was reprinted in India March 1942, BL, IOR, L/MIL/17/20/28.

209 Jeffreys, *Approach to Battle*, pp. 77-79.
210 Diary entries for 2-4, 6, 9 July 1943, NAM, 1976-03-93-52.
211 Notebook, Jan-Nov. 1943, NAM, 1976-03-93-59B.
212 Section on policy in notebook, Jan-Nov. 1943, NAM, 1976-03-93-59B.
213 Jeffreys, *Approach to Battle*, p. 203.

alert, with reasonable wireless telegraphy (WT), fieldcraft and battle drills. He indicated that Inskip and the DMT had clashed over basic training.[214] Savory's requirements for basic training included weapons training with rifle, bayonet, Bren and grenades; physical training to include games, swimming, field craft, battle drills, marching; orientation to include visits and demonstrations of other arms and fire control; and education and regimental history as well. Ultimately, the Regimental Training Centres did come under Savory's remit and Inskip contracted dysentery and left the role in 1944 when the Regimental Centres were centralised under Army Commands, ceasing the need for the Inspector of Training Centres, with the infantry coming under Savory's control.[215]

Savory made a number of observations from his visits on both other ranks and officers. In the Training Divisions, he recognised the importance of battle drills, battle inoculation, patrolling, basha building, river crossing, swimming, ambushes, reactions to surprise, blitz and boom barrages, malaria discipline, night work, battlefield organisation, tent discipline, WT and general alertness. Much of this was also relevant for officers who, in addition, needed knowledge of men, languages and villages, weapons training, patrol leading and planning and administrative plans of all kinds, liaison with VCOs, cooking own food, knowledge of battle drills and deliberate attack. When visiting the IMA, he noted the need that the 'instructors handbook must supercede all that's gone before. This is the Bible. An Order.'[216] He thought the IMA, OTS and Jungle Warfare schools muddled through on battle drill and this needed to be addressed immediately.

Savory wasted no time. As early as the beginning of July, he was addressing whether all infantry schools, such as those at Saugor, Raiwala and Sevoke, should come under his jurisdiction. At the Infantry School at Saugor, he questioned, interrogated and analysed all aspects of training. For example, he investigated how the school correlated with GHQ and Army schools and what was the teaching on carriers in jungle warfare and whether there was any guidance on the matter. He noted that battle drills on the parade ground were good and should be continued. He informed the DMT of this, as well as requesting further training pamphlets and asking for more small arms courses with the ultimate aim for further decentralisation, making the school more responsible and even taking the school to individual infantry units for training. Savory noted that the 2-pounder course was a 'washout' but wanted to coordinate 'reports from other travelling circuses'.[217]

214 Note for 8 July 1943, notebook, Jan-Nov. 1943, NAM, 1976-03-93-59B.
215 Infantry Liasion Letter No. 9, 4 August 1944, BL, IOR/L/WS/1/778 and https://www.britishmilitaryhistory.co.uk/wp-content/uploads/sites/124/2024/04/INSKIP-Major-General-Roland-Debenham-V3_1.doc.pdf accessed 8 July 2024.
216 Notebook, Jan-Nov. 1943, NAM, 1976-03-93-59B. *The Instructors' Handbook on Fieldcraft and Battle Drill (India)* was a reprint of the War Office training pamphlet written by Lieutenant Colonel Lionel Wigram and Major R. M. Kerr. It comprised seven chapters modified for India Command in 1943 which was intended to be read together with *Battle Drill for Thick Jungle*. See Moreman, *Jungle*, p. 102.
217 Ibid.

Savory's solution was to simplify the courses at Saugor with courses for rifles and Bren guns, with the object of abolishing rapid fire for rifles and the use of automatic fire with Bren guns respectively. Fire discipline was to be maintained and there were special courses for instructors that would in turn be disseminated across the Training Centres. Indeed, he thought the centres and infantry schools should all come under his command as currently there was 'too much "free for all"'. He saw the current battle courses as good and tough-going but questioned whether they were relevant to fighting in the jungles of South East Asia, calling them 'a glorified obstacle plus bullet and bayonet course'.[218]

Savory toured the training establishments and units at Saugor, Deolali, Poona, and Belgaum for the remainder of July 1943. He observed that the 5th Mahratta Light Infantry Regimental Training Centre was excellent and lectured at the OTS Belgaum. He was very keen to keep his knowledge up to date by visiting active battalions and discussing requirements with their commanding officers.[219] Thus, he inspected infantry units, such as the 4th and 5th Battalions of the 5th Mahratta Light Infantry, who he thought were well-drilled.[220] In addition, he visited the 25th Battalion, The Mahar Regiment, which was a garrison battalion who impressed Savory to the extent that they needed to be upgraded to an active battalion. He noted garrison battalion COs got paid less than active battalion COs and wanted to lay out the duties and training of a garrison battalion. He also met Captain David Wilson, who he considered a good type. Wilson was responsible for the Battle School for the British 2nd Division, demonstrating that Savory was also keen to learn how the British Army in India undertook training.[221] This tour also made him question the current basic infantry training pamphlet and whether it needed updating.[222] After the tour, he met up with the DMT about his findings. They both met with the American Colonel Francis Brink and, the following day, Savory discussed night operations with Brink.[223] Thus it was clear that Savory was keen to learn from not only lessons in Burma and practice across India, but also the American observations of the British, Indian armies and the US experience in the South West Pacific.

Savory and GHQ India were also intent on learning the lessons from the Australian Army experience of fighting in the jungle. As a result, at a tactical level, units were encouraged to stalk and consolidate – a lesson learnt in New Guinea – as well as protect reconnaissance units and spread Light Machine Gun ammunition throughout a section, keeping it in separate containers. Savory was involved in the decision to send fifty Indian Army officers to New Guinea in order to learn about the jungle fighting methods

218 Notebook, Jan-Nov. 1943, NAM, 1976-03-93-59B.
219 Note for 8 July 1943, notebook, Jan-Nov. 1943, NAM, 1976-03-93-59B.
220 Diary entry for 24-25 July 1943, NAM, 1976-03-93-52.
221 David Wilson, *Sum of Things* (Staplehurst: Spellmount, 2001), pp. 96-99.
222 This paragraph and the following ones draw upon Savory's notebook, Jan-Nov 1943, NAM, 1976-03-93-59B. See also *MTP (India) No. 19 Notes on the Training of the Infantry Recruit* (Simla: Manager, Government of India Press, 1941), BL, IOR, L/MIL/17/5/2261.
223 Diary entries for 30-31 July 1943, NAM, 1976-03-93-52.

employed there and in the South West Pacific Area generally.[224] On 20 November, Savory met Brigadier J.E. 'Jack' Lloyd for lunch, writing 'v. interesting re. New Guinea' in his diary.[225] Lloyd had been sent to India Command by the Australian High Command to aid the learning process. He had served in the Indian Army from 1918 until 1922, as well as having experience of fighting in the jungle and as an instructor of jungle warfare, having commanded 16th Australian Infantry Brigade on the Kokoda Trail, and been Commandant of the Tactical School at Beenleigh in Queensland respectively. He spent six months lecturing on the New Guinea operations to units, formations and training establishments across India.[226] The Australian Army, in a similar vein to the Indian Army, ensured that officers who had recent operational experience spent a period of time at training establishments 'to ensure that instruction was up to date and reflected the reality of combat'.[227]

As a result of these first two big tours, which took up most of July and August, Savory redefined his role. He wrote that his post was to lobby for the interests of the infantry as a whole, which would be achieved by constant touring, and maintaining good relations with formation and local commanders, the DMT and the Inspector of Training Centres. He also felt compelled to compare his role with the equivalent for artillery and armoured branches.[228] He now realised his role was to deliver trained men to battalions, run the infantry schools but simultaneously needed to define what a trained soldier was and what was the objective of the schools. Similarly, he needed to coordinate what was taught at the infantry schools with what was taught at all army schools. This would be achieved by experiencing and analysing battlefield infantry experience to formulate his policy, which would in turn be taught and disseminated at the training schools. His expanded role was to advise GHQ India on all infantry matters and to oversee the general interests of the infantry. His visits showed that there was a lack of instructors at the schools, 'both in quality and quantity', even though training establishments were expanding. One of his proposed solutions was to cut the number of schools or at the very least stop them overlapping. In particular, Savory thought WT training was ineffective and inefficient, with 75% effort wasted. His remedy was a travelling WT training team that would go around the Training Centres and training establishments, all the way up to Army and Corps schools. He recommended periodic WT inspection.

In his travels he continued to pose questions. For instance, at Poona, he asked what the instructors thought of the new Instructors handbook, which received positive feedback. When he visited the OTS in Belgaum, Savory made a few notes as to whether such matters as battle drills were being taught and if there was any instruction and practice on living in the jungle. He noted the use of the new handbook for *Battle Drill for Thick*

224 Moreman, *Jungle*, pp. 100-101.
225 Diary entry for 20 November 1943, NAM, 1976-03-93-52.
226 DMT's Liaison Letter No. 13, 7 October 1943, BL, IOR, L/WS/1/1302.
227 Threlfall, *Jungle Warriors*, p. 178. See also Jeffreys, *Approach to Battle*, p. 207.
228 Director of Infantry notebook, NAM, 1976-03-93-67.

*Jungle* and that surviving in the jungle was taught. These questions even extended to more social aspects as to whether Britsh and Indian cadets mixed, which they did. It was at OTS Belgaum that he picked up that the OTS were rarely visited by senior officers. He concluded that this needed to be remedied across the OTS and the IMA. As a result, the schools were included on the General Auchinleck's tours as Commancer-in-Chief India. Savory thought that at the OTS adherence to the syllabus was too strict and that periods allotted per subject were too rigid, with an upper and lower limit per subject to be applied by the Commandant according to the state of the efficiency of each class. Therefore, he endorsed a much more flexible approach.

Savory toured Assam and Shillong in August and kept in continual contact with the front-line commanders, such as Generals Slim, Cowan, Messervy, Briggs and Roberts.[229] Although he was not impressed by all formations, 48th Indian Infantry Brigade had a good reputation during the retreat from Burma and the original commanding officer Brigadier Ronnie Cameron was responsible for an important report on the lessons learnt in 17th Indian Division.[230] Indeed, Cameron became the Commandant of the Infantry School at Saugor in 1944. However, Savory was unimpressed when he talked to the infantry commanding officers in the brigade, commenting that they were 'a very unresponsive, dumb, lot!!'[231]

Savory continued to work very closely with the DMT and planned a tour with him for September, which included the OTS, 33 Corps and the North West Frontier. After they attended the Training Centre Conference, 24-28 August, they spent a day writing up pamphlets on patrolling and ambushing.[232] They coordinated tours for the next six months and wrote up training plans. One issue that was high on Savory's discussion agenda with the DMT was that the OTS and infantry schools were not producing well enough trained officers. In Savory's mind, the OTS should concentrate more on turning out trained platoon commanders, who can instruct their platoon in weapons, tactics, drill, physical training (PT) and set an example for their men with strict discipline. He also stressed that officers needed administrative skills in the field as well as in barracks and, lastly, they needed to be able to speak Urdu. He concluded that if officers commissioned from the OTS were trained as platoon commanders there would be less need for the Platoon Commanders course at Saugor.

It seemed that nothing was sacrosanct to Savory as he considered closing the Jungle Warfare Training Centre at Raiwala Bara. It was established in December 1942 by Major Angus Rose. Rose, along with a couple of Argyll and Sutherland officers – Ian Stewart, David Wilson and Company Sergeant Major Bing – who were evacuated from

229 See for example diary entries for 9, 29 July, 9, 24 August, 9, 10, 12, 13, 24 Sept 1943, NAM 1976-03-93-52. See also Director of Infantry notebook, September 1943-May 1944 with notes written up after a talk with Slim in September 1943, NAM, 1976-03-93-67.

230 Major General D.T. Cowan, 'Report on the Lessons of the Burma Campaign', 18 June 1942, TNA, WO 203/5716. See also Moreman, pp. 54-55.

231 Diary entry for 11 August 1943, NAM, 1976-03-93-52.

232 Diary entry for 30 August 1943, NAM, 1976-03-93-52.

Singapore to teach jungle warfare in India.[233] The Centre's role was to train reinforcements for Eastern Army but had never really functioned properly in its assigned role. Following the establishment of the Training Divisions, it was now tasked with training complete units or cadres in jungle warfare skills.[234] However, as Tim Moreman has pointed out, by 1944, the Jungle Warfare Training Centre played 'an increasingly important role…in preparing battalions destined for Burma', before relocating to Gudalur in August 1944.[235] Similarly, Savory contemplated the closure of Kitchener College, Nowgong, which had developed into an Inter-Service Pre-Cadet College.[236] Savory was unimpressed by the British NCOs at the Jungle Warfare School at Sevoke. Furthermore, he noted that after an all-day march the majority of officers 'fell short through lack of guts'.[237] He was concerned whether it was up to the same standard as its sister Jungle Warfare School at Shimoga. Ultimately, his concerns proved correct as, during 1944, the Jungle Warfare School at Shimoga trained most of the officers and NCOs in jungle warfare techniques, whereas the one at Sevoke closed in March 1944.[238]

By November 1943, a major initiative for the new directorate was battle discipline, which Savory considered paramount stating that 'All other discipline is the means towards this end'.[239] He considered punishments for breaches of battle discipline, such as bad fire-discipline, losing arms and equipment, shouting, smoking, or putting on lights during night operations, and bad hygiene. His considered methods of instilling battle discipline was accounting for the return of ammunition expenditure and courts of inquiry after each operation.

The two training divisions were operational towards the end of the year. Savory visited 39th Indian Division at Saharanpur in December.[240] He noted that more instructors were needed for the battle course and that there was a shortage of 2-inch mortars (which was not the case in 14th Indian Division), which he intended to bring up with the DMT. In turn, he visited 106th and 115th Indian Infantry Brigades, within the division, and observed that 106th Brigade had one machete per every three men whereas one in two

233 Jeffreys, *Appraoch to Battle*, pp. 145-146; Angus Rose, *Who Dies Fighting* (London: Jonathan Cape, 1944), pp. 144-145 and David Wilson, *Sum of Things* (Staplehurst: Spellmount, 2001), p. 80.

234 Field Marshal Sir Claude Auchinleck, 'Operations in the Indo-Burma Theatre based on India from 21 June to 15 November 1943, *Second Supplement to the London Gazette*, 27 April 1948, pp. 27-28; DMT India's Liaison Letters, BL, IOR, L/WS/1/1302 and Moreman, *Jungle*, p. 60.

235 Moreman, *Jungle*, p. 164.

236 Jeffreys, *Approach to* Battle, pp. 199-200 and Vipul Dutta, *Making Officers out of Gentlemen: Military Institution-Building in India, c. 1900-1960* (New Delhi: Oxford University Press, 2021), pp. 131-133.

237 Diary entry for 7 September 1943, NAM, 1976-03-93-52.

238 Moreman, *Jungle*, p. 164.

239 Director of Infantry notebook, NAM, 1976-03-93-67.

240 Diary entries for 19-21 December 1943, NAM, 1976-03-93-52. See also letter to his wife, 18 December 1943, NAM, 1976-03-93-63.

was required, and put that as an action point that he would deal with. For both brigades, he noted down Major Jim Corbett's name and address as an action point for the DMT. Jim Corbett became a noted conservationist but had previously been an expert on tracking down tigers in the jungle. It was thought that valuable lessons of jungle lore could be learnt and applied to operations agains the Japanese. His book *Man-Eaters of Kumaon* was recommended reading in the other training division.[241] Similarly, Savory visited 14th Indian Division twice in early 1944.[242] In addition, Savory made a thorough trawl of all the available jungle warfare doctrine such *The Jungle Book*, the 4th edition of Military Training Pamphlet (India) No. 9, which encapsulated the jungle warfare doctrine learnt in the previous three editions from the campaigns in Malaya and Burma.[243] Especially from the First Arakan campaign when the British and Indian troops came across the Japanese bunkers for the first time.[244] For instance, the training manual described the tactics needed for bunker-busting. It also popularised training pamphlets led by a professional production team employed by the Directorate of Military Training. As a result, it was more readable, with cartoons and photographs included, for the first time, to make it more appealing to the officers and soldiers. Indeed, the pamphlet was the basis of jungle fighting methods for the remainder of the Second World War and was the blueprint for two War Office manuals produced in 1944-1945 (Military Training Pamphlet No. 51, *Preparation for Warfare in the Far East*, June 1945, 2nd edition, and Military Training Pamphlet No. 52 *Warfare in the Far East,* December 1944) demonstrating that it was the Indian Army rather than the British Army who pioneered Jungle warfare doctrine. This doctrine was not just a top down process as it was added to and updated in the *Army in India Training Memorandum,* which was issued monthly and based on battle experience, particularly the divisional, brigade and even battalion training instructions that were produced to learn the lessons from operations. By 1943, this was in process across all Indian Army divisions, whether they were fighting in South East Asia or in western theatres such as the Middle East and the Italian campaign.[245]

As a result of Savory's hard work and lobbying, his staff grew. He wrote to his wife in October 1943: 'My responsibilities continue to increase and the work with it. I have had to be given a bigger staff: but I keep all paper-work down to the absolute minimum, as you may imagine. I *wish* I could get away for a bit, but I just cannot. I take Sunday off now and then but that is all.'[246] Savory noted in his diary that he had a 'long talk'

241 Report 14th Indian Division July 1943-Nov 1945, pp. 16-17, Private papers of Major General A.C. Curtis, IWM, P140.
242 Letters to his wife, 4 Jan, 17 Feb, 5 March 1944, NAM, 1976-03-93-63 and Director Infantry notebook, NAM, 1976-03-93-67. See also Jeffreys, *Approach to Battle*, pp. 163-166.
243 *Military Training Pamphlet No. 9 (India) The Jungle Book*, 4th edition (September 1943), BL, IOR/L/MIL/17/5/2250.
244 Tim Moreman, 'Debunking the Bunker': From Donbaik to Razabil, January 1943-Match 1944' in Jeffreys and Rose (eds.), *The Indian Army, 1939-47*, pp. 109-136.
245 Note on the *Jungle Book* followed by one on 25 Division Training Instruction in Director of Infantry notebook, NAM, 1976-03-93-67. See also Jeffreys, *Approach to Battle*, p. 210.
246 Letter to his wife, 24 October 1943, NAM, 1976-03-93-63.

with the DMT on 23 October and was taking 'over all infantry training!!'[247] The expansion included the appointment of a Deputy Director of Infantry, Brigadier Gane, who was responsible for infantry weapons, equipment and liaison letters. By 1944, he had four staff officers in his Directorate who also undertook tours, particularly to see which battalions were operationally fit. Brigadier Ian Stewart had played an important role in the development of jungle warfare doctrine and training in the Australian, British and Indian armies since his evacuation from Singapore in 1942. He visited Savory on 24 December with a 'plan for D[irector] of Inf[antry] to become a super D.M.T!!'[248] Not long later Savory wrote to his wife: 'My appointment is a new one and I have had to make it what it is. It is the kind of pioneering work that suits me…'[249] Not only was it pioneering but also hard work, with constant touring. A few days later he wrote: 'I get to my office at 9am and return home at 7.30pm and even then am never finished. However it is an interesting day and I never tire of it…'[250]

At a tactical level, Savory recommended that all automatic weapons be outlawed, revolvers abandoned and train soldiers of the importance of one man one round which would result in cutting down ammunition supplies. Economy of fire became very apparent in all the training literature. With regards to artillery, he recommended that it should be kept well back as the Japanese used very little artillery themselves. In its place, 3-inch mortars and grenades were to be carried. Savory described jungle as the country 'par excellence' for unseen offensives. Therefore, he recommended that carriers should not be used as they indicated actions. Both the cutting down of ammunition supplies and petrol simplified maintenance which would mean relying more on aerial dropped rations and dehydrated food carried by individual soldiers, sustained with the slaughter of animals and fish, thus cutting maintenance to a minimum. He argued the first objective of operations must be an airfield, achieved in combination with airborne troops and with guerrilla forces available to intercept reinforcements behind enemy lines. Savory realised this was only possible with complete air superiority, which was the case by November 1943.

In 1944, Savory continued to visit the front-line. During the Imphal campaign he consulted with Bill Slim at Comilla, Geoffrey Scoones at Imphal, as well as the divisional commanders of 5th, 17th and 23rd Indian Divisions.[251] For example, he noted in his notebook a discussion with Slim about the 8th Battalion, York and Lancester Regiment and the 1st Battalion, Wiltshire Regiment (Duke of Edinburgh's) needing to

247 Diary entry for 23 October 1943, NAM, 1976-03-93-52.
248 Diary entry for 24 December, NAM, 1976-03-93-52.
249 Letter to his wife, 1 February 1944, NAM, 1976-03-93-63.
250 Letter to his wife, 4 February 1944, NAM, 1976-03-93-63.
251 Savory remarked in his diary after visiting 17th Indian Division '(Punch in good form). Dinner 4 Corps (talked to Scoones till midnight. Punch's HQ attacked soon after my departure.' 20 May 1944, NAM, 1976-03-93-64. See also letter to his wife, 26 March 1944, NAM, 1976-03-93-63.

be relieved.[252] Slim was prepared to accept an Indian battalion in place of one and the 2nd Battalion, Green Howards (Alexandra Princess of Wales's Own Yorkshire Regiment) for the other.[253] Similarly, the 4th Battalion, 3rd Madras Regiment was 'not good' and needed replacing, with the suggestion that 2nd Battalion, Assam Regiment could be sent up to the front as they would be 'invaluable'. Savory also noted the 1st Battalion, Sikh Light Infantry had 'not only done well but bucked up other Sikhs in the Army'.[254] Along with Colonel Gradige, who was responsible for reorganising the reinforcement camps, they inspected the reinforcement camp at Comilla and 27th Reinforcement camp at Chittagong, which Savory labelled as efficient in his diary.[255] Gradige transformed these Reinforcement camps, which had originally been established in April 1943, along the lines of the camps in the Middle East and were designed to hold and continue training for 3000 troops. The instructors were from India, often with little operational experience. The ratios of instructors to soldiers were very low, with little direction for training, all resulting in poor morale and cases of ill-discipline. After August 1943, each camp was allocated to a particular division with the reinforcements adopting the divisional formation badge, which helped the soldiers feel that they were already part of the division and improved morale. Furthermore, realistic training was undertaken and discipline restored.[256] After this visit to Northeast India, Savory wrote to his wife: 'The Indian soldier has come right into his own again and is magnificent'.[257]

Savory kept up with his contemporaries both in the British and the Indian armies. For instance, he discussed the new infantry organization with Major General Thomas 'Pete' Rees, CO 19th Indian Division, on 1 July 1944. Over the summer he continued to consult with the DMT and revisit the front-line meeting infantry units that had fought at Kohima, as well as inspect training establishments and met up with Slim regularly.[258] In January 1945, Savory visited various regiments and the Infantry Training Centre in the UK, as well as meeting General Robert Adam and Major General Douglas Wimberley, Adjutant General and Director of Infantry at the War Office respectively.[259] Indeed, the following month, Wimberley visited India.[260] Then, in March 1945, Savory was visiting

252 The York and Lancasters were replaced by 2nd Battalion, Punjab Regiment from September 1944 in 51st Indian Infantry Brigade.
253 The Green Howards replaced the Wiltshires in 4th Indian Infantry Brigade from September 1944, having spent four months in 116th Indian Infantry Brigade training in jungle warfare in 39th Indian Division.
254 Director of Infantry notebook, NAM, 1976-03-93-67. Savory became Colonel of the Sikh Light Infantry regiment in 1946.
255 Diary entries for 17,22-23 May 1944, NAM, 1976-03-93-64.
256 Brigadier J.H. Gradige, 'How the Fourteenth Army was Reinforced', *Journal of the United Service Institution of India*. Vol. XXV, No. 321, October 1945.
257 Letter to his wife, 28 May 1944, NAM, 1976-03-93-63.
258 20 June, 18, 24, 29, 31 July, 1, 4, 24-25 August, 2 September entries for 1944 Diary, NAM, 1976-03-93-64.
259 Diary entries for 2, 18 Jan, 5 February 1945, NAM, 1976-03-93-85.
260 Infantry Liasion Letter No. 16, 29 March 1945, BL, IOR/L/WS/1/778.

the front-line again, and on the way he stayed with General Oliver Leese, Commander of Land Forces at South East Asia Command and later dined with Lieutenant General Philip Christison.[261] Both of whom he had met when he attended the Staff College at Camberley. He wrote to his wife: 'I find it very interesting knowing all the high commanders of this war, many of whom were contemporaries of mine at the Staff College or my instructors'.[262] This clearly demonstrates the importance of the connections made at Staff College.[263] The tours of infantry units and training establishments continued throughout 1945 and he liaised with senior officers such as Slim, Arthur Holworthy, Geoffry Scoones, Geoff Evans, Ouvry Roberts, Joe Lentaigne, Cyril Lomax, Philip Christison and George Wood.[264] However, Savory was not only highly thought of by his fellow senior officers and peers. Captain Dan Munro, who had served as his GSO3 and then later served with Slim, wrote to him in March 1945 that '...there were Generals and Generals, but nobody quite in your class. Still, if I have to be with anyone else, I would rather be with General Slim. He is a great man and one of the nicest in the world. He's so terribly kind to all those below him and rude only to those fairly high up!'[265]

## Infantry Reorganisation

After the disastrous retreat from Burma and the Fall of Singapore in 1942, it was clear that Indian formations were over-mechanised. As a result, 17th and 39th Indian Divisions were converted into light divisions, which comprised six infantry battalions in two brigades, with six mule companies and four Jeep companies each, in order to operate away from roads. Weapons were to be carried by the battalions, except the 3-inch mortars, which meant that more mules were used to carry ammunition. [266] The number of vehicles was reduced in a number of other divisions which were renamed Animal and Mechanised Transport (A & MT) divisions.[267] In 1943, rather than follow British Army infantry organisation, it was decided that Indian Army battalions would follow a six company organisation, comprising four strengthened rifle companies, with the headquarters (HQ) company divided into two – one concerned with fighting and the other with administration. In addition, the number of carriers was reduced but the strength of the battalion was increased to 866 (830 in 1941). Units carried sufficient supplies to

261 7-8 March 1945 Diary, NAM, 1976-03-93-85.
262 Letter to his wife, 4 March 1945, NAM, 1976-03-93-63.
263 See Frost, 'The British and Indian Army Staff College in the Interwar Years'.
264 Diary entries for 7, 11, 17 March, 8-9, 28, 29 May, throughout June & 21, 24, 25 July, NAM, 1976-03-93-63. See also Director of Infantry notebook, NAM, 1976-03-93-67.
265 Letter from Captain Dan Munro, Cameron Highlanders, to Savory, 28 March 1945, NAM, 1976-03-93-63.
266 See Marston, *Phoenix from the Ashes*, p. 86.
267 Army in India Organisation of Animal Transport and Mechanised Transport Divisions, BL, IOR/L/WS/1/1333.

fight, in line with Savory's ideas, with further supplies brought forward when needed. However, it soon became apparent that the light divisions had insufficient strength in numbers due to only two brigades in each division. These were increased by one platoon per rifle company – amounting to 993 all ranks. With the exception of the two light divisions, all Indian and British battalions were put on A & MT or MT organisation.

Then in 1944 after a conference at GHQ in Delhi on 26-27 May, during the Battle of Imphal, the differing divisions were standardised across the theatre. Similarly, along Savory's lines, carriers that had little tactical use were replaced by one man per section, adding one rifle platoon to the HQ company and reducing the transport to 41 mules and 12 jeeps and trailers. Other changes included the 3-inch mortar becoming the main infantry supporting weapon, in place of carrier borne Light Machine Guns and 3.7-inch howitzers. These changes simplified the overall infantry organisation, and the standardised division replaced the previous differing divisional organisations.[268] Savory highlighted the various infantry changes in the Infantry Liaision Letters and in a radio broadcast.[269] His notes for the broadcast gave the historical precedent of Malaya and Burma, where there was a heavy reliance on vehicles to an embarrassing level. The ideal was the minimum amount of transport with a standardisation across infantry battalions that meant they could adapt to all roles rather than having infantry battalions that could only be used for specialist roles. He concluded 'Bayonets take precedence', remarking that 'it must be remembered that the real infantry consists of the Riflemen who must have precedence both in quality and in quantity and that once their ranks have been filled to the numbers required the residue many be allotted for the so-called specialists' duties'.[270]

Previously in practice, a rifle section consisted of recently joined men from the training centres or those who were not capable of becoming specialists. Savory wrote: 'It is not an over-exaggeration to say that the tendency of our Infantry organization is to put our best men behind our worst men in the front…'[271] He concluded that the infantry had reached saturation point with regards to specialists, using an example from a questionnaire reply from the 5th Battalion, East Yorkshire Regiment on introducing the 95mm gun into the infantry: 'The Infantry B[attalio]n is already overloaded with supporting arms often causing an exaggerated emphasis to be placed on their training and selection of personnel at the expense of Rifle Coys which are of course the most important part of the battalion'.[272]

268 See 'Developments in Infantry Organisation 1939-44', Savory Papers, NAM, 1976-03-93-69.
269 Infantry Liasion Letters, BL, IOR/L/WS/1/778 and Broadcast: change in Infantry Organisation, NAM, 1976-03-93-69. For a useful overview of divisional organisation in the British Army during the Second World War see Paul Latawski, 'The British Corps and Division in the Twentieth Century: Historical Evolution and Doctrinal Context' in *Orchestrating Warfighting: A History of the British Army's Corps and Divisions at War since 1914* (London: Routledge, 2025), pp. 55-72.
270 Broadcast, NAM, 1976-03-93-69.
271 Savory, 'Infantry Organization, 5 February 1944, NAM, 1976-03-93-69.
272 Ibid.

In addition to reorganisation, Savory wanted to increase the prestige of infantry generally. He wrote up a paper in August 1944, which he sent to Lieutenant General Rob Lockhart, who was Vice Chief of the General Staff at the time. Savory emphatically outlined the importance of infantry. He wrote:

> In effect, the "Army' means infantry. It is not an exaggeration to say that the complete military machine (Signals, Supplies and Transport, Ordnance, Engineers, Artillery, Tanks and the Tactical Air Force) exists in order that it may assist the Infantry to fight its battles.
>
> And yet in the eyes of the public the prestige of the infantry compared with that of the supporting arms is low. Why?[273]

He went on to answer the question by mentioning that this had always been the case historically but one of the reasons in the current war was due to the 'photogenic' nature of other arms of service that helped shape public opinion. However, in numerical terms, the infantry had suffered the highest casualties in the First World War, compared to other arms which would be repeated in the current war and likely to influence opinion. Furthermore, the infantry was paid less than the other arms. Savory proposed a Corps of Infantry as 'our Infantry has never been able to speak with one voice. Its intense regimental spirit has militated against a strictly literal "esprit de corps". It has been a house divided to some extent against itself'.[274] He considered the infantry should have precedence in the army, with distinct uniform accoutrements and badges. More importantly, pay should be on an equal basis across the army, as in the Australian and American armies. He suggested that extra pay in wartime should be given to those in operational areas, with the infantry drawing double that of any other arm. This was in direct contrast to the current system, whereby specialists in the infantry and other arms were paid more than front-line infantry soldiers. In his covering letter to Lockhart, Savory qualified his remarks on a Corps of Infantry by noting that he wanted the infantry to have one voice with a permanent Colonel Commandant rather than a Director of Infantry that could be dismissed in economic downturns.[275] Although Savory's thoughts did not fully materialise, the pay and conditions of both Indian officers and soldiers improved under the stewardship of the C-in-C India, General Sir Claude Auchinleck.

273 Savory, 'The Prestige of Infantry', 23 August 1944, NAM, 1976-03-93-69.
274 Ibid.
275 Letter from Savory to Lieutenant General Rob Lockhart, 25 August 1944, NAM, 1976-03-93-69.

## Infantry Liaison Letters

The first Infantry Liaison letter was issued in December 1943, once Savory had been in post for six months but, more importantly, when he had the staff to facilitate the letters. They were distributed to all the Commands, the Staff College, infantry training centres at Poona and Saugor, the three Jungle Warfare schools, the IMA and the three OTS, the schools at Kakul and the various directorates at GHQ India, such as the Military Training Directorate. They were also sent further afield to the War Office in the UK, as well as equivalent military institutions in Australia and the US. There was a three-fold purpose to provide the infantry with short accounts of recent operations so that lessons could be learnt, to keep the infantry up to date with current developments in organisation, weapons and equipment, and to discuss all matters relating to the infantry. The plan was to issue the letters monthly down to brigade level with the intention they would be disseminated further down the chain of command.

Savory reiterated in the liaison letters that they were not training memoranda or an authority to demand more weapons or equipment, but at the same time requested feedback to improve the letters, as well as questions on the various topics within the scope of the Infantry Directorate. The letters were divided into five main sections with appendices: operations, organisation, weapons, equipment and miscellaneous. All the sections included lessons from further afield, such as the Australian experience in New Guinea. For instance, the liaison letter stated that 'automatic fire has become practically taboo' in the theatre: a subject that Savory had been reiterating ever since his experience in Eritrea. The weapons section discussed the requirement for infantry support in the jungle with mortar firepower. As a result, a strengthened base plate was produced for the 3-inch mortar, which increased the range from 1600 to 2570 yards. Similarly the 2-inch mortar was fixed with a 'bowed' plate reducing the weight to 11lbs but with the accuracy and range unaffected.[276] By March 1944, the strengthened base plates had been issued to all units in the Fourteenth Army.[277] In his tours, Savory had noted that five majors in an infantry battalion were now needed and this was promulgated in the first liaison letter, noting it was largely due to the heavy responsibility of rifle company commands as well as increasing the promotion prospects of infantry officers in line with other arms. Lastly, the liaison letter emphasised the importance of infantry and keeping experienced infantry soldiers as infantry, as the bulk of requests for extra regimental employment as batmen, provost, clerks and so on traditionally fell on the infantry, such requests would now be more evenly distributed throughout all arms.[278]

The second Infantry Liaison Letter came out on 1 January 1944. The distribution list was extended to include all Regimental Training Centres and training battalions. It

276 Infantry Liasion Letter No. 1, December 1943, Bl, IOR/L/WS/1/778.
277 Infantry Liaision Letter No. 5, 21 March 1944, BL, IOR/L/WS/1/778.
278 Infantry Liaision Letter No. 1, December 1943, BL, IOR/L/WS/1/778. See also Roy, *Sepoys against the Rising Sun*, pp. 228-229, 235-236, 239

included operational experience from campaigns in North Africa, Italy, Sicily, and 21st Army Group in Northwest Europe. The main lesson from North Africa was that 'the teaching of battle-drills is undoubtedly to be of the greatest value in instilling dash and determination'. However, the letter concluded:

> Battle Drill must be our servant, not our master. Their greatest value is to train troops to re-act offensively when surprised or when coming suddenly into contact with the enemy. Apart from this, Battle Drill are Basic Tactics capable of modification and development.[279]

The letter noted that all relevant training points in the letter would be added to the *Army in India Training Memoranda* in due course, as the 'object of these letters is to get the stuff to the troops quickly'.[280] The fourth liaison letter, which came out the following month, with the Training Divisions included on the distribution list, stated that operational detail would not be included in future letters as the *Battle Bulletins* were now publishing accounts of recent operations.[281] However, subsequent letters continued to include the operations section. In Savory's notebook whilst Director of Infantry, he made a note to publicise the role of 8/16th and 15/8th Punjab Regiments which was accomplished in the fourth letter, stating that these were training centres for Viceroy's Commissioned Officers (VCOs) with the 15/8th Punjab Regiment based at Jhansi and the 8/16th Punjab Regiment at Fyzabad. These were, in effect, the OTS for VCOs and the first time specific training was put in place for infantry VCOs.[282]

By April 1944, when Infantry Liaision Letter No. 6 was produced, it was widely agreed that there were now too many training pamphlets.[283] Scott Gilmore, an American officer who served in the 4/8th Gurkha Rifles, remarked in his memoir: 'We read the manuals, which by now were thick on the table packed with advice from two years of campaigning in Burma and the Pacific'.[284] The War Office had produced *Infantry Training 1944*, with Part VIII on Fieldcraft and Battle Drill replacing *The Instructor's Handbook on Fieldcraft and Battle Drill.* Similarly the Indian pamphlet *Infantry Section Leading 1941* Military Training Pamphlet (India) No. 14 was now obsolete. As a result,

279 Infantry Liaison Letter, No. 2, 1 January 1944, BL, IOR/L/WS/1/778.

280 Ibid.

281 *Battle Bulletin* No. 1, January 1944, BL, IOR/L/MIL/17/5/2241.

282 Infantry Liaision Letters Nos. 4 & 10, 17 Febuary, 9 September 1944, Bl, IOR/L/WS/1/778 and Director of Infantry notebook, NAM, 1976-03-93-67. Royal Indian Army Service Corps VCOs were trained at the School of Supply at Bareilly which was the first training school entirely for VCOs in the history of the Indian Army, see Jeffreys, *Approach to Battle*, p. 205. Previous attempts in organising training for VCOs included the Roorkee Training School where a small number of VCOs and NCOs were taught military surveying in the 1880s, see Dutta, *Making Officers*, p. 39.

283 Infantry Liaison Letter No. 6, 25 April 1944, BL, IOR/L/WS/1/778.

284 Scott Gilmore, *A Connecticut Yankee in the 8th Gurkha Rifles* (Washington: Brassey's, 1995), p. 173.

*Infantry Training 1944* was the doctrine of general approach for all infantry in the British and Indian Armies along with the special application of *The Jungle Book* and *Battle Drill for Thick Jungle*. The letter stated that a common doctrine was essential and should be taught at all training establishments. Nevertheless, the need for the continual updating of doctrine was stressed:

> It must be remembered that the tactical doctrine training of infantry will alter as the result of experience in battle. As time goes on some sections of Infantry Training Pamphlets will become out of date and Infantry Training Memoranda will therefore have to be published from time to time to give the latest developments in teaching and to keep various parts up-to-date. These Memoranda will include not only the latest developments as the result of experience in battle but alo special points dealing with the practical application of Infantry Training to any special theatre of war.[285]

Infantry Liaison Letter No. 6 reiterated that battle drill 'must be our servant and NOT our master', defining battle drill as ensuring 'a uniform standard of battle procedures throughout the Army. When every officer, NCO and man is taught the same procedure, the fullest co-operation is assured even when casualties occur and changes have to made'.[286] This letter had the widest dissemination to date, as they now went to all infantry battalions, Indian State Forces and Nepalese battalions, and reprints of the first five letters were produced for those who had not already received them.

Unsurprisingly, Savory's thoughts on infantry training and organisation made their way into the letters, with his paper on infantry organisation reprinted in an appendix in Infantry Liaison Letter No. 9.[287] Something that he was also keen on was the paramount importance of the rifle companies within infantry battalions. Infantry Liaison Letter No. 7 considered the tendency for some battalion COs to choose the best men for their HQ and administrative companies at the expense of the rifle companies, which was described as unsound. He was also keen to prevent infantry from doing more than its fair share of extra regimental duty. For instance, on the North West Frontier, infantry battalions complained of the 'milking' of their battalions to provide personnel for Provost units.[288]

Operational lessons and extracts continued in the letters from the campaigns in Italy, North West Europe, India, South East Asia and the US and Australian armies in the South West Pacific Area. Updates on weapons and equipment continued. For example, the 2-inch mortar was found to be of limited use as a platoon weapon in recent operations. Thus, it became a company weapon used primarily for smoke production. There were twelve per battalion and all future issues of the 2-inch mortar would have a spade

285 Infantry Liaision Letter No. 6, 25 April 1944, BL, IOR/L/WS/1/778.
286 Ibid.
287 Infantry Liasion Letter No. 9, 4 August 1944, BL, IOR/L/WS/1/778.
288 Infantry Liasion Letter No. 7, 29 May 1944, BL, IOR/L/WS/1/778.

baseplate fixed.[289] There was also clarification on the Jungle Warfare school at Shimoga which trained instructors, who then returned to their units to pass on what they had learnt, whilst the Jungle Warfare Centre at Gudalur trained complete units or sub-units. One of the problems at all the training centres was that, due to the shortage of available officers, instructors tended to stay too long at training establishments. Indeed, battalion COs were not keen to part with their experienced officers. Thus, a new scheme was established that appointments up to the rank of major would not serve longer than 9-12 months, Lieutenant Colonels and above not longer than 12-18 months, and Commandants of Regimental Centres and training units not longer than 24 months, with extensions only in special circumstances. Similarly, to increase the prospects of promotion, the rank of company commanders at the Training Divsions were all to be at the rank of major.[290] For instance, Brigadier Jonah Jones and Brigadier W. B. Thomas, both of whom had served in the retreat from Burma in 1942, had been commandants of the IMA and the Tactical Training Centre, Clement Town, Dehra Dun since 1942 and 1943 respectively.[291]

To enable acclimatisation for the war in Burma, one new initiative was to attach COs of battalions that were proceeding to Fourteenth Army for a three week attachment to a formation in theatre prior to the battalion movement to Burma.[292] In 1945, Allied Land Forces South East Asia Command (ALFSEA) appointed their own Brigadier Infantry, Brigadier Cyril Barclay, who worked with Savory and were planning to issue their own liaision letters.[293] Despite the war being practically over and that Indian soldiers were now fighting in the open plains of Burma, rather than the close confines of jungle warfare. At the same time, an announcement in the liaison letters stated 'Although the campaign in Burma is practically over and we will be fighting in a different type of country', ALFSEA wanted jungle warfare training to continue as 'the jungle calls for the highest standard of training'.[294]

## Man Management and other writings

A huge number of training pamphlets were produced or reprinted by GHQ India, but it is very rare to know who actually penned them. One exception was a lecture on man management that Savory had originally given at the Staff College at Quetta and then was issued in pamphlet form in June 1944 and distributed with two copies per company

289 Infantry Liasion Letters Nos. 9 & 15, 4 August 1944, 25 February 1945, BL, IOR/L/WS/1/778.
290 Infantry Liaision Letter No. 16, 29 March 1945, BL, IOR/L/WS/1/778.
291 *Indian Army List*, October 1944.
292 Infantry Liaision Letter No. 17, 28 April 1945, BL, IOR/L/WS/1/778.
293 Barclay wrote a number of regimental and wartime histories after the Second World War.
294 Infantry Liaision Letter No. 19, June 1945, BL, IOR/L/WS/1/778.

to all arms.[295] It was the culmination of his time as Director of Infantry and his career to date. The pamphlet drew upon his extensive battlefield experience during the First World War, the North West Frontier and different theatres during the Second World War. He defined man management in military terms as making men physically fit for, and in, battle and then to restore them mentally and physically afterwards. On the first page, he emphasised the importance of training: 'First of all comes training. A well-trained man knows that he is a better man than the enemy and makes him mentally fit for battle. This the greatest of all the commandments…'[296] He then went on to stress the importance of fighting against boredom, good relations between officers and men, discipline, leave, comfort, saluting, turn-out, mail, pay and physical aspects of keeping men fit for battle. Savory continued that the standard of discipline should be twice as strict for officers as those for soldiers and he reiterated his high standards of saluting and turn-out that he had previously taught at the IMA in 1932. He wrote 'My own idea about saluting is not that it is an action by a subordinate to his senior but that it is a greeting between two brother officers'.[297] He continued that not to salute due to the lack of noticing was still unacceptable, as '…one of the biggest things we are teaching our troops now in jungle warfare is constant alertness, constant observation and constant readiness…'[298] He concluded the section, 'I regard good turn out as the outward and visible sign of an inward and spiritual soldier'.[299] He empahsised that this was particularly important in the jungle where standards can drop, but countered this in jungle warfare with the slogan "From Ratcatcher to Guardsman", indicating that both the enemy and the army can look like ratcatchers in the jungle but, once out for rest and recuperation, should be dressed like a Guardsman. Thus, it followed that good relations between officers and soldiers were equally essential, commenting:

> If you mix with your men and really felt to know then you will notice one day when they salute you that they smile at the same time although they do it unconsciously. Once you have got that, you know that you have got the confidence of your men which is something worth working for. I often wonder if we British Officers are not sometimes too aloof from our men, a bit apt to sit apart in our messes and so on. I remember seeing a Chinese General in Imphal after the Chinese troops had withdrawn from Burma, and I might add that they withdrew in extremely good order, and were an example to some of our units. I was interested to to see this General living almost in the middle of his men with just enough cover round him

295 *A Lecture to Infantry Officers on Man Management* (Delhi: Chief of the General Staff (India), 1944), Savory Papers, NAM, 1976-03-93-69. The following paragraphs are drawn from this pamphlet.
296 Ibid. p. 1.
297 Ibid. p. 5.
298 Ibid.
299 Ibid., p. 6

> for privacy, and he appeared to me to have the confidence of his men to a very marked degree.[300]

The general was General Sun Li-Jen who commanded the Chinese 38th Division.

The next section was on how to keep men fit in battle as it 'is the most exhausting ordeal, both physically and mentally, that a man can be called upon to undergo'.[301] Thus, it was essential to keep troops fresh before going into battle as well as before patrolling. One essential was the need for fresh food and hot tea before action. Savory gave the unorthodox example in the pursuit of the Italian forces in East Africa, when the commander only had sufficient transport for three companies and instead sent the cooks ahead so that when the troops arrived after the long march they were greeted by a meal awaiting them. Battle discipline was another area that Savory continually mentioned in his notebooks as Director of Infantry but also in his earlier Second World War career, particularly in Assam in 1942-1943, remarking here that it 'is a difficult thing to define except to say that discipline in battle is the be-all and end-all of all discipline.'[302] He mentioned fire discipline and courts of enquiry for the loss of arms and equipment. Another lesson learnt in Assam in making men fit for battle was anti-malarial discipline. He concluded the section that 'Commanders must always realise that their presence during action in the forward areas is inspiring'.[303] This was very much done by divisional commanders in the Burma campaign, such as Major General Francis 'Frontline Frankie' Festing who commanded 36th Division and Major General Thomas 'Pete' Rees, CO of 19th Indian Division, amongst other division and brigade COs who led their formations from the front.

The section on restoring men after battle is much shorter, recommending a period of recovery followed by putting soldiers in the bigger picture of what they have been involved in. Then the preparation starts all over again for the next phase of battle. Sections from the pamphlet also appeared in Infantry Liaison Letter No. 9.[304]

Savory asked Ian Stewart for his opinion on the pamphlet, which was very positive, remarking 'It is really admirable, and I got quite excited when I found all my pet points coming out!' Although Stewart continued:

> But admirable as your pamphlet is it will not achieve much unless it is given verbally and personally. I would strongly urge that you give that lecture to the Tac[tical] Tr[ainin]g Centre every course – in fact I am impertinent enough to say that it is your job!...For I hold (contrary to most senior though not junior officers) that the task of that place is not only to teach but to inspire. It can be done – it was done at

300 Ibid., p. 3.
301 Ibid. p. 8.
302 Ibid. p. 14.
303 Ibid. p. 16.
304 Infantry Liaision Letter No. 19, June 1945, BL, IOR/L/WS/1/778.

> the School of Inf[antry] at Home…The place (Clement Town) itself could be better equipped in "atmosphere" – climate, countryside, battle realism.

As always, Stewart was strident in his views, going as far as to suggest that the Viceroy should visit the School just as the Prime Minister had spoken on 'leadership and service' at the School of Infantry in the UK.[305] Savory did give the lecture to the Staff College at Quetta and elsewhere, such as the 6th Gurkha Rifles Regimental Training Centre on 5 June 1944.[306] Indeed, as the pamphlet was distributed down to company level, it had much wider coverage than some of the Infantry Liaision Letters for example.

Savory wrote up his thoughts on the wider preparation for war and what made a soldier fight. For example, he questioned the practicality of *Field Service Regulations*, which was the common doctrine across all British and Commonwealth armies at the beginning of the Second World War.[307] All officers knew the contents in order to pass the various examinations but he thought, 'They are of such wide application and to some extent vague that I feel they are can be of little use to the ordinary soldier'.[308] Savory was an advocate of battle drill, which meant men were trained so thoroughly that as a result they instinctively took the right decision in battle. He compared jungle warfare with fighting at night, which the Indian Army had trained for prior to the war and in theatres such as North Africa for campaigns in the Western Desert.[309] However, he did differentiate for the element of surprise in the jungle between night and day. At night time, soldiers should sit or lie down and await orders in complete silence whereas during the day soldiers should go straight for the enemy or a tactical feature near the enemy when surprised. Other lessons he hightlighted from recent fighting included that knowledge of the enemy was essential, which had been lacking in the Retreat from Burma. He emphasised the need for rest and food before any action and that soldiers should never abandon their weapons. He instigated that after every action a court of enquiry be held to account for arms and equipment. He concluded that strict discipline should be adhered to, giving the example:

> I have recently seen an example of a Gurkha Jemadar who led his men back here from the Irrawaddy in ten days' march with practically no food, being followed up part of the time by the enemy. Those men when they arrived back were tired but in good order. They had their arms and equipment with them, and their bivouac

305 Letter from Ian Stewart to Savory, 22 July 1944, NAM, 1976-03-93-69.
306 See diary entry for 24 October 1943 where he gave lecture at the Staff College at Quette, '1100-1300 steady going. Quite a success I think! (bit ill prepared)', NAM, 1976-03-93-52 and diary entry for 5 June 1944 when he gave the lecture to the 6th Gurkha Rifles Regimental Training Centre, NAM, 1976-63-93-64.
307 Delaney, *Imperial Army Project*, p. 288.
308 Savory, 'Some basic factors in War', NAM, 1976-03-93-69.
309 Jeffreys, *Approach to Battle*, pp. 49, 96.

> when I saw it soon after their arrival was a model. That can only be done by strict discipline.[310]

Probably helped by one of his other principles which was 'Never Show Fear', writing that 'war is never as dangerous as it sometimes appears to be'.[311]

Morale was an essential factor in war and in the Burma campaign was epitomised by Slim's spiritual, intellectual and material foundations.[312] It is interesting to compare them with Savory's thoughts on 'Morale in Battle'. As a professional Indian Army officer, Savory was very keen on the officers code, which he described as never show fear, always be better turned out than your men and do everything better than your men. One factor that differed from Slim, but was one of Savory's particular obsessions throughout his career, was the smart turn-out of officers. For instance, he was unimpressed by the wearing of suede shoes by officers. One of the ways Savory thought that morale could be improved was by improving the standards of turn-out in the British, Indian and US armies in India.

Much of his thinking was a constant throughout his career, such as fire control, which should be learnt in training as it was vital, but often disintegrated on contact with the enemy due to the excitement of battle. He reiterated that automatic fire with Light Machine Guns should be the exception, stating that the 'single shot Bren is the answer'.[313] Similarly, single shots were to be used by the Bren Gun in an anti-aircraft role and mounted on the hood of a truck on the move. He emphasised cool headedness when he wrote 'Soldiers must be taught to regard a battle in the same light as any other parade. Complete silence is vital, yelling and shouting do no good. Teach COOL HEADEDNESS. It cannot be over emphasised'.[314] He stressed the speedy evacuation of wounded and thought there was a gap in water supply between the water truck and individual water bottles. Indeed, supply from the rear to the front-line and vice versa could be improved. For new troops, Savory recommended gradual acclimatisation to war and kept all soldiers informed about an action and made sure standards were maintained after the battle. He wrote 'It is the will to win and the determination to carry out your task in spite of everything the enemy may do that wins wars'.[315] He finished off the piece with some older points, including that slit trenches should be dug at once, a point also made very clear in Infantry Liaison Lettter No. 1.[316] Other observations included recognition of troops with the use of easily recognisable signs such as white armbands, control of Mechanised Transport and administrative organisation behind the battalion.

310 Savory, 'Some basic factors in War', NAM, 1976-03-93-69.
311 Ibid.
312 Field Marshal Sir William Slim, *Defeat into Victory* (London: Cassell, 1956), pp. 182-190.
313 Savory, 'Morale in Battle', NAM, 1976-03-93-69.
314 Ibid.
315 Ibid.
316 Infantry Liaison Letter No.1, December 1943, BL, IOR/L/WS/1/778.

Savory was not keen on the sending back of undesirable officers to Regimental Training Centres, as well as too much collective training, which meant that the training of soliders suffered, with a lower confidence in their weapons, resulting in lower morale. Savory thought the training of officers was too rushed and suggested shorter tours of longer stays. He recommended meritocracy within the officer corps and the disbandment of units that were consistently failing, concluding that 'we are fighting for our lives *not* for democracy'.

The receipt of mail was one of the big factors in keeping up morale. This was very apparent in Savory's own correspondence with his wife throughout his military career. Even though there are few examples of his wife's letters, he is very candid and affectionate in his correspondence. There is little new in Savory's writing on man management, war and morale but rather a culmination of all his operational, training and command experience. However, he always made all the principles and examples relevant to the war in Burma and jungle warfare generally.

## PAIFORCE

Although Savory's role as Director of Infantry (later Major General Infantry) had been tremendously important, he wrote to his wife, 'I shall not be sorry to leave my present job in which I feel I have done as much as possible during the two years of my tenure'.[317] He relieved Lieutenant General Sir Arthur Smith as GOC Persia (Iran) and Iraq Command (PAIFORCE), reporting to General Sir Bernard Paget, in Cairo.[318] He wrote to his wife, 'It is of course a command of the greatest responsibility, and an area for which I shall be answerable is immense'.[319] The soldiers under his command were largely Indian Army, but his main task was to organise the repatriation of British soldiers, which he achieved in the six months in post. Not long after his appointment, in October, he became advisor to Paget on all matters affecting the Indian Army across the Middle East.[320]

Whilst in post, Savory was asked to give a lecture on infantry to the officers of the Iraq Army. He started: 'In my opinion the keynote of all infantry organisation, armament, equipment, training and fighting should be simplicity. In fact simplicity is, to my mind, one of the great rules of warfare'.[321] The lecture encompassed all he had learnt throughout his career in the infantry and in particular as Directory of Infantry, including much of his thoughts on man management for example. He told the officers that when they left Staff College to take up staff appointments, the three rules for soldiers were basic,

317 Letter to his wife, 13 August 1945, NAM, 1976-03-93-72.

318 For more on PAIFORCE see Ashley Jackson, *Persian Gulf Command: A History of the Second World War in Iran and Iraq* (New Haven, Yale University Press, 2018).

319 Letter to his wife, 13 August 1945, NAM, 1976-03-93-72.

320 Letter to his wife, 7 October 1945, NAM, 1976-03093-72 and 'PAIFORCE Autobiography', NAM, 1976-03-93-74.

321 Lecture on Infantry, NAM, 1976-03-93-77.

section and platoon training. The equivalent for an officer was co-operation with other arms, good training and administration skills and 'be better than his men at all they are called upon to do'.[322]

Savory thought this would be his last job, writing to his wife, 'I cannot help feeling that time for me to retire will be when my present appointment expires, and that is what I would like to do; but if I am *asked* to stay on afterwards in the interests of the Indian Army I May do so'.[323] The situation was looking unlikely, as his old friend 'Piggy' Heath wrote to him complaining that 'It seems that senior appoitments in the East have over-favoured the British Service'.[324] However, in March 1946, he was asked to replace Lieutenant General Ralph Deedes as Adjutant General. He wrote in an autobiographical account 'so my next appointment was going to be the one which will test me very hard indeed'.[325]

## Adjutant General

The role of Adjutant General was neatly defined in the Defence Headquarters handbook issued to all those who joined GHQ India, as:

> responsible for raising, organising and maintaining military forces and their reserves, and for the distribution of Units, Officers and personnel (other than Officers above the rank of substantive Lieut-Colonel). He is also responsible for the general policy as to leave, repatriation, promotions, discipline and pay and allowances; the general morale and welfare of the troops, education, demobilization and resettlement of personnel; the control of prisoners of war; for all matters affecting the health of the Army in India (the Director of Medical Services acts as the Adjutant General's adviser in this respect; and also for martial and international law in its defence aspect (the Judge Advocate General being his adviser in this respect).[326]

Savory wrote to his wife, on taking up the post, 'I find that my particular responsibilities are probably as great as they have ever been in this appointment, and I take them up with a deep sense of responsibility coupled with a determination to keep cheerful and to rise…to every occasion.'[327]

His wide-ranging remit, for example, included involvement in suppressing the Royal Indian Navy (RIN) Mutiny in February 1946.[328] The Mutiny started at the signal school

322 Ibid.
323 Letter to his wife, 2 October 1945, NAM, 1976-03-93-72.
324 Letter from Heath to Savory, 7 October 1945, NAM, 1976-03-93-74.
325 'PAIFORCE Autobiography', NAM, 1976-03-93-74.
326 *Defence Headquarters* (New Delhi: War Department, March 1945), p. 19.
327 Letter to his wife, 8 March 1946, 1976-03-93-80.
328 Letter to his wife, 15 March 1946, 1976-03-93-80.

at HMIS Talwar in Bombay (Mumbai), when several sailors were court-martialled for insubordination after racial abuse by the CO, Commander King. It spread to over 10,000 men, 26 ships and ten naval barracks as well as rioting in Bombay, Calcutta (Kolkata) and later in Karachi and other cities. It was put down by British and Indian soldiers but 1,000 people were arrested, 1,000 injured and 200 killed.[329] Savory called it an 'unpleasant affair' and noted in his dairy that he consulted with the Admiral Godfrey, RIN. It had become clear that the British officers in the RIN were out of touch with their men, with the result that a number of Indian Army officers were given temporary commissions in the RIN.[330]

On 13 March 1946, Savory saw the Willcox Report, commenting that is was 'already much out of date'.[331] The committee had been established in November 1944 to look at India's defence requirements after the war. It was chaired by Lieutenant General Henry Willcox and included the later notorious Brigadier Enoch Powell and the future Field Marshal and first Indian C-in-C, Brigadier Kodandera Cariappa.[332] Some of the conclusions of the report, however, were incorporated in the Indian Army after independence.[333] The future of South Asia, and the army in particular, was paramount during Savory's time as Adjutant General. He wrote to his wife on 24 March 1946:

> Today is a fateful day for India and possibly for the Empire. Lord Pethwick-Lawrence and his cabinet committee arrived in Delhi at mid-day and are now in the Viceroy's House half-a-mile away from where I am writing this letter. Tomorrow they start their long series of conferences with Indian political leaders of all opinions and with princes and the governors and all the rest. It looks as if India may well have her independence this year; a very critical year; and my role will be to help guide the Indian Army through the transition (under guidance of the Auk) in a spirit of calm discipline. There may be trouble. There is bound to be, with so many contrasting opinions but I have no doubt we will be able to keep it under control. It is a great thing to be called upon to play one's part in such great times.[334]

Unfortunately, his words did foreshadow the future. Savory was definitely involved on the 'fringe (the outer fringe) of the inner ring' during the very difficult time of the run up to independence.[335]

329 Alan Jeffreys, 'Wars of Decolonisation in South Asia: The Indian Army, 1945-47' in Kaushik Roy and Michael Charney, *Routledge Handbook of the Global History of Warfare* (London: Routledge, 2024), pp. 442-443.
330 Letter to this wife, 15 March 1946 and diary entry 14 March 1946, NAM, 1976-03-93-88 and 89.
331 Diary entry 13 March 1946, NAM, 1976-03-93-89(2).
332 Powell gave his notorious 'Rivers of Blood' speech on immigration on 20 April 1968 in Birmingham and consequently was dismissed from the Conservative Party shadow cabinet.
333 Jeffreys, *Approach to Battle*, pp. 197-199.
334 Letter to his wife, 24 March 1946, NAM, 1976-03-93-80.
335 Letter to his wife, 29 June 1947, NAM, 1976-03-93-80.

The growing violence appalled Savory, he wrote that the Calcutta riots: 'produced 20,000 casualties in three days. The Army stopped them killing each other off in greater numbers.' He continued 'it is the Army alone which stands between order and chaos'.[336] The riots spread to East Bengal, Bihar and the United Provinces. The British government decreed in 1946 that British Army units could only be deployed in India as 'aid to civil power', if British lives were at risk. This meant that virtually all peacekeeping duties in 1946-1947 fell upon the Indian Army. On 31 January 1947, the Army Commanders, Messervy, Tuker and Lockhart met up with Savory to discuss the future of the Indian Army, 'We came to the conclusion that with the British officers now about to start leaving at speed, its future was indeed dark; and that we must do all we can to help Indians take over and run a good show, but how?'[337] Consequently, Savory wrote up a paper with some very pessimistic predictions, such as the inevitable collapse of the Royal Indian Navy and Royal Indian Air Force, the withdrawal of Indian troops from Burma, which would affect the country's internal security. The Indian Army faced breakdown after independence and the imminent disintegration on the division of India, a view shared by Auchinleck and other senior officers.[338] He also noted that Indian officers were becoming communally minded, drunk on the prospects of early promotion and forming cliques.[339] He was greatly saddened by the death of Lieutenant Colonel Dewan Ranjit Rai, the CO of his old regiment 1/11th Sikh Regiment, who was killed in the fighting in Kashmir in 1947 when the regiment was flown to Srinagar and fought near Baramula. Rai had been a cadet at the Indian Military Academy in 1932 when Savory was an instructor. He wrote 'I liked and admired him: a fine character and a great loss'.[340]

Although Savory was a forward-thinking military officer, this did not always translate across to his views on India, which he called a 'benevolent despotism' that was unsuitable for democracy but with many freedoms except for defence, foreign affairs, ecclesiastical department and reserved powers. However, throughout his career, he never seems to have been particularly keen on the British in India. He wrote to his wife in June 1943, 'I feel lost in a cantonment, as I play no tennis, polo or bridge! How I hate Anglo-India-dom!' and then wrote in 1946 that when he retired he was not keen in seeing too many Anglo-Indian friends as 'most of them bore me'.[341] The new job certainly created a certain amount of stress, as he wrote to his wife: 'I propose when I do go out to mix more with the Indians. It is only right that I should: and in any case I now have many Indian friends'.[342] However, a month later he wrote: 'I do NOT like India really. I long for my

336 Letter to his wife, 25 August 1946, NAM, 1976-03-93-80.
337 Diary entry 31 January 1947, NAM, 1976-03-93-89(3).
338 Philip Warner, *Auchinleck: The Lonely Soldier* (London: Buchan & Enright, 1981), p. 214.
339 'Results of 20 February 1947', NAM, 1976-03-93-82.
340 Letter to his wife, 29 October 1947, NAM, 1976-03-76-80.
341 Letter to his wife, 25 June 1943 and letter, 27 April 1946, NAM, 1976-03-93-63 and 80.
342 Letter to his wife 24 March 1946, NAM, 1976-03-93-80. There is a photograph of the family of Lieutenant Colonel (later Major General) Syed Shahid Hamid, the first Indian Private

own country though I have apparently a reputation for being a "friend of India".[343] This became a recurring theme in his correspondence, following it up in his next letter: 'The Indians call upon us to "Quit India" and little do they realize how glad most of us will be to quit. It is only a sense of duty that keeps most of us in this country and the fact that many of us are not allowed to go in any case!'[344]

Just before independence, Savory wrote 'India is finished so far as the Army is concerned, and Frank [Messervy, C-in-C Pakistan Army] and Rob [Lockhart, C-in-C Indian Army] have my sympathy for the new tasks they have undertaken.'[345] The situation in the Punjab was critical, as Savory wrote:

> Things in the Punjab are very bad, with the Sikhs going quite mad over the boundary question. Lahore is in ruins and the countryside is anarchy. The troops (all Indian) have been remarkable, but one wonders how much longer they themselves will be able to stand the communal strain.[346]

Savory questioned his time in India: 'It is sad to leave India in this state with the Indian Army torn asunder and declining under one's eyes in morale and efficiency. One wonders what one has achieved during one's years in the country?'[347] He initially reported that the support was immense for the Mountbattens being driven in Delhi on 15 August 1947 with the new Indian flag flying had been very supportive, quoting an American reporter commenting that 'The British have been in Indian for 200 years and they have not conquered the country until to-day'.[348] He thought Mountbatten had performed a 'psychological miracle'.[349] At the same time, Savory and his fellow senior officers were well aware of Mountbatten's faults and how little he knew and understood the Indian Army.[350] However, a few months later Savory concluded on leaving India that the British mission in India had failed.[351] Especially as the violence had escalated in the Punjab, which became more and more apparent in Delhi, and near to where he lived, when he witnessed the corpses at the railway station, the panic of all the Muslim servants, the

Secretary to FM Auchinleck, in Simla flanked by Auchinleck and Savory in Mishal Hussein's *Broken Threads: My Family from Empire to Independence* (London: 4th Estate, 2024), p. 6.

343 Letter to his wife, 14 April 1946, NAM, 1976-03-93-80.

344 Letter to his wife, 27 April 1946, NAM, 1976-03-93-80.

345 Letter to his wife, 7 August 1947, NAM, 1976-03-93-80.

346 Letter to his wife, 24 August 1947, NAM, 1976-03-93-80.

347 Letter to his wife, 13 September 1947, NAM, 1976-03-93-80. See also Hamid, *Disastrous Twilight*, p. 231.

348 Letter to his wife, 17 Augsut 1947, NAM, 1976-03-93-80.

349 Ibid.

350 Detailed at length in Andrew Roberts's essay on Mountbatten in *Eminent Churchillians* (London: Weidenfeld & Nicholson, 1994), p. 109. See also John Kiszely, *General Hastings 'Pug' Ismay: Soldier, Statesman, Diplomat: A New Biography* (London: Hurst, 2024), p. 214.

351 Diary entry 12 December 1947, NAM, 1976-03-93-89(4).

huge numbers of refugees and the growing lack of food.[352] He wrote 'we British can do nothing much except try to keep the two Dominion Armies stable and stop them becoming violently communal. It is all very humiliating. Nothing appears in the Press which is severly muzzled under the new regime more than under us, except in war.'[353] Savory was knighted by the Viceroy, Field Marshal Lord Wavell, on 8 March 1947.[354] His wife Myrtle described the ceremony in a letter to her daughter, Dorothy, concluding 'All this must sound rather unreal to you, with massacres going on not many miles from Delhi, with little food and no coal at home and the British Empire daily weakening.'[355]

Savory was much impressed by Auchinleck, C-in-C India, writing: 'He is a remarkable man. His mental energy, enthusiasm, good temper and driving power are all immense. How he has managed to stand up to the strain of the past years I cannot think. He just lives in and for his job'.[356] Auchinleck, in turn, was very appreciative of Savory's work and support. He told his wife, Auchinleck 'took me aside, before lunch, and thanked me for my work as A.G. saying that we have been a happy combination and that he was glad he selected me'.[357] Indeed, according to Shahid Hamid if the Indian Army had remained as an entity Savory was in line to be the next C-in-C to replace Auchinleck.[358]

In retirement, Savory kept up his connections with India and military history. He served as Colonel of the Sikh Light Infantry from 1946 until 1956. He had championed the regiment and agreed to become Colonel, even though it would prevent him from Colonelcy of his own Sikh Regiment.[359] In the UK, he was Deputy Lieutenant for Somerset and was chairman of the County Territorial Forces Association. Along with Auchinleck, Messervy and others he was involved in the Indian Army Memorial room at Sandhurst.[360]

352 Letters to his wife, 24, 28 August, 4, 10 September 1947, NAM, 1976-03-93-80.
353 Letter to his wife, 28 August 1947, NAM, 1976-03-76-80.
354 Major General Shahid Hamid, *Disastrous Twilight: A Personal Record of the Partition of India* (London: Leo Cooper, 1986), p. 123.
355 Letter from Myrtle Savory to Dorothy, 8 March 1947, NAM, 1976-03-93-80.
356 Letter to his wife, 21 April 1946, NAM, 1976-03-93-80.
357 Letter to his wife, 26 November 1947, NAM, 1976-03-93-80 and diary entry for 25 November 1947, NAM, 1976-03-93-89(4).
358 Hamid, *Disastrous Twilight*, pp. 268, 292. Although Savory thought Lieutenant General Sir Arthur Smith was the most likely candidate and wrote to his wife 'You need not worry about me being that', see letter to his wife, 15 August 1946, NAM, 1976-03-93-80.
359 J. D. Hookway (editor), *M & R: A Regimental History of the Sikh Light Infantry 1941–1947* (Privately published, 1999), p. 28.
360 The Indian Army Memorial Room remains today and the Indian Army collection was a precursor to the National Army Museum.

## Conclusion

This extended essay has concentrated on Savory's Second World War career and his important role as Director of Infantry in particular. This is the first time that this part of his service has been written about in forensic detail. Savory, as Director of Infantry, enabled that all infantry training across India was carried out along the same doctrinal lines. He made sure that lessons from the front-line were continually incorporated into the doctrine and instigated across the training establishments, not least by frequently visiting the front-line and liaising with the commanders like Slim. From his own experience, he realised that jungle warfare was primarily an infantry affair. Savory ensured that the infantry in India were manned, equipped and trained to successfully reinforce the largely Indian Army-dominated Fourteenth Army to defeat the Imperial Japanese Army in the campaigns in Northeast India and Burma during 1944-1945. His reforms and reorganisation also supported all infantry such as those soldiers earmarked for the Italian campaign during the same period.

Savory was a soldier-scholar through not only penning his reminscences of his earlier career in the Indian Army, particularly in the Gallipoli campaign, but also his very well-received book on the Seven Years' War. Indeed, his papers will hopefully provide a rich resource for generations of future historians. Savory is important for his training initiatives within his regiment and battalion, his stint at the Army School of Education, his essential input into the Indian Military Academy and finally his crucial two years as Director of Infantry. One of the reasons he has been bypassed until recently is that he only a played a smaller part in the Second World War campaigns and is very rarely the only senior officer involved and therefore often gets overlooked. However, it is rather through his career as a whole and his development as an officer that his real significance comes to light.